DELUSIONS OF A DICTATOR

DELUSIONS OF A DICTATOR
The Mind of Marcos as Revealed in His Secret Diaries

William C. Rempel

Little, Brown and Company
Boston   Toronto   London

First Edition

Unless otherwise stated, all photographs are courtesy of the Lopez Museum in Manila.

Library of Congress Cataloging-in-Publication Data

Rempel, William C.
     Delusions of a dictator / the mind of Marcos as revealed in his
   secret diaries / by William C. Rempel.
           p.   cm.
     ISBN 0-316-74015-2
     1. Philippines—Politics and government—1973–1986.   2. Marcos,
   Ferdinand E. (Ferdinand Edralin), 1917–   . I. Title.
   DS686.5.R43   1993
   320.9599—dc20   92-27531

10 9 8 7 6 5 4 3 2 1
MV-NY

Published simultaneously in Canada
by Little, Brown & Company (Canada) Limited

Printed in the United States of America

For Jason and Lara

Contents

Acknowledgments

This book would not be possible without the vital contributions of people who cannot accept my thanks publicly. At considerable risk, politically and professionally, they opened the Marcos diary to this American journalist with only one condition on its use: that those who provided access to the pages would never be identified. They must know I am deeply grateful.

The first diary stories were published in the *Los Angeles Times,* my professional home for twenty years. Many colleagues and editors contributed to the journalism that was the foundation of this book, but I am most indebted to the assistance and friendship of national correspondent Richard E. Meyer. My thanks also to Tim Rutten, Nina Green, and D'jamila Salem.

In Manila, I received gracious assistance from the Lopez Museum research staff. Philippine journalist Kristina Luz Rose was an invaluable guide and research assistant. I am also very grateful for the time and consultation contributed by Philippines historian Belinda Aquino of the University of Hawaii at Manoa.

Special thanks to writer Jeffrey Robinson, whose enthusiasm

sparked this project; to its shepherds, Robert Ducas, Roger Donald, and Irv Goodman; to Barbara Pierce, whose editorial counsel and encouragement were special gifts; and to Lara and Jason, who spent too many weekends watching Dad write.

Author's Note

This book is a historical narrative that draws extensively on information and insights made possible by the diary of Philippine President Ferdinand E. Marcos. The Marcos journal serves both as a source of specific detail and, even when it is not quoted directly, as a guide for this author's interpretation of Marcos's thoughts, motivations, and character. As a historic record, the diary is not always accurate or objectively sound, so the author has relied upon many independent sources to corroborate or correct the record. These include the recollections of key figures obtained through extensive interviews by the author in the Philippines and the United States; other Malacanang Palace documents and papers obtained by the author during five years of covering the Marcos story for the *Los Angeles Times*; old news accounts published in the Philippine and foreign press, and the books and articles of numerous historians, journalists, insiders, and other participants in the events covered by this manuscript.

W.C.R.

The Diary: An Introduction

In the regal isolation of Malacanang Palace, President Ferdinand E. Marcos dreamed of a place in history alongside the world's great figures. From the volumes that filled his impressive library he studied the lives and politics of Winston Churchill and Adolf Hitler, Charles de Gaulle and Napoleon Bonaparte, Julius Caesar and Alexander the Great. And he listened to voices calling him to greatness. One night in a dream, he said, God told him to save his country. "You are the only person who can do it. . . . Nobody else can," whispered the heavenly voice. Or was it, instead, the still small voice of his own titanic ambition? So obsessed was he with the judgment of history that he fantasized about the glowing eulogies and heroic epitaphs that could one day pay tribute to his life:

> I often wonder what I will be remembered in history for. Scholar? Military hero? Builder? The new constitution? Reorganization of government? Builder of roads, schools? The green revolution? Uniter of variant and antagonistic elements of our people? He brought light to a dark country? Strong rallying point, or a weak tyrant?

But who would render that verdict? That was the rub. Historians? Marcos did not trust them. They might be influenced by his critics. Indeed, some of them *were* his critics. "History," he insisted, "should not be left to the historians." He preferred the model of statesman-writer Churchill: "Make history, and then write it," Marcos said.

Therefore, driven by a passion for history and his desire to influence its perception of his life, Marcos created his own contribution to the historic record: a presidential diary, a decidedly odd document blending history and myth.

It was handwritten in English on pages of palace stationery, his penmanship usually neat, his prose often Olympian. The result is replete with self-serving, even utterly false, recreations of key moments and events. Often, it offers illusion as fact, paranoia as genuine menace, personal ambition as the will of God. But always, even through the inventions and exaggerations, it documents in unprecedented fashion the flawed personality of a contemporary political ruler, its pages revealing the transformation of a democrat to a despot.

Consequently, the Marcos diary provides history with an extraordinary view of a rarely witnessed event: the advent of a dictator.

To tell this story of Ferdinand Marcos, *Delusions of a Dictator* revisits a tumultuous period in Philippine history — the last one thousand days of democracy under the republic's sixth elected president. It is a story based on analysis of the diary, aided by independent historical records and extensive interviews. It is, of course, barely a glimpse of what eventually would be the corrupt and repressive twenty-year Marcos rule. But it is a telling glimpse of history being shaped by one world leader's towering ego, nagging paranoia, and cunning politics.

The diary pages were discovered almost by chance about a year after Marcos and his family fled the Philippines in 1986 for exile in the United States. Investigators for the new government of President Corazon Aquino, seeking to trace some of the purported billions of dollars looted from the Philippine national treasury by Marcos and his cronies, came upon a cache of nondescript cardboard cartons in a neglected corner of the Malacanang compound. Inside, was history — thousands of pages of diary and other presidential documents apparently abandoned in the rush to pack jewels, gems, and financial instruments that were carted off to Hawaii by Marcos and his aides in the bellies of two jumbo jetliners.

The diary was seized by the Philippine government, which still possesses the original manuscript. Few copies have been permitted outside the government vaults since its discovery first was disclosed by this author, writing for the *Los Angeles Times* in 1988. Photocopies of the diary and other related documents were obtained from Philippine government sources in Manila and elsewhere who still cannot be identified.

Officially, the Marcos diary was classified "secret" by the Aquino government for national security reasons. Consequently, among the approximately 2,500 pages obtained are scores of missing pages withheld by the sources to protect Philippine national interests. But most of the document is intact, as is the story it tells.

Marcos began his diary at the pinnacle of his political career — on the eve of his second term, January 1, 1970. Barely fifty-two years old, he had just achieved what no Philippine president before him had ever attained: reelection. And by an apparent landslide vote.

But one early morning, alone with his diary, he reflected on life. And it came to him, like a shiver in the dawn:

> I am president. I am the most powerful man in the Philippines. All that I have dreamt of I have.
>
> More accurately, I have all the material things I want of life — a wife who is loving and is a partner in the things I do, bright children who will carry my name, a life well lived — all.
>
> But I feel a discontent.

It was a discontent that would haunt his nation, alter history, and beget a new generation of Philippine martyrs and heroes.

DELUSIONS OF A DICTATOR

PROLOGUE
Friday, September 22, 1972

The superstitious sensed trouble in that sultry Manila evening, the howl of dire portent in the distant chorus of mournful dogs and the otherwise inexplicable eruption of cackling chickens. Ancient stories told that prowling spirits raised such clamor. Old people might have recognized the signs, but not eleven-year-old Luis "Boyet" Mijares. He played on a minimotorcycle near his house, oblivious of all concerns, happy there had been no school that Friday thanks to the bomb threats. Children called it an unexpected holiday. Parents called it terrorism. As crimson crept across the sky over Manila Bay and the city slipped deeper into shadows, the cacophony of animal wails seemed to intensify. Finally, a worried elder couple called out to the boy. Listen. Heed the omens, they warned. Speaking quickly in Tagalog and their native Ilocano dialect, the anxious neighbors urged Boyet to hurry home. Those distant sounds were whispers from the heavens that something terrible lurked beyond the twilight.

A few miles away at Malacanang Palace, the gracious colonial-era residence of Philippine presidents, Boyet's father, Primitivo "Tibo" Mijares, heard only one voice — the disapproving voice of The Boss.

"Those people move so sluggishly . . . !" Ferdinand Marcos muttered into an open intercom speaker, pointedly broadcasting his irritation so it would not be missed by the unseen aide at the other end. The impatient president of the Philippines sat fiercely erect behind his desk, his four-inch platform shoes concealed beneath it. He wanted to speak immediately to his secretary of defense, Juan Ponce Enrile. And he was annoyed by the delay.

Tibo had seen it before. "Sir," as much of the president's staff called him, was not one to be kept waiting. Even cabinet members learned quickly not to take too much time expressing their own ideas during meetings. Such meetings primarily were intended to convey the president's ideas to the cabinet. Mijares was the proverbial "fly on the wall," a journalist of sorts, writing for the Marcos-controlled *Daily Express*. More important, he was the president's ghostwriter. The regular Marcos column in the *Express* came from all the hours Tibo spent at the president's side. Tibo's extraordinary palace access made him privy to high-level secrets. Still, Tibo Mijares had only an inkling of the plots and intrigues waiting in the night.

"Sir — ?" An apprehensive aide was back on the intercom. Enrile seemed to be away from his office. They were trying to find him. The president pondered the cluster of silent red telephones arrayed before him and waited. Enrile was supposed to be at Camp Aguinaldo, the Pentagon of the Philippines. Some of the red phones were direct lines to those offices. The others linked the president to every major military camp in the country. The new communications system, financed with foreign aid money from the United States, put all key military officials in easy reach — except, at that moment, for the secretary of defense.

These were particularly unsettled times for Marcos and for the Philippines. Political criticism was deafening. The peso was slumping. Commodity shortages had set off panic buying in urban grocery markets. But among the surplus commodities were rumors: of plots to assassinate the president, of Communist rebel plans "to liquidate" Manila business leaders, of secret alliances between opposition senators and subversive groups, of CIA meddling, of agents provocateurs from the military spreading violence and fear, of plans for a military takeover of the government. Nightly bombings had become as predictable as sunset, although most exploded harmlessly and shattered little more than glass and nerves. Finally, the maelstrom of terror swirled even around Manila's children with the forced closure of schools that morning in the face of bomb threats. In an open letter to her president, already set in type for publication in the *Manila Chronicle*'s Saturday morning editions, Patty, a local sixth-grader, demanded of Marcos: "What are you going to do about the situation?"

In fact, the president was looking for his secretary of defense on that Friday evening to deal with what he, too, called "the situation." On matters of political delicacy Ferdinand Marcos confided in no one more than Juan Ponce Enrile. The most influential member of his cabinet, a man Marcos addressed as "Johnny Ponce" when he was pleased or as "Secretary Enrile" when he was not, Enrile had been Marcos's personal lawyer before The Boss became president. The young Harvard-trained attorney moved immediately into the cabinet. Always Enrile was particularly solicitous for the president's safety, whispering warnings when he detected the slightest hints of conspiracy against him. It was to Johnny Ponce that Marcos first confided his most intimate political dream, a secret plan spelled out in documents locked away in the president's bedroom safe.

"Sir — ?" There was relief in the intercom voice. Enrile finally was on the line. Marcos seized the phone.

"Secretary Enrile? Where are you? You have to do it now — Yeah — Yeah — The one we discussed this noon. We cannot postpone it any longer. Another day of delay may be too late."

The president paused. He had started the day alone with his diary, writing in the dark hours of early morning about his own dishonesty. He had lied to political allies from Ilocos Norte, his home province. He had lied to the American ambassador. He had told them all that he had no immediate intention to take the action that, in fact, he now was ordering. Of course, there would be no apologies. Not in his diary. Not to allies or ambassadors. His was a divine mission. And God's will be done, even if it required a few tactical lies for security's sake.

On the telephone Marcos resumed in English, then Ilocano: "Make it look good. Maybe it would be better if somebody got hurt or killed —" Mijares could not hear the defense secretary's reply. An involuntary shiver welled up from deep within him.

"Okay, Johnny, go ahead. And be sure the story catches the 'Big News' and 'Newswatch'— and call me as soon as it is over."

By now, evening shadows reached across Malacanang's lush gardens and the dark Pasig River just below the palace veranda. First Lady Imelda Marcos often was not happy with the river so near to the open veranda. At times it had an unpleasant urban-industrial bouquet. Sometimes it had the stench of an open sewer. This night the Pasig was sweet again, flushed by heavy rains that had flooded much of the city and the countryside. Imelda prepared for a dinner across town with foreign journalists. The president doubled her security and sent the bulletproof car.

At Manila Metropolitan Police headquarters, on United Nations Avenue across from the Hilton Hotel, the usual crowd of police beat reporters converged on the chief's office at day's end, before the first round of news deadlines. The city was quiet. Too quiet, said Brigadier General Gerardo Tamayo. "I don't like it, boys." But to the journalists no news simply was no news. A *Manila Times* reporter, on the phone to his city editor, said: "Don't expect any earthshaking story from our end."

All over town the business of government was shutting down for the weekend. Delegates to the scandal-plagued constitutional convention were the first to go home, adjourning early out of weariness from weeks of raucous battles, harsh accusations, and bomb scares. All were tarnished by a vote-buying scandal. This was no way to rewrite a constitution. Finally, a bruising fight to defeat, at least for now, proposals to ban the Marcoses from trying to stay in Malacanang. The president's second term would expire in a year, and term limits in the current U.S.-model constitution barred his reelection. Cynics everywhere wondered how Marcos would try to elude the restrictions. It was a favorite topic of debate and banter at the Senate, where some of the president's leading rivals held office. The most popular of these was Benigno "Ninoy" Aquino, the pudgy whiz kid of the opposition Liberal party and virtually every pundit's favorite to succeed Marcos in 1973. On Friday, the only Senate business remaining was setting the tariff quotas, a tedious exercise left to a congressional conference committee that would meet all night, if necessary, at the Hilton Hotel. Reporters desperate for a hint of interesting copy clustered around Aquino who, as usual, obliged. The senator regaled them with lively criticisms of the president. Laughter echoed through the near-empty chamber.

Night draped the putting greens and fairways of Wack Wack Golf Course when a distant burst of machine-gun fire rattled out of the darkness. Then another. And another. How many rounds? A dozen? Maybe twice that? There was no one out on the course. No one to see what or who was the target. Perhaps the answer would be in the morning papers, or on Channel 9's "Newswatch."

The palace was darker than usual when press secretary Francisco "Kit" Tatad came looking for The Boss. He was going home to his bride of less than two years as soon as he debriefed the president on afternoon meetings with media executives. Tatad found Marcos in the dimly lighted State Dining Room, waiting to watch a movie. With the three children away at school, the after-dinner movie was not the customary family event. The president was alone, but the press secretary was not invited to stay for the film, or to report on his meetings.

"Kits!" The president greeted him eagerly. For some reason The Boss always referred to Kit as if he was plural. It didn't bother him. "You go see Johnny. There are some things you will have to work on together tonight." Marcos sent him to telephone the secretary of defense. It threatened to be another long night at the office. Kit reached Enrile almost immediately at Camp Aguinaldo. "You wanted to see me?"

"You know —" Enrile began in a voice betraying no emotion —"I have just been ambushed. No one was hurt, but my car is wrecked." Kit gasped at the news, delivered with such coolness, so matter-of-fact. The president must be informed immediately. Enrile agreed. Kit rushed back to interrupt the president's movie, blurting out: "Secretary Enrile has been ambushed!" Marcos only half turned. "Is that so?" He asked nothing more. Is that so? Is that so! For a moment Tatad wondered why he was the only one so excited by the news. But then he had to hurry out to Camp Aguinaldo. As his car pulled away from the palace, Tatad looked back. There seemed to be more security guards. Then he recognized the car of a prominent radio news reporter fall in behind him as he drove out through the gates. Kit had to smile. What irony. They were headed for perhaps the biggest story in Philippine history, but the Philippine press would not be free to report it.

Finally, Manila was dark.

Marcos retired to the Study Room just before 10:00 P.M. and

asked an aide to fetch his diary. At 9:55 the president scratched an entry on page 2,332, describing how Enrile's car had been attacked about two hours earlier by armed assailants waiting in ambush near Wack Wack, how the defense secretary's car was riddled with bullets, how Enrile escaped harm because he luckily was riding in the trail car with his bodyguards. The fact that it was a staged attack, that Enrile simply was making it "look good," was not noted. And Marcos scribbled one more sentence: "This makes the martial law proclamation a necessity."

Diary lies and half-truths . . . a staged provocation . . . finally, a dire presidential decree. Dogs and sirens howled all over Manila. This time, the phantoms were visible. They had names pinned to their uniforms. They carried arrest warrants signed by the secretary of national defense.

In smoke-filled room 1701 at the Hilton Hotel, a sharp rap on the door interrupted conference committee debate over tariff quotas for zinc bars. It was about midnight. Senator John "Sonny" Osmena opened the door to a constabulary officer who saluted him smartly, then stepped inside. Colonel Romeo Gatan had a brown manila envelope for Ninoy Aquino. Sonny, standing where he could read its contents over Ninoy's shoulder, turned cold. He focused only on the words "I hereby declare martial law. . . ." The colonel spoke softly to Aquino. "I'm here to take you, sir."

There had been time for flight. Ample warnings. Go to the hills, some had urged. Go to California. But go. Get out of Manila. He was first on the president's enemies list, everyone knew. His popularity made him a very dangerous man to an unpopular president. But Aquino rejected exile or the life of a fugitive. "If martial law comes, my place is with my people." Indeed, it had come. And two hundred armed troops waited in the lobby, basement, and corridors outside to make this first and most important seizure of the night. "Gentlemen, I am being arrested." Aquino smiled to his colleagues. He seemed apologetic. No resistance. No rhetoric. Then, taking his first steps to martyrdom, Aquino disappeared through the doorway of room 1701.

Word of the Aquino arrest crackled over radios and walkie-talkies, signaling Malacanang that it was safe to proceed. Immediately, fleets of freshly painted blue government cars moved into the streets. Swarms of uniformed men with machine guns swept through the city, raiding newspaper offices and television stations. An editor was dragged off to jail in his pajamas. A columnist was clubbed with a rifle butt. Presses stopped. Television screens went black. At radio station DZHP where the hourly newscast was about to go on the air, reporting Aquino's arrest, troopers burst into the studio and ordered employees to go home. The 2:00 A.M. news was preempted by silence.

It was the dog that awoke professor Hernando Abaya and his family, well after two o'clock. They peered out to see shadows moving in their garden courtyard. Old Laddie reacted with angry, uncontrollable barking. One of Abaya's daughters tried to phone for help. The line went dead. Outside, a man in military fatigues threatened to break open the front door. He said he was a lieutenant. *"Bakit ba?"* called out the bewildered professor in Tagalog. "What is it?" The shadow at the door replied, "Martial law, sir."

For Philippine democracy, this was the far side of twilight. This was everything terrible the omens could have premonished. This was the night of the dictator.

CHAPTER ONE
The First Coffin

He was born an Ilocano, an accident of history that defined the character of Ferdinand Edralin Marcos as surely as if he had been born a Scotsman in Great Britain or a Sicilian in Italy.

For generations, inhabitants of the sun-scorched coastal provinces of Ilocos Norte, Ilocos Sur, and La Union — farm families mostly — learned to get along with less water, less money, and less comfort than their countrymen in other, lusher, regions of the big island of Luzon. Consequently, the Ilocandia region bred tough, proud, independent stock who confronted the vicissitudes of nature with the same resolution they engaged any enemy. Over the centuries Ilocano farmers with crude plows had tilled dry, rocky fields to force food from the reluctant earth; and with sharpened bamboo stakes they had battled Spanish and American colonial troops. The rather stern code of the Ilocano, then as now, regards honor and loyalty as divine virtues, waste and ostentation as cardinal sins, and any menacing act or personal insult as an invitation to violence.

Such an "invitation" was received by the Marcos family of Ilocos

Norte, in September 1935. It was delivered to Ferdinand's father — in a coffin.

During the late 1920s, Congressman Mariano Marcos served the second district of Ilocos Norte, but his six-year political career ended abruptly with a stunning upset election loss in 1931. The family blamed a neighbor in their town of Batac, a political novice named Julio Nalundasan who ran last in a three-way race but split the vote. The elder Marcos lost by fifty-six votes and for the next year suffered not only unemployment but acute depression. He tried a political comeback in 1935 when America's Philippine colony was reorganized as a commonwealth. The second district congressional seat was open and Mariano Marcos faced Nalundasan again, this time in a two-man duel. Marcos lost. But that was not the last insult.

A victory party at Nalundasan's home, only a few hundred feet from the Marcos house, spilled out into the street. Someone put a coffin in the rumble seat of a car, and two men climbed inside the open box. One man was labeled Gregorio Aglipay, the losing candidate for president; the other was labeled Mariano Marcos, whose political career was now clearly dead. The high-spirited throng of revelers paraded the coffin through several villages in a mock funeral cortege that ended back in Batac, in front of the Marcos home. Horns honked. A few inebriated musicians played an uneven dirge. The revelers feigned sorrow and wiped their eyes of imaginary tears. The crowd jeered: "Marcos is dead; long live Nalundasan." In Ilocandia, where there is no such thing as an honorable defeat, the Marcos humiliation was exquisite. Young Ferdinand, home from law school in Manila where he was a sharpshooter on the University of the Philippines pistol team, stayed within the walls of the Marcos compound and shared the family shame in silence.

The next night howling storms lashed Batac. The moonless, overcast night later would be recalled in court as "black as sin." After dining with friends, Congressman-elect Nalundasan stepped out to a washbasin on his porch to brush his teeth, his tall frame illuminated by a lantern. From out of the damp shadows of rain-drenched banana plants a single shot exploded. Nalundasan fell dead, shot in the back. The murder weapon was a competition pistol with an eight-inch barrel. And four years later, in the Laoag Court of First Instance, Ferdinand E. Marcos was convicted of pulling the trigger. He was sentenced to a prison term of ten to seventeen years.

In jail, Ferdinand drafted his own 830-page appeal to the Supreme Court, studied for the bar examination, and played Ping-Pong on a table provided by the mayor of Laoag, Roque Ablan, Sr. During the years between the shooting and his trial, young Marcos had completed law school and graduated with honors. While still in jail he passed the bar with a record high score. Ferdinand had been in jail nearly one year when the Supreme Court agreed to consider his appeal. In October 1940, Ferdinand Marcos had his first client: Ferdinand Marcos. Dressed in the white of innocence, from his sharkskin suit to his shoes, Marcos appeared before the black-robed justices. But even before the appeal was fully argued, presiding Associate Justice Jose P. Laurel interrupted the proceedings. He said he did not believe the word of a key eyewitness, who had testified that Ferdinand had insisted on doing the shooting himself because he feared that an uncle, who also had volunteered, might miss. The same witness also had said he accompanied Marcos and his uncle to Nalundasan's home just before the shooting.

With the eyewitness testimony rejected, the case against Marcos collapsed. The conviction was overturned. Marcos was free. The next day young Marcos was back at the Supreme Court, this time to be sworn in as a lawyer. Justice Laurel administered the oath.

But after beating the murder charge, Marcos had little time to launch his career. War loomed in the Pacific. Less than a year after his Supreme Court victory, Marcos was called into the army in November 1941. He was a third lieutenant attached to the 21st Philippine Infantry Division when Japanese invasion forces under Lieutenant General Masaharu Homma came ashore at Lingayen Gulf, north of Manila.

By his own account, Marcos was a war hero of legendary dimension — more war medals than Audie Murphy, praise from General Douglas MacArthur for helping Bataan hold out so long, a recommendation for the U.S. Congressional Medal of Honor, founder of the *Maharlika* guerrilla unit, a victim of torture and multiple combat wounds.

Most of the Marcos claims were sheer fantasy, originally created to further his exaggerated claims for compensation from the United States, but they played an important role in his postwar political ascent. Marcos the War Hero was to become a persistent and persuasive campaign image. Later, American officials from President Lyndon B.

Johnson to Vice-President George Bush would salute the war record invented for those compensation forms. Meanwhile, United States military records rejecting the Marcos claims and raising serious questions about his conduct in the war would remain buried in Washington archives for forty years. Among those documents, in fact, was an arrest order issued by an American guerrilla officer accusing Marcos of wartime racketeering.

The end of World War II brought with it the official end of American imperialism in the Philippines. In ceremonies attended by General Douglas MacArthur at Luneta Park on July 4, 1946, the United States formally surrendered all claims to the island nation. As a crowd of 300,000 cheered and bands played the national anthems of the two countries, the Stars and Stripes was replaced by the sun-blazoned flag of the new Republic of the Philippines. "A nation is born," proclaimed Paul V. McNutt, last United States high commissioner and first American ambassador to the Philippines. And MacArthur declared: "Let history record this event in the sweep of democracy through the earth as foretelling the end of mastery over peoples by force alone. . . ."

What it did not signal, however, was the end of America's strategic interest in the Philippines. A Military Bases Agreement signed in 1947 gave the U.S. a ninety-nine-year lease on twenty-two military sites, including the air base at Clark Field and the deep-water navy base on Subic Bay. By the early 1950s, the cold war and the emergence of Red China combined to make the Philippines and the U.S. military presence there increasingly important elements of Washington's Communist-containment strategies in Asia. That prominence would continue through the Vietnam war era. At the same time, as it recovered from the devastation of war and Japanese occupation, the Philippines seemed eager to keep close ties with its former colonial master, for both military and financial security.

A new republic needs new political leaders, and one of the first in line was Ferdinand E. Marcos. After the war he joined a prominent Manila law firm, reestablished his residency in Ilocos Norte, and began to build a political organization. In 1949, he won his first congressional election.

During three terms in Congress he became chairman of the Import

Control Committee, where rumors first linked his name to bribes and payoffs. He denied them.

At the time, Marcos lived with a Philippine beauty, a former Miss Press Photography named Carmen Ortega who worked in the import control section of the Philippines Central Bank. The couple had already published an engagement notice in the newspapers when, in April 1954, Marcos was introduced to another beauty queen — the "Muse of Manila," Imelda Romualdez of Leyte.

Imelda had come to the Legislative Building to pick up her cousin, the speaker pro tempore of the House, who was delayed by business on the floor. While waiting in the cafeteria, she was somewhat embarrassed to be introduced by a reporter to the brash young Congressman Marcos. She had worn a simple housedress and slippers. When she stood to greet him, Marcos was stunned by her beauty. He was taller by barely half an inch. As they would later tell the story, he immediately proposed marriage. She laughed.

The next day, to dispel any notion that he was jesting, Ferdinand sent Imelda a symbolic Ilocano love message — two roses: one a closed bud representing his young love for her, the other in full bloom representing the love he hoped would blossom between them. After an eleven-day courtship, they were married.

The civil ceremony was followed about a month later by a huge church wedding in Manila on May 1, 1954. At the invitation of President Ramon Magsaysay, the wedding reception was held in the gardens of Malacanang Park, just across the river from what already was the object of Ferdinand's deepest desires — the presidential palace.

The Marcos wedding was more than romance. The Romualdez family was wealthy and politically well connected. Imelda was one of the poor relations, but still her name had substantial political currency. Her relatives would make valuable political allies. In short, she was beautiful and she was from the right family. It was a perfect marriage.

But Imelda, the beauty queen from the provinces, was not comfortable in political brawls or in the public spotlight. She was stricken by insecurity. Even her home was no haven. Supplicants at her door beseeched her husband at all hours. Political caucuses took over her dining room. She suffered headaches and chronic exhaustion. One night in 1958 Imelda's brother Benjamin "Kokoy" Romualdez was summoned to her bedside. He found her "cold, pale, motionless and hardly breathing." The diagnosis: a nervous breakdown. She was flown to New York City for psychiatric treatment. It appeared that Ferdinand might have to make a choice between Imelda and his political ambitions. Instead, Imelda returned from New York three months later a changed woman — less inhibited, more assertive. Rather than shrink from politics and public life, she pursued it, becoming a student of government and political gamesmanship. This was the future "Iron Butterfly" stepping from her cocoon to be, for better or for worse, a true partner in politics with Ferdinand.

Next stop was the Senate. In 1959 Ferdinand took on the majority Nacionalista party and a slate of Senate hopefuls secretly supported by the U.S. Central Intelligence Agency to get more votes than anyone else in a twenty-two-candidate race for eight open seats. Marcos, one of only two Liberal party candidates to win, emerged as a prominent figure in speculation over who would make a presidential bid in 1961. Significantly, the Ilocos precincts went heavily for Marcos in his first nationwide race, providing an early glimpse of "the Solid North" that was to be a fiercely loyal bastion of Marcos political support to his last days.

Now forty-two, Marcos was confident he could parlay his dazzling Senate victory and the Solid North into a successful campaign for the presidency. He had barely taken his Senate seat when he began maneuvering for the presidential suite at Malacanang.

In 1961, Marcos arrived at the Liberal party's presidential convention with campaign buttons, cases of pesos and an acceptance speech already written. To win favor with delegates, Marcos distributed boat tickets to those traveling to Manila from the distant Visayas islands and Mindanao in the south. But that gesture was trumped at the last minute by his rival who handed out airplane tickets. Then, in convention backrooms, Marcos could not hold his support. A deal was sealed: the nomination would go to Diosdado Macapagal, then vice-president to rival Nacionalista President Carlos P. Garcia.

Marcos had been outmaneuvered. His father had always advised him never to get into a fight unless he was sure to win, but this time his ambition had gotten ahead of his preparations. Marcos had to accept defeat. He may have brooded privately, but publicly he went along with the party decision. He served as Macapagal's campaign manager and president of the party. Macapagal, in turn, pledged to serve only one term and then step aside for Marcos. After getting to Malacanang, however, Macapagal changed his mind. He would run for reelection. Marcos, needing very little coaxing from the Nacionalista Romualdez family, jumped parties. In 1965, it would be Macapagal versus the newest Nacionalista. This time, Marcos was ready for the brawl.

The Nacionalista convention was held at the aging Manila Hotel, where MacArthur once had established his headquarters. Marcos operatives wined, dined, and entertained delegates with cruises on Manila Bay, trips to fashionable nightclubs, and full-course dinners featuring chicken garnished with peso-stuffed envelopes. Leaving nothing to chance, hotel operators were paid to see that the Marcos foes had extra problems with the already unreliable telephone system. Then he set out to forge a critical alliance with the wealthy, aristocratic family of Eugenio "Ining" Lopez, Sr., proposing Ining's brother Fernando as his vice-presidential running mate.

The close-knit Lopez clan published one of the country's most influential newspapers, the *Manila Chronicle,* and controlled the Meralco holding company that owned Manila's electric utility company, an oil refinery, a construction firm, and the nation's second largest bank. Few families could rival the Lopezes for power, prestige, and money. There was one problem: Fernando Lopez was not interested in being vice-president.

It took an uninhibited Imelda to salvage the alliance. Going alone to the Lopez suite she cried, dropped to one knee, and pleaded with him to accept the nomination. He did. "She made people feel important, even when they were getting hustled," said Lopez's nephew, Eugenio "Geny" Lopez, Jr.

If there was one man in Manila that Marcos feared at the time it was Ining, the Lopez family don. Like Marcos, he had the instincts of a brawler. "He was another Marcos, actually," said Ining's son, Geny (pronounced Henny). "When he went into a fight, he threw everything into it. He didn't try to protect anything. He was a very bad enemy, but a very good friend." It was to assure the friendship of Don Eugenio Lopez, Sr., that Marcos pursued Fernando as his running mate. And for a time, it worked.

The Lopez-owned *Chronicle* eagerly supported the Marcos-Lopez ticket, as did other major publications with less obvious conflicts of interests. In the propaganda war, Marcos was a clear winner. A fawning biography by American author Hartzell Spence, *For Every Tear a Victory*, came out in time for the campaign. It cast the mythical Marcos war exploits as history. Those images also burst onto theater screens later in the campaign when Marcos backers released a docudrama film depicting him as a war hero and loyal son.

The campaign began in earnest in January 1965, with a harrowing boat ride to the small island of Romblon, off Mindoro. Ferdinand and Imelda were to crown a local fiesta queen. As the winds grew and the seas churned, Imelda feared for their safety. Ferdinand quipped: "Don't be scared. A good girl like you will not die this way." Imelda was not reassured. But they landed safely in Romblon, politicked at the fiesta, and then, while touring the town, encountered a large snake that slithered across their path. Their Romblon escorts cheered. A good omen, they insisted. Finally, Imelda felt better. They both did. Ferdinand and Imelda were always grateful for good omens.

Meanwhile, the CIA also watched for omens, for signs of trouble in the nation that was becoming an increasingly important staging area for U.S. troops and equipment bound for Vietnam. In Manila a nationalist youth movement was attracting middle-class and affluent university students. The *Kabataang Makabayan* (Patriotic Youth), known simply as the KM, was founded by a Maoist English instructor at the University of the Philippines, Jose Maria Sison. He led student protests critical of the U.S. role in Vietnam, the presence of American bases on Philippine soil, government corruption, and unpopular school policies. Similar demonstrations were common in the United States. But on the eve of Philippine elections, the CIA saw signs of growing cynicism throughout the country. Omens of unrest, even instability.

"The Philippine electorate craves efficient and honest government and increasingly feels it does not get it," CIA analysts reported to Washington in October 1965. They detected a general condition of "discontent and lawlessness" fed by widespread rural poverty, vast class differences, extensive unemployment, and pervasive graft, corruption, and favoritism in government and business.

The Marcos campaign appealed to the pent-up frustrations. As November neared, Ferdinand pounded away at his slogan: "This nation can be great again!" He opposed sending Philippine troops to

Vietnam. The Civil Liberties Union endorsed him with virtually no dissent. Meanwhile, Imelda was organizing some of Manila's most prominent society matrons as Marcos volunteers to serve at parties and receptions, to answer phones, to run errands. They wore blue dresses and came to be known as "the Blue Ladies," a name forever associated with the coterie of women who traveled, shopped, and partied with Imelda.

Out on the stump, the Ferdinand-and-Imelda act was a big hit. In a booming baritone he preached nationalism and government reforms, promised new roads and schoolhouses, pledged to root out corruption and give land to the peasants. She looked beautiful and sang soprano. Sometimes they sang together. Marcos called her his secret weapon. He pulled out the same old line at one stop after another: "I will give you everything you want — except my wife!" The crowds loved it.

And Imelda showed no signs of the earlier shy, even frightened, young wife from the provinces. She strode boldly into crowds of outstretched arms eager to touch her. At each village on the campaign trail she sought out the busy market plazas to maximize her exposure to crowds. There, she learned to start with the fruit and vegetable vendors before moving to the meat sellers, always saving the fish vendors for last so that her hands would not smell of fish from the first handshake. Imelda, the student of politics, was showing a gift for the game. By some estimates she was worth one million votes. Marcos won by 670,000. It was not quite the sweeping victory of Marcos's dreams, however. He lost to Macapagal in Tarlac, the province of a popular young Liberal party governor named Benigno "Ninoy" Aquino, Jr.

Marcos was sworn in as the sixth president of the republic on December 30, 1965, delivering stirring oratory that American guests compared to John F. Kennedy's. Marcos declared that the country had given him "a mandate for greatness." Imelda played the Jacqueline role. Exuding understated elegance, she wore a simple beige *terno*, the traditional Philippine gown with butterfly sleeves. She was beautiful. Their three children were beautiful. They were, trumpeted the press, "the Kennedys of the Philippines." And this was Camelot on the Pasig: Day One.

In the Luneta Park audience for the occasion was U.S. Vice-President Hubert H. Humphrey, then the highest-ranking American official to attend a Philippine inauguration. Other countries sent budget and petroleum ministers. But Humphrey was on a mission, rounding up support for Lyndon B. Johnson's Vietnam policy. Marcos was key, notwithstanding his campaign pledge to keep Filipino boys out of the war. That pledge would be among the first casualties of the new presidency. By summer Marcos would commit two thousand noncombat troops to Vietnam, prompting a grateful LBJ to call him America's "right arm in Asia."

Manila's new First Family did not immediately occupy Malacanang Palace after the inaugural balls. There was remodeling to be completed. And omens to analyze. The Marcoses were unsure which suite of rooms to choose for the family's bedrooms. Imelda was especially concerned because all the presidents who had occupied one wing of the palace had died in office; all the presidents sleeping in another wing had been defeated in bids for reelection. Omens. They had not even slept a night in the presidential palace when, already, Marcos was thinking of reelection.

Imelda entertained Muriel Humphrey, escorting the vice-president's wife on tours of Manila that could not avoid the inevitable sights and stench of poverty. It embarrassed Manila's new First Lady. Frequently, she tried to draw Mrs. Humphrey's attention away from an unpleasant sight long enough for their car to slip past, leaving troubling scenes of misery and decay to the rearview mirror.

The new Marcos administration set out quickly to alter the physical and political landscape of the Philippines. Construction equipment rumbled up and down Luzon — but especially in Ilocos Norte, where loyalty at the polls was rewarded with miles of cement pavement and the best roads in the republic. Bridges went up. And small schoolhouses, literally by the thousands. In rural areas, irrigation projects delivered water desperately needed for food production. Days after the inauguration Imelda launched a multimillion-dollar cultural center project in Manila, soliciting contributions from business leaders. Some, including Ninoy Aquino, called it coercing contributions. Success was so swift that she was ready for ground-breaking ceremonies barely ninety days into the new administration. There was a hitch. Another omen. The event would have occurred on the Ides of March. Ceremonies had to be delayed.

Less visible at first were reforms of the armed forces of the Philippines. Marcos had inherited a small military force, poorly trained, poorly equipped, and poorly paid. Some warlords in the provinces maintained more efficient private armies as security against local bandits — or sometimes to settle disputes of a more personal nature. A wise warlord took good care of his army. Marcos, who never had his own private army, now was commander in chief of the nation's armed forces. Immediately, he set out to rebuild it, reorganize it, and restock it with more and better weapons. It was his favorite project. To celebrate his first birthday in Malacanang, the president reviewed the troops in colorful parades that over the years became an annual tradition. It was an excuse for more oratory. Lavishing praise as well as personal attention on the soldiers and officers, he extolled their virtue as defenders of Philippine democracy. And he improved their pay. A wise president took good care of his army.

But a bigger and better military was a more expensive military. So were roads. And irrigation networks. And electrification projects. Philippine veterans of World War II were clamoring for better benefits. There was a rice shortage. Marcos needed money. Coincidentally, Washington needed Marcos, a Southeast Asian leader supporting the Johnson administration's Vietnam policies.

A Marcos state visit to Washington was brokered by Imelda's brother, special envoy Benjamin "Kokoy" Romualdez, who presented LBJ with the mounted head of a wild water buffalo, a hunting trophy supposedly shot by President Marcos himself. Mindful of Ferdinand's youthful arrest record, some State Department aides promptly dubbed the unfortunate beast "Nalundasan."

In Washington, Marcos told a joint session of Congress that he was criticized back home for being "much too pro-American." He conceded it might be true. He spun dubious tales of his World War II heroism and told the U.S. Congress that he and other Filipino fighters had "gambled everything — life, dreams and honor — on a faith and the vision of America when all was lost. . . ."

By the time he flew back to Manila, Marcos the wild buffalo hunter had bagged more than $125 million in aid commitments for everything from new Philippine army engineering battalions to Imelda's new cultural center. It was only the beginning. Months later President Johnson would conclude that he had fallen in with a blackmailer.

The United States had made possible the most thorough renovation of the Philippine military since World War II. But contrary to

Johnson's wishes, the troops did not go to Vietnam. Most did not even leave Luzon. Instead, they went to work on road projects, helping to build highways between Manila and Ilocos Norte — and, in the process, building a platform for future Marcos election campaigns.

As he approached midterm, Marcos was riding a crest of unprecedented popularity and power. A rice production program, spearheaded by his executive secretary, Rafael Salas, had in little more than a year turned chronic rice shortages into a surplus that would make the Philippines a rice-exporting nation by the end of the first Marcos term. The press heaped praise on Salas, calling the Marcos chief aide "the little president." Marcos found himself sharing credit with a staff assistant for an enormously successful program that promised equally enormous political dividends. Their relationship soured. Marcos intended to run for reelection in 1969 as the president of rice and roads. It was a platform only big enough for one.

The Marcos political juggernaut was tested first in the midterm senate and local elections of 1967. It was a devastating display of power. With one exception, Nacionalista party candidates won every senate race. The lone Liberal victor, the youngest senator ever elected, was Tarlac's thirty-five-year-old former governor, Ninoy Aquino. He was fast becoming the bane of Malacanang.

A popular orator, masterful storyteller, and gifted negotiator, the cocky and self-assured Aquino first gained fame as a teenaged journalist covering the war in Korea for the *Manila Times*. Later, back home working both as a journalist and an adviser to President Magsaysay, Aquino helped mediate the surrender in 1954 of a notorious peasant leader who was the military commander of the *Hukbalahap* rebels. Aquino was twenty-one at the time. A year later he became the youngest mayor in the Philippines when his hometown of Concepcion launched his meteoric political career — a career that almost ended before it began. A discouraged Ninoy had decided to quit the race until his mother, failing with appeals to family pride, finally accused him of cowardice. "You're afraid!" she proclaimed. Ninoy stalked back out onto the campaign trail. Never let it be said that Benigno Aquino, Jr., was afraid of anything — except, perhaps, his mother.

As mayor, and later as provincial governor of Tarlac, Ninoy continued to negotiate with remnants of the peasant insurgent *Hukbalahaps*, or Huks. He also conferred with other radical groups, from strident land reform advocates to armed disciples of a Maoist revolution. Despite its geographic proximity to traditional Huk strongholds, Tarlac experienced relatively little conflict during Aquino's tenure. Always in reserve, should Aquino's considerable persuasive skills fail, was his own private army. If necessary, it enforced the peace — or dispensed justice. He once personally tracked down and arrested a rape suspect at gunpoint. Governor Aquino also built health clinics, irrigation systems, and schools throughout his province. It was an enviable record of regional success that made him an all-but-invincible political power at home.

In Tarlac, Ninoy Aquino had been the nemesis of local Marcos allies. In the Senate, he emerged as a dangerous rival to the president. Aquino came to Manila with designs on Malacanang. Never again would democracy feel quite so comfortable or the presidency quite so secure to Ferdinand Marcos.

For the Marcos administration the honeymoon was nearly over. After two years in office, despite the road-building and rice-growing programs, the country's most serious economic problems remained intractable. Crime rates soared in Manila, a problem only amplified by sensational newspaper headlines. Rumors of waste and corruption were starting to get more attention from columnists and political foes. Marcos remained enormously popular, but for the first time rumbles of criticism could be heard over the din of applause.

The Civil Liberties Union that had endorsed his election now worried about Marcos's increasingly apparent determination to expand the armed forces, warning that militarization threatened "the great traditions of political democracy, we could be risking our survival as a free and sovereign people." Noisy and sometimes destructive student demonstrations against the war in Vietnam and American ties increased, though markedly less violent than antiwar riots in the United States. Students called Marcos a *tuta* (lap dog) of the Americans.

Political criticism in the press began to feel more like personal attacks. Imelda's prized cultural center came in for ridicule as a costly and ostentatious white elephant. Word that a prominent artist was sculpting a life-size statue of the First Lady prompted suggestions she was "immortalizing herself." In editorial columns and cartoons, she was dubbed "Imelda the Fabulous." It was not a tribute. After the president announced plans to construct the nation's longest bridge between the islands of Samar and Leyte, dedicating the project to Imelda as a birthday present, the press panned it for serving regions with no roads, as a bridge "linking jungle to jungle." Wasteful pork barrel, complained critics of what came to be called "the Love Bridge."

But just as the criticisms began to sting, another presidential campaign season loomed. Nothing could make Ferdinand Marcos feel better than winning a fight. And he was ready. He had money. He had "Rice and Roads." He had Imelda. He had the Solid North. And he had friends eager to help.

Late in 1968, a group of Marcos's golfing partners put together a movie company to help the president's campaign. Their plan was to make a full-length Hollywood feature film about Marcos the war hero. It could be on the nation's screens before Election Day in November 1969. Their aim: a money-maker, a myth-maker, a vote-maker. They would call it *Maharlika*, after the president's romanticized guerrilla unit.

The front money came from Potenciano "Nanoy" Ilusorio, a close friend for more than thirty years. The tall, affable businessman, whom Marcos called "Calbo" (Baldy), had coached "Ferdie" on the university boxing team and loaned him his Packard convertible to squire college dates. Ilusorio flew to Los Angeles and with director Paul Mason thumbed through a casting catalogue looking for a leading lady — an actress to play Evelyn, the wartime sweetheart of Marcos the guerrilla fighter. Scanning the pictures of starlets, Ilusorio was interested in two things: her looks and her salary. He settled on a former Nashville church organist who had done bit parts in soap operas and B-movies. She had a pretty face and, most important to the frugal Ilusorio, an attractively low salary. The only question was whether she was too mature for the part. By Christmas Dovie Beams, thirty-six on her birth certificate but twenty-four on her Hollywood bio, was on her way to Manila to star in what would turn out to be much more than a movie.

At about the time of Dovie's arrival in Manila, a group of eleven Maoist revolutionaries was meeting secretly in a remote region of Pangasinan province one hundred miles north to form the new Communist party of the Philippines. Its founder, Jose Maria Sison, a member of the leftist KM student movement, called for armed struggle to overthrow a government he said represented only the interests of American imperialists and wealthy Philippine landowners. But it was a call to revolution by a ragtag band of unarmed ideologues, more audacious than menacing.

Meanwhile, a few peasant insurgents still active under the Huk banner were looking for help in their faltering struggle to force land reforms or mount a peasant uprising. The Huks originated during the American colonial period prior to World War II, opposing the feudal concentration of landownership. They fought a fierce guerrilla campaign against the Japanese. After the war General MacArthur refused to send U.S. troops against them, saying that had he been born a Filipino peasant he, too, would likely be a Huk. But in the 1950s, forces of the Philippine republic, with American CIA assistance, captured or killed top Huk leaders and drove remnants of the rebel groups into the mountains. The Huks were virtually extinct by 1969. Among those that remained were a number who had retired to simple banditry or criminal protection rackets. The CIA compared the Huks who operated outside Clark Air Force Base to gangsters of the Al Capone era in Chicago. Internecine conflicts resulted in Huk leaders fighting or betraying each other. One who retained his revolutionary zeal was Bernabe Buscayno of Tarlac, the one they called "Commander Dante."

In another round of secret meetings, Sison and Dante agreed to join forces — the ideologues and the fighters. Thus was born in March 1969, the New People's Army. It was a misnomer. The NPA was hardly an army. It began with thirty-seven guerrillas sharing thirty-five guns. In 1969, that was the sum of what comprised "the Communist threat to the Philippines." Nonetheless, a bogeyman was born.

The presidential election campaign of 1969 had a significant new element: the helicopter. Ninoy Aquino had used it earlier in his successful Senate race. Now, Marcos rode the mechanical whirlwinds from island to island, swooping down in bursts of swirling dust and debris to meet isolated villagers. Some had never traveled on anything faster than the plodding carabao, the domesticated water buffalo that powered their carts and plows.

Marcos could visit a dozen towns in a day, often speaking without benefit of microphones or amplification systems, his baritone seldom wavering. He avoided cold drinks, sipping only tap water, he said, to protect his throat. But he did suffer one campaign injury at a helipad in Negros Occidental when he was jostled by an eager crowd and sprained his ankle. Pain interrupted his campaigning. Nothing else did.

Certainly not the noise of student protesters — prompting occasional clashes with security forces. At a speech to graduating officers of the Philippine Military Academy, the president mentioned, as if in passing, that one option for dealing with unrest was to impose martial law.

Nor "the Salas crisis" — set off when his popular executive secretary abruptly resigned and moved to New York. A flurry of press accounts speculated about a rift in the administration, about meddling by Imelda and her brother Kokoy Romualdez, about the suddenly doubtful future of the vaunted rice program. Publicly, Salas said only that he was taking a job with the United Nations. Privately, he confided his most troubling discoveries of sweeping administration corruption to one man: Ining Lopez, the powerful owner of the *Chronicle* and brother of the vice-president. With that, the seeds of a titanic feud were sown.

But the Marcos reelection was never in doubt. His Liberal party opponent, Sergio Osmena, Jr., was a lackluster senator with strong support only on his home island of Cebu. His father had been the last president of the commonwealth, losing in his bid to become the first president of the republic in 1946. Marcos sent the son to a similar defeat. It was the margin that surprised many: nearly two million votes. Hints of fraud grew to loud accusations. It became clear that Marcos was not content with certain victory. He had stolen enough votes to record a landslide.

Huge sums of money went into the campaign. Osmena would have spent more than he did except that on the weekend before Tuesday's election Marcos suddenly declared that Monday would be a bank holiday. Consequently, on the last day of the campaign Osmena could not withdraw any cash from his accounts. Meanwhile, Marcos kept the pesos flowing to the last hour. By the time he appeared on television to declare a victory that he said "speaks well of the future of our political institutions," the incumbent had spent more than $50 million. It would soon be apparent that one victim of that spending orgy was the suddenly ailing Philippine peso.

Inauguration Day, December 30, 1969, dawned with threats of

showers and demonstrations. The arrival of U.S. Vice-President Spiro T. Agnew a day earlier had been marred by a riotous reception on Roxas Boulevard outside the U.S. embassy. Someone hurled an explosive device at Agnew's car. It went off harmlessly. Police charged into a crowd of about six hundred to arrest two university students. The truncheon-wielding riot squad injured several youths and some journalists. Agnew was getting accustomed to angry receptions. His acerbic verbal assaults on U.S. antiwar activists as "an effete corps of impudent snobs" had made him a lightning rod for criticism in the States. He dismissed the Manila incident as the work of a few rambunctious students. But the demonstrations embarrassed Marcos.

At noon on the Luneta Park grandstand, however, Marcos noticed only the demonstrations of loyalty, respect, and affection. World leaders stood in his honor. Military units strutting to martial music saluted him. A camera captured Imelda's adoring glance. He stepped to the podium to a thunderous ovation from tens of thousands of spectators who had transformed Luneta's grassy expanse into a sea of friendly faces.

Marcos began his second inaugural address: "When I first assumed the presidency, we found a government at the brink of disaster and collapse, a government that prompted fear before it inspired hope; plagued by indecision, scorned by self-doubt, its economy despoiled, its treasury plundered, its last remaining gleam shone to light the way to panic. But panic we did not."

He assured his nation that the Philippines had passed from beneath "that terrible cloud" and was on its way to recovery; that even a nation with a legacy of poverty could be rich in dignity and freedom; that neither wealth nor power would purchase privilege; that a difficult future required the people and their leaders to have big dreams.

The second inaugural, like the first, had echoes of Kennedy-esque oratory. In the heart of his speech Marcos put a twist on the words of assassinated U.S. Senator Robert Kennedy when he told his audience: "There are too many of us who see the things as they are in this world and complain. Let us instead see the things as they should be and aspire. Let us dream the dream of what could be and not the dream of what might have been. There are many things we do not want about our world. Let us not just mourn them. Let us change them."

Finally, in a rousing conclusion that brought another round of thunder from the crowd, the president boomed: "We shall prove . . . the wave of the future is not totalitarianism but democracy."

It was a triumphant day, despite an occasional glimpse of protesters. A day at the pinnacle. A dizzying schedule of pomp and festival continued into New Year's Eve. The days of crowds and spectacle, of anthems and oratory, all came down to one last inaugural ball, a party in the Forbes Park estate of Ining Lopez to honor the president and visiting foreign dignitaries. Champagne toasts. Music. The sweet bouquet of success in the air of a tropical winter's evening.

Just as the new year approached, Ferdinand and Imelda slipped away from the elegant crowd, retreating to family and the stillness of Malacanang where the children — Imee, Irene, and Bongbong — waited to greet 1970 with a clutch of sparklers and fireworks. It would be a small party in the garden by the palace fountain — Spiro and Elinor Agnew the only outside guests. At the stroke of midnight the sparklers ignited. Dark waters of the fountain reflected the hissing sprays of orange and yellow glitter, harmless fire, falling around the feet of children and world leaders. In the echoing garden of Malacanang, the new decade was ushered in with a shower of sparks and laughter.

It was January 1, 1970. Ferdinand Marcos was going to bed the twice-elected president of a democracy. The apparent beloved leader. Pride of Ilocos Norte. Toast of Manila. Hero of the Philippines. America's "right arm in Asia." Devoted father and husband. It was a moment to savor — and to record. Before turning out his bedside lamp, the president reached for a pen and a sheet of palace stationery. And he wrote:

> I start a daily written record of my second term in office as president. . . .

It was page one of the presidential diary. And page one of an extraordinary chapter in the chronicles of power.

CHAPTER TWO
Another Coffin

He saw the crowd first. A blur of placards and raised fists beyond the portico of the Legislative Building. He paused in the shadows of soaring Corinthian columns atop the stone steps to survey the scene. Beyond a cordon of helmeted riot police sprawled twenty thousand young demonstrators, engulfing the House of Congress, spilling out into P. Burgos Boulevard, making a spectacle of their demands: to investigate vote fraud, to create a nonpartisan constitutional convention, to reduce American influence in the Philippines, to hasten land reform for the poor.

Then the crowd saw him. "Marcos!" the cry went up. The president's anxious security men edged closer, urging Ferdinand Marcos down the steps toward a waiting limousine. "Marcos, puppet!" some shouted. "Marcos, puppet!" others joined. Immediately, the epithet became a chant — twenty thousand voices taunting in unison.

Suddenly, a large black object appeared, rising from the mob, supported overhead by dozens of extended arms. It passed from one set of hands to the next, finally on a course straight for the cluster of presidential security forces. Police and security guards strained to identify what looked like a black torpedo skipping through a sea of shirt sleeves. The black box was a coffin.

Ancient Filipino corpses, embalmed and scented with herbs and perfumes, were escorted to their final resting place in similar coffins borne by villagers who, along the way, chanted the glories and virtues of the dearly departed. But the boisterous crowd outside Congress on January 26, 1970, was in a mood to bury Marcos, not to chant his praises.

Instinctively, riot police moved to intercept the oncoming coffin, their truncheons raised as they advanced on the crowd. A collective cry of disapproval and anger exploded, and with it came a rain of stones and bottles. In that last instant before the crude missiles descended, in that last instant before flesh and glass were shattered, what was left of Camelot ceased.

It had been a stormy honeymoon for the reinstalled administration since the first day of the new year. The economy was so bad that Marcos had ordered a halt to all public works projects and was resisting strong international pressure to devalue the peso. The press, especially the *Manila Times* and the Lopez family's *Chronicle*, blamed him for the mess. The landslide vote count was generating more skepticism than respect. Roger "Bomba" Arienda, the most popular political commentator on Manila radio and television, attacked it as "the rape and death of Philippine democracy." Osmena had filed a formal appeal to overturn the results. Criticism was coming even from the Church, where priests who worked with the poor published an open letter to the president urging action to ease the plight of peasants.

In the first week following his inauguration, a frustrated but self-righteous Marcos complained about the general state of society, writing:

> But I have been asking myself why has the world become so vile, so materialistic, so dirty. All is pragmatism, selfish and unedifying. Why is there no more tenderness — all sex? Why is there no more charity — all malice?

Despite the increasing vehemence of verbal and political attacks on his administration, Marcos was not prepared for the physical violence that confronted him outside Congress on January 26. He had just delivered what he regarded as the very best of his annual State of the

Nation speeches. Inside, he had received an ovation from the predominantly Nacionalista members. Outside, he encountered the jeers — and then worse.

Caught on the open steps as the fusillade of rocks and bottles crashed around them, the presidential party surged for the limousine door. Imelda fell behind. Colonel Fabian Ver, the president's boyhood Ilocano friend and dour chief of palace security, tried to shield Marcos. Another bodyguard was hit above the left eye, splattering blood on Ver's white barong. He shoved the president toward the open car door. As Marcos recalled in his diary that evening:

> I could not go into the car as Imelda kept standing on the stairs. Col. Ver tried to push me inside but I ordered the First Lady to be fetched and put inside first. Since she could not be pulled by anyone, I had to do it myself. I am afraid I pushed her into the car floor much too hard. Anyway, I bumped my head behind the right ear against the car's door side and twisted my weak right ankle again. We moved out under a hail of stones.

The president's departure did not end the violence. Indeed, it intensified. Riot squads pursued fleeing students. Fighting raged for more than two hours, a frenzy of beatings and blood-letting that stunned the nation. The press decried what it called excessive police force against unarmed demonstrators. Public sympathy for the students spread.

For many students the demonstrations had been a lark, a slightly daring but reasonably harmless way for rebellious youths to assert themselves in a society that still exalted the role of elders. They called their rallies "the parliament of the streets," but few were dedicated ideologues like the KM's Jose Sison. And few really believed they might be assaulted by their government. Many were children of the oligarchy, the sons and daughters of the richest and most influential families in the Philippines, some sharing a collective guilt for their comfort in a land of hopeless poverty. Most were unaccustomed to harsh treatment, but the truncheon was no respecter of wealth or position. Their shock, and subsequent anger, from seeing friends and classmates clubbed to the verge of death transformed the student protest movement. Out of their outrage were born new radicals. Out of the violence was born more violence.

In Malacanang that afternoon, Marcos watched televised news coverage of the riots. The disturbing images on his screen seemed ill omens for his political agenda, a threat to his private dream — a dream that the Philippine people would clamor for his leadership, would demand as if in one voice that he remain in office beyond the constitutional limit of two consecutive terms.

Already, plans for a constitutional convention were well under way, and it seemed likely that a new national charter would be drafted sometime during his second term, a document that could simply eliminate the current limit in time for Marcos to campaign again in the 1973 election. Another possibility was creation of a new form of government. Under a British-model parliamentary government controlled by the Nacionalista party, Marcos might be able to serve indefinitely as a prime minister.

Barely inaugurated to his second term, Marcos again was thinking ahead to reelection. Still, a rewritten constitution offered no guarantee of a Marcos election victory. What if the flickering television pictures represented flickering popular support for the president? What if criticism in the headlines reflected criticism in the countryside? Before the riotous aftermath of his State of the Nation address, Marcos had taken solace in the assurances of friends, acquaintances, and visitors such as Richard M. Nixon's biographer Earl Mazo.

> [H]e says Imelda and I are so high above the newspapers and the crowd now that we should not be concerned what the papers print, because if it is bad, the people will not believe it anyway.

And he found comfort in the kind remarks of those who greeted him during public appearances. After an early January 1970 Rotary Club speech about new economic policies, Marcos noted:

> I can feel the confidence surging back to our people. Standard remark was: "We did not know this was being done. We are glad he is president." Soft-soap, but gratifying.

On the other hand, Marcos loathed criticism. In fact, when he stepped out of Congress for what turned out to be the first stage of a street riot, the president still was smarting from what he considered a hostile opening prayer. It was one thing to read his alleged shortcomings in headlines printed for public consumption. It was particularly galling to hear them enumerated before Providence. Furthermore, the proceedings in Congress were being broadcast over loudspeakers to the streets.

"With us into this hall, O God, we bring the growing fears, the dying hopes, the perished longings of a people . . . ," intoned Father Pacifico Ortiz, Jesuit head of Ateneo de Manila University and a life-long advocate for the poor. He solicited divine guidance to make the streets safer from crime, the countryside safer from goon squads, the poor safer from the ravages of spiraling prices, to spare the nation from revolution. His prayer began with all heads reverently bowed. It ended with Marcos erect, glaring at the clergyman. Afterward Marcos wrote:

> The invocation . . . was in poor taste. It castigated the government, referring to . . . how the citizens were ready to fight for their rights even in the barricades. . . . I hope he is happy with what he has helped to bring about.

In considering who was responsible for the riots, Marcos looked beyond the riot squad, beyond his own administration policies, beyond questionable campaign results, beyond the spirit of rebellious youth. He blamed nonstudent extremists for exploiting the youthful demonstrators. He blamed the press for poisoning public sentiment. And, finally, he blamed the prayer of a priest.

In the sanctuary of Malacanang Marcos called in press secretary Kit Tatad to analyze how the media were going to treat the story, to consider its impact on the government. The president was tense. Tatad had never seen that. The conversation lapsed into long periods of silence. Marcos brooded, gazing past Tatad. The muscles in his jaw twitched. He talked to himself, a mumble inaudible to the young aide. Then he nodded as if responding to himself.

Tatad was astonished, troubled. This was a president normally cool and calculating in every crisis. A leader who never revealed anxiety to a subordinate. But as darkness settled over Malacanang that night, this was a changed man. Confused. Anxious. A leader who never would recover completely from that unexpected and profound encounter with fear and humiliation on the steps of Congress.

Late in the day a grim Marcos huddled with Colonel Ver and other security advisers. The latest intelligence reports blamed a small group of radical KM students for starting the violence. What about the coffin? It turned out to be cardboard. It belonged to "Bomba," the political commentator Roger Arienda. Marcos knew him well. The same coffin had been an anti-Marcos prop for one of his previous evening shows on Channel 11.

Another report troubled him more, especially in light of the day's violence. It was the American rumor. The one suggesting that the U.S. embassy was secretly supporting advocates of a coup attempt against Marcos. Shades of Saigon, 1963? Marcos saw images of assassinated South Vietnamese President Ngo Dinh Diem. Lyndon Johnson had called Diem the "Winston Churchill of Asia." Then the CIA had backed his overthrow. On this night, America's "right arm in Asia" was feeling especially insecure. Diem's collapse had come after his popularity plunged amid street riots and police beatings of middle-class and affluent student protesters.

The president's advisers quietly recommended stern measures. Marcos mulled it over. Retiring for the night, the troubled president was sure of one thing: It was time to polish up what he called "the emergency plan."

Morning restored the president's energy and veneer of confidence. He was on the offensive, meeting with top police and constabulary officials to order a critique of riot squad conduct. He also wanted all criminal charges dropped against any students arrested the night before. Diem had made no such gesture of peace and reconciliation.

At 10:45 that morning, Tuesday January 27, Marcos received American Ambassador Henry A. Byroade. A relative newcomer to Manila, Byroade was the tall, dashing career diplomat known as "the John Wayne" of the foreign service. President Richard M. Nixon had sent him to the Philippines five months earlier, just in time for the presidential campaign. Byroade had a reputation as a ladies' man and a maverick, popular attributes for any man in the macho Philippines. And popular attributes with Marcos who identified with the same traits. He and Byroade seemed to hit it off well from the outset, but Marcos had his reservations. Remember Diem! Despite the message of placards calling him a *tuta* of America, Marcos nurtured a deep distrust of the United States. Confronting Byroade with the coup rumors, Marcos was "a little relieved" by the ambassador's response:

> He seemed stunned and said he was greatly concerned. . . . He said as long as he & Nixon were in position we would not be fighting Americans.

Next, to deal with the troublemakers. Arienda, the political commentator, was summoned to Malacanang for an evening meeting with the president. A swaggering, pugnacious character — acutely aware of his own popularity — the man Manila knew as "Bomba" arrived with a tape recorder in one hand and a pistol contemptuously jammed into his hip pocket, by his own account "the picture of a rebel and a spoiled mediaman." A presidential aide blanched on seeing the gun. Marcos ignored it. Coffee was served. The president scowled. "What happened yesterday, Roger?"

The moderate National Union of Students of the Philippines (NUSP) had organized the demonstration primarily to dramatize concerns about next year's constitutional convention. Their message was intended for the president and for lawmakers of all partisan stripes: "Keep your hands off our constitution." They demanded a nonpartisan convention. They feared the president would use it to remove term limits. Other groups, including the radical KM crowd, had joined the rally. But it was a peaceful demonstration — until the coffin appeared. Arienda's coffin.

"Ah . . . !" Marcos seemed amused. "I see you're not through protesting, uh — what did you call it in the last election? The rape and death of democracy!" The two men smiled. Arienda could not help himself. He was enjoying the attention. After nearly an hour of increasingly amiable conversation, Marcos got to the point. "Can't we be friends . . . ?" It had been an odd contest. Another attempt by the president to neutralize opposition with charm and an offer of his powerful friendship. Marcos often met critics one-on-one. He trusted his charm. Arienda feared it. "Mr. President —" he said slowly, with a tone of conciliation. "You are not and have never been a personal enemy. . . ." Marcos seemed pleased. They shook hands.

The next night "Bomba" appeared on television to deliver his regular commentary — his first since the riot, his first since the private meeting in Malacanang. Had the president's appeal turned critic into friend? More student demonstrations were being planned and Marcos was looking for ways to defuse the anger, both in the streets and in the press. Would the Arienda meeting help?

"Two days ago I heard a group of students, the *Kabataang Makabayan*, yelling 'down with fascism,' the television commentator began, his dark features filling the screen. "I didn't know what that meant until I saw a policeman hit a student — and keep on hitting and hitting him, even after he was down." Into his measured tones crept the unmistakable tinge of anger.

"Now I know the meaning of fascism. And I shout with contempt at the people up there — Fascists! You are all fascists!" The commentator was raging now, pledging to be in the streets with his young *kababayan* (countrymen), vowing that "no amount of superior fascist force can frighten us. No one can stop the power of the parliament of the streets!"

Marcos braced for more criticism. He began to wonder about his ability to maintain law and order, about the loyalty of his military, about his own personal safety. Rumors became demons. A soothsayer predicted the president would be assassinated before April by "a light-skinned man wearing a suit." Marcos ordered security improved at the palace. He drafted a list of his enemies. He brooded about the future. And he wrote:

> The pattern of subversion is slowly emerging. The danger is now apparent to me but not to most people.

It was the counsel of loyal aide Colonel Ver that the president "meet force with force and that the conspirators be eliminated quietly before they prejudice our country and democratic institutions." That held some appeal to Marcos. He noted in his diary that he was considering the option of preemptive arrest to seize suspected plotters. But he feared unleashing a wave of uncontrollable violence. He chose to wait.

Meanwhile, the notion of authoritarian control posed more than theoretic appeal. If violence intensified or attempts were made to assassinate or topple him, he could declare martial law, he wrote. He could then round up and arrest all the suspects. And who were they? On January 28, 1970, who was on the president's list of suspected subversives?

Yellow journalists and "pink intellectuals, writers, professors and students and fellow travelers." On the night that "Bomba" shouted "Fascist!" at him through his television screen, the president's diary entry predicted more violence and unrest:

> I am certain this is just the beginning. The newspapermen I have on my list are busy placing the government in disrepute and holding it in contempt before the people . . . [resulting in] the slow chipping at the people's confidence in government authority.
>
> If we do not prepare measures of counter-action, they will not only succeed in assassinating me but in taking over the government.
>
> So we must perfect our emergency plan.

Despite the outburst of violence and unrest, despite the assault on his popularity ratings, Marcos found satisfaction in one aspect of the tumultuous events. Student demonstrators, he noted, seemed to want a parliamentary form of government. It was characteristic of Marcos the lawyer to turn adversity to advantage. He embraced the students' goals.

> If I want to be perpetuated in power, this is the easier way to it, with a constitutional provision that there shall be no elections unless a majority of all members of a unicameral legislature should adopt a formal resolution asking for such elections — and the powers of the Prime Minister are those of the President now.

On January 29, faculty members from the University of the Philippines marched on Malacanang to deliver a manifesto. It blamed the Marcos administration for a "pattern of repression" exemplified by the brutal police response to demonstrators outside Congress. Marcos invited a delegation to his office. But his first efforts to charm misfired. "This manifesto is not written in the best English," he lightly scolded, considering his remark an attempt at humor. "I thought it would start some laughter," he said later. No one laughed. They were offended.

Incensed by their impudence, Marcos accused them of suborning violence and fostering subversion. He expressed disappointment that his alma mater had become "the spawning ground of communism." He wondered aloud if one particular professor in the room had directed fellow members of the Bertrand Russell Peace Foundation to prepare Molotov cocktails for a demonstration scheduled the next day. Marcos read from a supposed intelligence report on his desk concerning the pacifist-oriented peace group and the professor. The delegation was infuriated. The tense session ended with a gesture of conciliation, however, when one teacher stood and said she had faith in the administration's goodwill. Acrimony clung to the moment, but Marcos smiled. The meeting adjourned.

The president's last chance to cool seething passions and temper dissent before Friday's massive student rallies was to negotiate directly with the students. He did not relish the prospect. He was tired of being rebuffed. And politics aside, he was rankled by students chanting obscenities so loudly outside the palace in recent days that they were keeping his family awake. Nonetheless, Marcos consented to granting the students a presidential audience. Better to parry words than weapons.

Late Friday afternoon, January 30, Edgar Jopson and his student delegation were admitted to Malacanang. Already, demonstrations were under way across the Pasig, at the scene of Monday's riot outside Congress. With every moment it seemed to gather size and energy. The crowd was nearing fifty thousand. Marcos understood that the protesters would not march on the palace, a concession by moderate leaders to minimize chances of another bloody confrontation with police.

The student leaders were escorted up a wide flight of stairs to the second-floor landing just outside the reception hall. There, Marcos kept them waiting. A large nineteenth-century oil painting by Filipino artist Juan Luna dominated the waiting area, the dark canvas of *El Pacto de Sangre* depicting the ritual of a blood contract, the pledge of eternal loyalty sealed by the symbolic spilling of blood. In fact, it was spilled blood that had brought the students to the second floor of Malacanang.

Edgar Jopson, president of the National Union of Students of the Philippines, was a management engineering student and top scholar at Ateneo, the Jesuit university. His father owned a grocery chain in Manila. Marcos liked bright young students. He had been one himself. And he knew Jopson's father. The president entered the meeting hopeful of conciliation. He would demand only that demonstrations be peaceful. A show of mutual respect should help matters.

Barely were the amenities of introduction concluded, however, when Jopson thrust a sheet of paper onto the desk in front of the president. The students clustered before his desk seemed overeager for his reaction. They showed no awe for the office of president. Marcos glanced at the paper. "You sign that," he heard Jopson demand. More impudence!

Jopson and his companions insisted that the president declare in writing that he would not seek a third term in Malacanang. It was not a polite request. With calculated calmness, Marcos shrugged. The constitution already barred another term. Other student voices, sarcastic and impatient, demanded that he leave the constitutional convention alone, that he endorse no changes to eliminate term limits. An angry Marcos smiled. Coolly, he assured his guests that, as he had said in many public forums, he had no intention of seeking another election.

"We don't believe you!" Jopson shouted. Other ragged voices agreed. The group was getting unruly. One insult to presidential dignity followed another.

"I don't believe you either!" Marcos retorted, turning angrily on the grocer's son. "Why are you so arrogant? Is this what the groceries produce?"

Yes, he was the son of a grocer, Jopson snapped back. But "at least my father is an honest grocer." Could Marcos claim to be an honest president? Insult upon insult. They had come not to listen, but to lecture. Again, they demanded a signed declaration. Marcos exploded.

Before they were ejected, other students called for a recess. After the break, his composure restored, Marcos assured the students that he would be willing to sign such a declaration someday — but only voluntarily. "I won't do it under coercion."

"But do you promise not to run again?" pressed the students. Marcos said he would not even answer the question. "I know you already have little respect for me and would have even less if I so much as gave weight to your arrogant demand." There was nothing more to be said. Marcos called in the palace photographer to record handshakes and smiles.

Across the Pasig the massive crowd of fifty thousand outside Congress had talked enough to each other. The speeches had grown more indignant, more contemptuous. Fascism and abuse of authority, themes of the day, had only one target. "Malacanang!" a voice called from the crowd. Another voice echoed the shout. It erupted as a thunderous chant: "Malacanang! Malacanang! Malacanang!"

At that moment, outside the palace where high fences lined the perimeter of Malacanang's spacious grounds, a small group of leftist *Kabataang Makabayan* students kept a vigil by candlelight. As they clustered near the palace gates, their flickering candles cast dancing shadows on the centerpiece of their demonstration — a black box with a sign inscribed: "Democracy."

The coffin was back.

CHAPTER THREE
Night Frights

Ferdinand Marcos heard the commotion on his way to a late dinner alone, as was common, in the family dining room. Shouts of alarm and explosions somewhere out in the darkness surrounding Malacanang. Firecrackers? Gunshots? Grenades? He pushed open a window to investigate. Immediately, it was clear the booming reports came from something more substantial than firecrackers. Pillboxes, most likely. The newspapers and his military advisers called them pillboxes — small containers or balls of aluminum foil filled with gunpowder and sometimes metal scraps. Homemade grenades, crude but potentially harmful.

The president, still dressed in his customary barong after the rancorous meeting with students, stood at the window trying to see the source of an ominous glow on Jose P. Laurel Street, the broad avenue running along the Malacanang perimeter. If it was a bonfire, the flames were a little too close to the residence for comfort.

Marcos sent an aide to call gate security officers for a report. Another was dispatched to see that Imelda and the children stayed together in one room where they could be located quickly. They might be forced to evacuate the palace.

Plink! One of the glass lamps atop the palace wall was struck by a slingshot marksman. *Plink! Plink!* More were being broken. Someone in the palace hit a switch and the entire bank of mercury vapor lights suddenly went dark, plunging the grounds into deep shadows. Then a different kind of light sailed over the walls — a fiery Molotov cocktail, smashing into the grounds and spilling liquid flames.

Marcos felt uncommonly vulnerable. If his guards gunned down rampaging students, the political backlash could be severe. Nor was he confident of his military's loyalty. Some were suspected of having friendly relations with Ninoy Aquino and various other political rivals, of the right and the left. And what if the CIA was behind the trouble? Government agents who infiltrated demonstrations earlier in the day reported seeing Americans in the crowds. Who could be trusted?

The president summoned his closest friends: Colonel Fabian Ver, the chief of palace security, and Juan Ponce Enrile, then his justice secretary. Top military aides also were called. At first he could locate neither Ernesto Mata, his secretary of defense, nor General Manuel Yan, his military chief of staff. The president wondered who might be plotting against him.

Meanwhile, out on Jose P. Laurel Street the siege of Malacanang escalated. A Manila city fire crew tried to hose down a bonfire with a weak spray of water, but demonstrators commandeered their truck. Then, to cheers from the crowd, the truck groaned toward the locked iron doors of Gate 4. The big truck hit the gate, backed up and rammed it again and again. Finally the truck broke through as palace guards retreated. At first, only a few students followed into the palace grounds. Guards fired warning shots over their heads. Then, hundreds of shrieking, rock-throwing students poured through the breach. In moments, the northern half of Malacanang, with its administrative office building and palace medical clinic, was overrun. Glass shattered. The fire truck burst into flame.

Next, Gate 3 came under assault, posing a more serious threat to the immediate security of the palace's nearby residential quarters. A constabulary major called the president from the palace grounds. "Permission to fire on the intruders," he requested. Marcos hesitated. Could he imagine how the newspaper photos would look? Of bodies strewn around Malacanang? Of dead children on the doorstep of the president? "Permission granted to fire your water hoses," he finally responded. "Pour as much water on them as you can." Tear gas was held in reserve. Prevailing winds were toward the president's quarters. Troops were ordered to push the demonstrators back but not to fire any shots at students inside the palace walls. There must not be a Malacanang massacre.

At that moment, Manila seemed on the brink of revolution or civil war. Marcos struggled to understand the animosity of the crowd, the venom of press criticism, the frustrating growth in popularity of his political rivals. Had he not won election only three months before? How could he explain such a precipitous loss of public support? It must be the Communists. Perhaps it was time for a cataclysmic show-down.

The president disappeared into his private chambers for a few moments of solitude. When he returned, he no longer wore his customary barong. Now, dressed in military fatigues, he was the commander in chief — ready for a fight.

A group of Ilocano congressmen rushed into the palace. They had heard about the rioting on radio news bulletins and had come immediately to offer moral support. And machine-gun support. They arrived with bodyguards and weapons of their own. The group, including congressmen Roque Ablan, Jr., of Laoag and Floro Crisologo of Vigan, stayed near the Marcos family. The palace was transformed into an armed garrison. Soldiers. Security guards. Congressmen. Private bodyguards. Even Justice Secretary Enrile carried a machine gun. At one point press secretary Kit Tatad scanned the assembled palace crowd and realized he was the only man in sight without a uniform or a gun.

The squawk of walkie-talkies was incessant, with commanders on the grounds reporting conditions outside and requesting orders from the president. Eventually, water hoses and truncheons drove the students back through the damaged gate and into the streets. The palace no longer was under siege. But the war of the streets was only beginning.

Mendiola Avenue is a major side street leading away from the palace. It literally begins at the Gate 4 entrance to Malacanang and extends northwest through "student row" and the university district of Manila's old San Miguel neighborhood. Over the next few hours, Mendiola Avenue and old San Miguel became a battleground where the relatively polite rules of Malacanang no longer applied. Not all the shots went overhead. No longer was the water hose the weapon of choice. Hundreds of helmeted Metrocom riot police moved into the streets, joined by military troops held in reserve.

The violence started slowly. Taunts. Vandalism. Rock throwing. Someone poured gasoline on the street and lit it. Finally, a shot rang out. "They're shooting us down!" someone yelled. The crowd broke. Screaming students fled up Mendiola Avenue, leaving a trail of broken glass and damaged cars. "Revolution! Revolution! Down with Marcos!" the crowd shouted. The acrid aroma of burning tires blended with the choking vapors of tear gas. Cries of protest mingled with screams for vengeance. Fear and anger shared the shadows.

At an overpass called Mendiola Bridge, one of the most prominent demonstrators in the crowd, "Bomba" Arienda, pulled out a carbine, raised it in classic revolutionary style, and declared: "This area is liberated. Get the Fascists out!" The television personality and political commentator whom Marcos had tried to woo just days before was, at that moment, raving for the president's ouster. And waving a gun.

To most of the thousands of students running through the dark streets and alleyways of San Miguel, this had begun as something less than an ideological conflict. If war was an extension of diplomacy, then street demonstrations were an extension of intellectual debate. The crowds included radicals espousing armed rebellion, but most were moderates with strong democratic values. Most advocated peaceful reform through a constitutional convention. In campus debates, radicals and moderates battled one another. In the streets, radicals and moderates had a common foe: Ferdinand Marcos.

For students, this was an exhilarating period, a time of chaos and ferment when nothing was sacrosanct. There was a youthful passion for sometimes vaguely understood but strongly felt ideals — and for the sheer romance of rebellion. "We made love in the bushes then marched out to face our martyrdom in the streets," recalled radical student leader Nelson Navarro. It was a time, he said, when "in the words of the poet, everything was possible . . . and to be young was very heaven."

Then came the night of January 30, 1970, and the "Battle of Mendiola." History may never know who fired the first shots. Some protesters, like Arienda, were armed. But very few. Some of the president's own agents secretly infiltrated the student crowd and were among those encouraging violence. The diary shows that one of those secret agents, a palace informant named "Joe" whom the president mentioned often in his journal, was spotted inciting violence. Friends of Marcos, disturbed by what they witnessed but unaware that Joe was an undercover operative for the palace, reported his activities to the president. In their account to Marcos, recorded a few days later in his diary, the president's friends informed him that Joe was "urging students to attack at Mendiola and plying them with whiskey from a jeep without any [identifying license] number and loaded with whiskey bottles." But in his diary account of the incident, Marcos made no reference to Joe's Malacanang ties.

Whatever the ultimate provocation, a pitched battle finally erupted that night over control of Mendiola Bridge, a strategically meaningless concrete structure nonetheless adopted by the students as their "Maginot line," their front line of defense, their last line of retreat. There, the game of demonstration became a casualty of violence.

From the beginning, Marcos had much more to fear politically than physically from the students. There was no question his armed guards and the Metrocom police could withstand any assault by rock-throwing, placard-waving, pillbox-tossing vandals. But it was characteristic of Marcos to guess at hidden meanings in every message, to suspect a plot in any plan. Behind the student movement, he was sure, lurked sinister and exploitive forces. He could not forget Diem.

Sometime during the night the most troubling report arrived. A detachment of army regulars from Laur in Central Luzon had reached Manila and was headed for the palace. Marcos had not called for reinforcements. Could this be the coup? The president left nothing to chance. He ordered Ver's loyal palace guards and the Philippine Constabulary troops of his school chum General Vicente "Banjo" Raval deployed in defensive positions outside the palace. It was a false alarm. The army regulars had intended to come to their president's rescue in the tradition of the horse cavalry: flags flying, guns blazing. They arrived too late for the fighting — but in time to give Marcos the fright of the night.

Meanwhile, violence spread through the streets of Manila, bursting out of San Miguel into the commercial district of Quiapo, the area then commonly called "downtown Manila." Shoppers and moviegoers found themselves in the crossfire of armed troops and brick-throwing rioters. Buses, taxis, and jeepneys [a peculiar Filipino cross between a taxi and a tram] were commandeered. Some were overturned and burned. Bandits and street thugs joined the chaos, looting stores.

Back in Malacanang, Marcos still could hear the distant sounds of gunfire around 1:00 A.M. when he convened a meeting of top military advisers. Chief of staff General Yan had just arrived from a social engagement. After being contacted in exclusive Forbes Park, he had rushed to Fort Bonifacio to borrow a uniform and share a ride with army commander General Rafael "Rocky" Ileto. Inside the palace, Ileto noticed Defense Secretary Mata alone in a corner. He also noticed that Marcos still seemed shaken. The president wanted to strike back: to mount a counteroffensive against the radicals, to impose a 6:00 P.M. to 6:00 A.M. curfew, and to suspend the writ of habeas corpus in order to arrest suspected subversives without warrants. He even raised the possibility of declaring martial law. No one seemed willing to challenge the president's drastic proposals.

It fell to Ileto to try discouraging such action. The army, he told Marcos, was understaffed, poorly organized, and inadequately armed — it was simply too weak to guarantee success if significant resistance should occur. Ileto's army-reorganization plan, including a requisition for about eight thousand M-14 and M-16 rifles, had been languishing on the president's desk since the last days of the 1969 election campaign. His U.S.-model army-reorganization plan was the product of his West Point education and more recent military-affairs studies the year before at the University of Pittsburgh, a plan originally intended to help the army deal with lingering Huk problems. Without its implementation, Ileto insisted, the army was in no position to enforce martial law — the threat of which, he privately hoped, would ease with the passing of time and the current crisis.

In the president's private study, General Yan endorsed his army chief's caution. Defense Secretary Mata also seemed reluctant to take drastic steps. But no one directly opposed the president's plan.

No prudent person ever directly opposed any plan of Ferdinand Marcos. Wise aides or bureaucrats — even old friends — learned to be creative in expressing any view contrary to the president's. (Once, when Marcos refused to appoint a judge to the Supreme Court because of potentially explosive rumors of the jurist's extramarital affair, a mutual friend prevailed on the president to change his mind — not because he was wrong to be concerned, the friend hastened to assure, but because it made good political sense to appoint a man who already had learned his lesson and was unlikely to be similarly embarrassed while occupying the bench.) "You could never tell him he was wrong," says longtime friend and golfing crony Potenciano Ilusorio. "You could only suggest that there might be other ways to analyze the same information." In using such a tactic the night of the "Battle of Mendiola," General Ileto may have prevented an immediate declaration of martial law.

Before a smoky dawn arrived to end "Black Friday," four students fell dead from gunshot wounds. One was a young actor who before that night apparently had done nothing more daring than perform nude in a university production of the musical *Hair*. He was completely unknown to student leaders of all factions. But in the police floodlights on Mendiola Bridge he became an instant icon, a sainted member of the student movement: he was forever after one of "The Four Martyrs."

In his diary the next night, Marcos reflected on the violent events of Friday, January 30, with some impatience. Not over the incidents so much as over the frustrating limits on his response. Noting additional meetings with his military advisers as well as with political leaders, he wrote:

> Most felt there should be no repression. So I have had to delay the suspension of the privilege of the writ of habeas corpus. We will await developments. . . .
> In the meantime I can only gnash my teeth and wait.

He expressed pity for "the citizenry caught in the crossfire" of riot violence. But at the same time he recognized potential political advantage: perhaps people would sympathize more readily with the president if they were all victims of the same vandalism and destruction.

If such public sympathy existed, however, it was not reflected in the attitudes of Manila publishing executives. Called to the palace on Saturday to hear a discussion of the president's options, they made it clear that repressive measures would get no endorsement in their pages. Chino Roces of the *Manila Times* "seemed hostile" to the president, and Teddy Locsin, Sr., of the *Philippines Free Press* seemed too sympathetic to the demonstrators' goals of reform. Of Locsin, whose influential weekly news magazine had endorsed Marcos in both presidential elections and only days before had named him "Man of the Year," the president groused: "I had forgotten that he had always written sympathetically of Mao Tse-tung."

But Marcos ended his final January entry on a stoic note. He would be patient. Although the publishers and others warned that a campaign to arrest every suspected Communist leader might incite further violence, might turn Manila slums into jungles of subversion, he would not be dissuaded. Not indefinitely.

> If I let these fears deter me from fighting communism, then we are lost. But I must continue to restrain myself lest we lose the support of the people by a stance of tyranny.

CHAPTER FOUR
The Total Solution

That one traumatic week in January 1970 had left Ferdinand Marcos a deeply troubled man. Humiliated by the students who challenged him in the streets and privately frightened by the prospect of a coup, he felt weak and vulnerable. For the next three weeks, Marcos was a virtual prisoner of Malacanang, afraid to venture beyond its walls, anxious about the loyalties of everyone around him. He tried on new bulletproof vests and prepared for more serious assaults on his presidency.

Emergency remodeling projects were launched throughout the palace. The president's basement gymnasium was converted into a bunker, a fully stocked shelter with baffled walls to withstand mortar attacks. Outside, armored gun emplacements were constructed at the gates. The lawn west of the veranda was cleared and lights were installed, making it a helicopter landing zone. Overnight, new fences went up. Instant foxholes pockmarked the lush grounds. Press aide Kit Tatad, who grew increasingly concerned about the president's phobic isolation inside the palace, noticed new palm plants and shrubs on his daily walks around Malacanang. One morning when he stopped to take a closer look at some of the latest palace flora, he found it concealed "a machine-gun nest."

But it was not so easy for Marcos to construct defenses against other demons that plagued him: criticism, suspicion, and feelings of impotence. He had lost control. Student demonstrators, most of them not much older than his own children, ignored his pleas for moderation. They mocked his words, his authority, his very name. In Manila, where many affluent and middle-class families left for the provinces after the riots and looting of "Black Friday," there was doubt about the restoration of civil order. And the Four Martyrs of Mendiola loomed over the political landscape like menacing spirits.

When Congress reconvened on the Monday after the riots, the reeling Marcos suffered a devastating verbal broadside from his most eloquent and popular rival, Liberal party senator Ninoy Aquino.

"Four Filipino students are dead, Mr. President," Aquino began in his speech on the Senate floor. "They were shot, not by strangers, but by their own countrymen; not by invaders, but by the soldiers of their own government, by the guards of their own president. They were young students, not grizzled rebels — innocent, unarmed, defenseless. They were gunned down while fleeing from the presidential security forces, not while assaulting Malacanang and the president. . . ."

It was a defining moment in what was to become a titanic rivalry between two powerful and charismatic men, a moment that encapsuled their clash of philosophy, ambition, and oratory. Marcos was the target of student demonstrators; Aquino became their champion. Marcos was contemplating legal strategies to extend his term beyond the constitutional limit; Aquino had designs on succeeding him in the next election. Marcos spoke of restoring order; Aquino spoke of tolerating disorder.

"The greatest sin we in this chamber can commit today, Mr. President, is not to tolerate disorder by the youth but to allow them to be cowed and coerced," Aquino thundered from a Senate lectern as a gallery of journalists scribbled in notepads. "To allow our youth to be frightened will be a sin against our people, a sin against history, a sin against our future.

"To some historians, Black Friday will doubtless become the symbol of violence and vandalism. But to many students, it will represent a turning point that should have its place among the great moments of our history, when the Filipino youth rose out in righteous paroxysm against the machinery of a police state.

"It was a night when, armed only with slingshots and their idealism, they confronted foot soldiers of the Establishment armed with the most modern weapons of death. . . . They had laid siege on Malacanang not as the seat of government but as the factory of privilege in the Philippines. . . .

"The deaths of these four students have ushered in a revolution — not a revolution of arms but a revolution of ideas."

Aquino already had said enough to enrage the president. But he went further, turning to issues of graft, corruption, and fraud that would dog Marcos to his grave. That day on the Senate floor, Aquino made them part of his bill of indictment against the president and his administration. Like a Marc Antony speaking over Caesar's dead body, Aquino decried the vandalism, the damage inflicted by students estimated at 250,000 pesos (about $50,000). For this, he said, the nation was shocked. He, too, was shocked.

"But I ask, is the nation equally shocked by the excesses of its leaders? The students destroyed 250,000 pesos' worth of property Friday night, but these leaders have pillaged and ravaged the Republic down to its last dollar!

"Yes, the students broke some Malacanang gates. But is this the reason to break student legs and student arms? And what about the leaders who forced open the gates of the Philippine National Bank and the Central Bank for their private looting?"

Aquino said he was shocked also by the violence — not by the violence of the youths against property, but by the crushing force brought to bear against the students by heavily armed troops in armored personnel carriers. And in a declaration that roused cheering from the packed gallery and removed any hopes for bipartisan unity in the crisis, Aquino concluded:

"I stand with the students, Mr. President — not with Malacanang's tools of violence, not with Mr. Marcos's bloodthirsty troops. They are the fomenters of violence, the harbingers of unrest.

"Yes, Mr. President, we are gripped by crisis, a crisis fraught with danger to us all. But not the crisis born of the imagined conspiracies and conspirators of Mr. Marcos. Our crisis, sir, is a crisis of aspiration among our young and a crisis of conscience among their elders. How shall we respond?"

Rejecting any notion that he or his policies might be unpopular, Ferdinand Marcos responded as he commonly did — by finding someone else to blame. When there were complaints about corruption in his administration, Marcos blamed midlevel bureaucrats. The stumbling Philippine economy, staggering from his excessive election campaign spending, he blamed on the U.S. recession and American bankers who, he said, "have nothing but dollars for hearts." He caught a cold and blamed it on Imelda. Responding to the student riots, Marcos publicly blamed leftist subversives. Privately, he blamed his political rivals. In his diary he wrote:

> It seems clear now that the demonstrations and riots are engineered by the Liberal Party. . . .
> We must unmask these would be anarchists hiding behind children.

Marcos viewed the Aquino-led Liberals as his most urgent threat. In fact, it was his belief, apparently based on an amalgamation of rumors and suspicions, that the Liberal party intended to launch a coup attempt in July. And he had a feeling, he wrote, that Huk sabotage was going to occur and that it would be masterminded personally by Aquino. The diary shows that Marcos often had these "feelings" — feelings that some plot was in the making, that something significant was going to happen. He claimed, in fact, to have the gift of clairvoyance and telepathy, what in the diary he called his "strange capacity to receive messages."

He was sure that a group of retired military officers was plotting his assassination, but it is not clear how much he was relying on intelligence data or his own prescience. There was also, of course, the soothsayer's pending prediction that he would be the target of a light-skinned assassin in a business suit sometime before April.

Intrigue multiplied around him. In the streets, passions still ran high. Marcos saw no signs of relief from the unrest. Alone in the sanctuary of his study, where day and night the sounds of construction on new security installations reminded him of his personal vulnerability, he studied his books about Napoleon, Hitler, and communism. He brooded about who was to blame for his troubles. And he worried about losing public confidence. Marcos wrote:

We must calm everybody down as the rumors of a revolution are wide-spread and the rich of Forbes Park have fled their beautiful homes. . . . After the calm, we can then attend to the enemies of the Republic one by one.

In fact, as Marcos became increasingly preoccupied with determining who were the enemies of the Republic, his popular support was plummeting. But few Filipinos, least of all the proud and feisty Ilocano president himself, could have realized that barely a month after his triumphant inauguration Marcos already was well on his way to becoming the most unpopular chief executive in Philippine history. "The first president to be reelected and the first president to be stoned!" crowed a Liberal party senator.

It was against this backdrop and during his long February days of self-confinement in Malacanang that Marcos seemed to discover anti-communism as the antidote for his ailing political fortunes. Communist subversion, he would argue, was the single greatest threat to Philippine security, the common enemy of the president and his people, the justification for decisive — even drastic — emergency action.

The president's earliest views on communism seemed to parrot the anti-Communist jargon of the 1950s. He expressed them in a three-page diary entry on February 1, 1970, that he titled "Why I Am Fighting Communism." In a portion of that entry — ladened with irony when read in the light of history — Marcos wrote:

[C]ommunism does not allow such simple liberties as freedom of thought, speech and religion among many others. There is no such thing as dissent or debate or dialogue. . . .

Communism is a totalitarianism or a dictatorship by the elite who have acquired power through force, killing, murder and coercion. . . .

Correspondingly, the common people that communism is supposed to serve do not have any share in government nor in decision-making. Communism does not allow such simple processes as an election or voting or political campaigns. Everything is dictated by the few or the man on top who got there by force and violence. . . .

Communism ostensibly seeks to eradicate the ruling or influential oligarchies. But it succeeds in only replacing them with a worse group — the ruling or influential cliques and elites who actually rule without the approval or consent of the people.

It was true that before February 1970, Marcos consistently had taken anti-Communist positions. And he had earlier voiced concern about leftist insurgents. During his first term he had ordered his army and constabulary forces into an aggressive seek-and-destroy campaign against the scattered Huk bands of central Luzon. In successful negotiations with President Lyndon Johnson for millions of dollars in U.S. aid he had portrayed himself as an anti-Communist to exploit American concerns about Communist expansion in Southeast Asia.

But Marcos had not emerged as one of the outspoken voices of anticommunism in the Pacific. He was no Chiang Kai-shek. Indeed, his support for America's policy of Communist containment in Vietnam was sufficiently tepid that he finally incurred the wrath of a frustrated LBJ, who once stormed at a State Department official: "If you ever bring that man near me again, I'll have your head."

Suddenly, Marcos was a pulpit-pounding anti-Communist, preaching the evils of Marx, Mao, and Lenin with the fervor of a born-again believer. His conversion clearly was politically calculated — forced upon him, he conceded in his diary, by violent and militant students. On February 6 he wrote: "It has saddened me to be driven to the refuge of anti-communism and pro-Americanism."

In formulating his political and personal philosophy on the Communist menace, Marcos was influenced by the voices of history and contemporary political theorists — such disparate voices as Adolf Hitler and American conservative Jeane J. Kirkpatrick (who some years later would be President Ronald Reagan's ambassador to the United Nations).

From Kirkpatrick, who wrote an introduction and edited a collection of essays by other authors called *The Strategy of Deception*, a study of Communist party tactics around the world, Marcos embraced the thesis that Communists "in practice are less doctrinaire than expedient," that their only goal is to seize power. Marcos said democracies should not be fooled.

From Hitler, whose euphemistic and chilling "Final Solution to the Jewish Question" became the blueprint for the Holocaust, Marcos devised what he called the "total solution to the communist problem." The Marcos *total solution*, like the Nazi *final solution*, was envisioned to begin with mass arrests. He also wrote:

> I feel that ultimately we must have a confrontation with the commu-
> nists in this country. And that their eradication as a threat to our free
> way of life may be one of my main missions. . . . Now we have an
> opportunity — perhaps the only opportunity to liquidate the move-
> ment in one clean sweep — if we plan it well enough.

Marcos realized that he could more easily justify wholesale arrests
and the suspension of such constitutional protections as free speech
and legal due process if such actions were preceded by substantial
provocation — massive sabotage, for example, or an assassination attempt against the president. Destructive street rioting was another
possible provocation. A little more violence and vandalism, he mused
in the diary, "and I can do anything" to restore order.

Announcement of another major student rally, scheduled for February 12 in nearby Plaza Miranda, threatened more street distur-
bances — more violence and vandalism, more potential provocations
for implementing the *total solution*. And there were more warnings of
plots and intrigues, including one from a student activist who met
privately with the president on Sunday afternoon, February 8. Afterward, a receptive Marcos wrote:

> [He] warned of a takeover by the Jesuit-fascist-CIA combine. We really
> should warn our people of this.

As the next demonstration date approached, Marcos attended to
other pressing problems — the economy and his cabinet. Since the
night Malacanang was attacked, he had regarded Defense Secretary
Mata as "a security risk." Marcos, who rarely even sipped alcohol, said
Mata was drunk that night. The president turned over the defense
portfolio to close friend and aide Juan Ponce Enrile as part of a major
cabinet reshuffle completed on February 8. In his first term, Marcos
had impressed many with appointments of skilled technocrats. Now,
under fire, he was surrounding himself more with people he could
trust.

Meanwhile, outside the palace, a currency crisis was strangling the
economy. The nation's dollar reserves had been virtually exhausted
since the election. The peso's value was plunging on the black market.
Prices were rising. Conrad, the palace barber, a Marcos sounding
board for matters pertaining to the common man, told the president

that money was getting very scarce in Manila. The president's efforts to get loans through the International Monetary Fund were hung up by preliminary demands for peso devaluation. For Marcos, such tense times were particularly ill-suited for a potentially destabilizing surge of inflation.

Marcos turned to U.S. Ambassador Byroade for a measure of reassurance, asking if the Americans would support him in the event he had to fight Communist subversives. "He said they would," Marcos wrote. The beleaguered president also was concerned about what he regarded as the all-too-friendly relations of the Americans with Liberal party leaders, the critics he privately regarded as agents of subversion. And he worried about the CIA.

Byroade was quick with reassuring gestures. He offered American stores of tear gas to Marcos and agreed to try diverting five U.S. military helicopters destined for Vietnam and Thailand to the Philippines. And he extended the invitation of President Nixon to meet at the Western White House in San Clemente during the late summer. Marcos accepted, but all agreed to keep it secret for a time to minimize chances the news might precipitate anti-American demonstrations in Manila.

Still holed up in Malacanang on the eve of February 12, anticipating a highly charged student rally at Plaza Miranda, Marcos wondered if there would be enough violence to justify exercising his emergency powers. If not, he could "recast the plans for a total solution" to accommodate a prolonged and tedious legal battle. Clearly, that was not his first choice as he awaited developments at Plaza Miranda.

Plaza Miranda is a teeming public square in the heart of downtown Manila, reeking of filth and flowers and the pungent odors of sizzling food over open flames. Makeshift vending stalls dispense herb cures for every ill, amulets to thwart any evil, and chains of sweet-scented blossoms for those who come to venerate Jesus at the shrine of the Black Nazarene in the old Quiapo Church on the square. Here, too, is the unmistakable aroma of politics. Even in the modern era of televised campaigns, no serious politician would dare stand for election without coming face-to-face with the sweating public, the vocal masses, in the crucible of Plaza Miranda. The real test of any government policy was whether it could be defended at Plaza Miranda — the Hyde Park of Manila, the Peoria of the Philippines.

On February 12, 1970, the plaza was packed. Students, radicals, journalists, union members, peasants from the provinces, undercover security agents. The secret agents of Malacanang wore badges, of sorts — Band-Aids, prominently displayed on their foreheads — for quick and easy identification to any truncheon-wielding riot police.

As crowds and angry rhetoric filled Plaza Miranda, an Ilocano delegation streamed into Malacanang — congressmen, senators, governors, and their teams of armed bodyguards. If trouble came, they were ready and eager to help their president. If trouble did not come, they were willing to instigate it. Marcos said he dismissed their offer, noting in his diary that night: "I dissuaded them from infiltrating the demonstrators and inflicting harm on them."

But the president did have a request. Just as Hitler had dreamed of a Bavarian mountain redoubt, Marcos wanted an Ilocandia redoubt — "a last bastion, just in case" — from which to fight back if Communists drove him from Malacanang. He asked his northern political allies to "cache arms and ammo," and he disclosed a plan to double immediately the runway length at Laoag Airport in Ilocos Norte to accommodate military jets. The revolution may come during this administration, he warned. It was time to prepare for a military confrontation with the Communists.

No revolution would begin that night, however. At Plaza Miranda there were speeches filled with fighting words, but the action was peaceful. Student deaths had hardened anti-Marcos sentiment, but it also seemed to have injected a new soberness into the protest movement. Voices in the crowd that called for violence went unheeded. It was suspected that some who cried for blood wore Band-Aids on their brows.

Indeed, the peace was bittersweet for Marcos. That night he confided in his diary:

> For a time I secretly hoped that the demonstrators would attack the palace so that we could employ the total solution. But it would be bloody....

Marcos was growing a little more confident. On Sunday, February 15, he ventured out of the palace to speak before a Manila labor convention. The sound of applause gave his morale a badly needed boost. It was only the second time in two weeks that he had made a brief trip beyond Malacanang. He wrote that he intended to do so again soon. But he did not. Press secretary Tatad fretted about a serious public relations problem. People were starting to talk. Was Marcos afraid?

The president's paranoia clung to the palace like tropical humidity. Imagined plots and conspiracies were being sighted everywhere, some by the obsequious in pursuit of favors, some by worried family and friends. The president's mother, Josefa, sent him a letter warning of rumors she heard that Vice-President Lopez was plotting to kill him. Meanwhile, aides whispered suspicions about one another to the president. Colonel Ver privately accused one of the president's cabinet members, Labor secretary Blas Ople, of being a Communist leader and secretly orchestrating media attacks on the government. Marcos even encouraged such groundless speculation, noting that he agreed to keep an eye on his labor secretary. And he wrote:

> Blas is an enigma. . . . But it is best he is in the palace when there is a crisis. Then we can neutralize him or use him.

Not surprisingly, people around Marcos suddenly seemed compelled to reassure him of their own personal allegiances. The commanding general of the air force, Jose Rancudo, came for lunch at the palace and to swear undying loyalty. In fact, the general promised Marcos that if other elements of the military turned against the president, the air force immediately would send F-5 fighter jets into the air and, "within ten minutes," would blast key army installations. Three days later, Rancudo installed a direct communications link between his Fifth Fighter Wing headquarters and the president's Malacanang study. Marcos relished overt signs of devotion. About Rancudo he wrote:

> He said he is willing to fight even the Americans if necessary. I hurried to add that the Americans were on our side.

The temptation of authoritarian control still weighed on Marcos despite the apparent easing of street violence — and despite the latest intelligence information indicating that the New People's Army was not much of a threat, either. The Sison and Dante–led Maoist radicals lacked arms and were capable of manufacturing only crude, homemade bombs — a sign to Marcos that they were not getting any outside help from the People's Republic of China or from other foreign sources. Marcos was a little disappointed. Frankly, the NPA did not pose a significant enough threat to justify emergency measures. So, Marcos wrote: "We should allow them to gather strength, but not such strength that we cannot overcome them."

Political allies were pressing Marcos to take sterner measures against the student activists. Even peaceful street demonstrations were hurting business throughout Manila. Many union workers and taxi drivers, angered by price increases, openly sided with students in anti-Marcos rallies. As the president prepared reluctantly to sign an order setting the peso afloat in world currency markets, many Nacionalista party leaders wanted to blame the nation's economic crisis on the students. Over one private dinner at the palace, a group of Ilocano congressmen was blunt: they wanted the student movement crushed even if that required inciting violence by some means in order to justify a harsh military response. In his diary Marcos reported:

> The congressmen (about 15) who visited me are all agreed, the peaceful demonstrations are debilitating and the disorders must now be induced into a crisis so that stern measures may be taken.

More violence did come. During the night and early morning of February 18 and 19, rampaging demonstrators, many wearing white bandannas, attacked the American embassy compound shouting "Yankee, go home!" and "Imperialist pigs!" They hurled stones and fire-bombs, tore a large U.S. seal from an exterior brick wall, broke windows, and burned a guardhouse. Ambassador Byroade called Marcos for assistance, but the president — apparently preoccupied with concerns about an attack on Malacanang — referred the ambassador's urgent request to Manila Mayor Antonio Villegas. Finally, Byroade was forced to use his small U.S. Marine security detachment to repel the mob with tear gas grenades. The rioting then resumed in the nearby middle-class business district of Ermita, where stores, hotels, and restaurants were vandalized and firebombed.

American response was swift and angry. Byroade filed a formal protest the next day, deploring the "dereliction of responsibility for the security of the diplomatic mission of a friendly foreign government." And in a separate statement after meeting privately with Foreign Secretary Carlos P. Romulo, the U.S. ambassador expressed concern that the American embassy was "being treated as a defenseless hostage, routinely available for physical abuse." Byroade complained that no Philippine law-enforcement officers arrived until forty-five minutes after the embassy attack.

Not mentioned in those public statements was the suspicion in some circles, including the U.S. diplomatic corps, that Marcos welcomed and maybe even steered the violence toward the embassy and the Ermita commercial district. Was Marcos trying to generate more support for a crackdown on demonstrators? Public sentiment for "sterner measures" definitely was growing in some sectors of Manila. The Chamber of Filipino Retailers was demanding more government protection. Latin American ambassadors gave Marcos the impression that they "are all for a dictator coming out of this confusion." Conrad, the barber, said the people supported tougher tactics.

On Friday, February 20, Byroade and embassy official James Rafferty called on Marcos to express their concerns directly. The president was apologetic about the embassy damage, but rejected any official blame. He seemed amused by suggestions that he had schemed to entangle the United States in the demonstrations that so far had focused most of their hostile energies on Marcos.

> Those crazy Americans for a time thought that I had deflected the rallies from Malacanang to the U.S. Embassy to get them involved. Ridiculous!

On the same day that Byroade and Rafferty called on the palace, the *Manila Chronicle* broke the first detailed story that Marcos was privately considering imposition of martial law. Marcos welcomed the coverage. It was his trial balloon. He told the *Chronicle* that he would resort to martial law only "if it would redound to the upholding of our democratic institutions." But the Lopez-owned newspaper blasted "the evil of martial law" in a front-page editorial. And columnist Ernesto Granada attacked the president as "snake-like." The personal attack was not so welcomed. And the president's growing enemies list made room for columnist Granada. "He probably knows he is suspected as a communist by me," Marcos wrote, invoking the same trumped-up allegation the president often used to disparage the motivations of his critics.

Days passed with only sporadic violence. Another demonstration outside the U.S. embassy seemed to attract fewer students than Philippine security agents. It was peaceful. The protesters were "losing their steam," Marcos concluded.

It was time to heed Kit Tatad's increasingly urgent advice: resume routine travel, be seen outside the palace, act confident. Marcos chose to go north, to bask in an Ilocano welcome, a carefully planned counterdemonstration of personal and political support. Every official, from governors to mayors, turned out for the public exhibition of unity with their native son. For Tatad, it was more of a relief than a major public relations score. Finally, the president was out of his Malacanang bunker. For Marcos, it literally was liberating. He felt safe for the first time since he was stoned by the crowd outside Congress a month before. That night, February 25, he wrote:

> Very overwhelming affection and trust — so completely different from Manila.
>
> Rode in an open car — convertible with the top down. Imelda as usual was mobbed affectionately.
>
> Must go to the provinces more where the atmosphere is more representative of the nation.

After another spate of street demonstrations in Manila, the student movement went into virtual hibernation. The allure of the so-called revolution was no match for the attraction of spring vacation. Schools emptied. Streets emptied. Just as Marcos was beginning to feel that he could take tough action against the students, they were gone. No violence. No threats. And consequently, at least for the moment, no *total solution*.

Denied the impetus of external events to justify sterner measures against antigovernment groups, Marcos turned inward — looking for other signs, listening for other voices. He had another one of those feelings. Call it clairvoyance or telepathy or his self-described "strange capacity to receive messages," but in the waning days of what came to be called the *First Quarter Storm*, Marcos had a very real feeling of anticipation. A feeling of destiny. He wrote:

> I have that feeling of certainty that I will end up with dictatorial powers if the situation continues — and the situation will continue. . . .

Then, too, flickered the first glimmerings of a messianic flame. Marcos had entered the dark period of the *First Quarter Storm* as a politician "driven to the refuge of anti-communism" by his critics. But he emerged from the ordeal with a transformed self-image — from victim to savior. On March 9, 1970, Marcos wrote:

> I still feel that my greatest contribution to the country will be saving it from communism. . . . And I would [be] guilty of dereliction of duty if not cowardice for not facing up to it and rooting it out while I had the opportunity and the power.
>
> So I am decided that I must risk even the future of my family so as to save our freedoms and individual dignity. The issue has become this simple and brutal. It is a matter of survival. It is a matter of daring or not — on my part.
>
> And I decide to dare.

But who were the Communists that Marcos dared to battle? If they were the few dozen armed subversives scattered through the mountains of central and northern Luzon, then his own diary entry a few days earlier seemed contradictory. Writing on February 22 about "our unanimous assessment" of the subversive threat, Marcos noted that while NPA guerrillas could harass and sabotage, they were incapable of mounting a significant assault.

Clearly, the president's list of Communists included much more than the roster of avowed ideologues and party members, more than the armed insurgents. In fact, his definition was broad enough to include virtually any critic.

Marcos wrote, for example, that he considered journalists and university faculty members as "fellow travelers" of Communist subversives. He regarded some liberal clergymen as "ambivalent do-gooders" who were being used by the Communists. He was being told that Ninoy Aquino was plotting with the Communists to overthrow him; that his last opponent, Sergio Osmena, Jr., was plotting to have him killed. In short, students, teachers, journalists, priests, political rivals — all were included in one sweeping Marcos definition of subversives, all potential targets of the *total solution*. The enemies of the republic were, he concluded, "all those who have in any way helped in the cause of communism."

It was a definition with profound implications for the president's critics. How could any of them escape accusations that their attacks on Ferdinand Marcos, whether in the streets or Congress or the press, undermined the political stability of the administration? And in so doing they were, by design or not, helping the cause of revolutionary groups with the same goal.

After making public statements that radical Jesuit priests seemed to be encouraging violence, Marcos agreed to meet with Father Pacifico Ortiz, the Ateneo University rector whose invocation before congress on January 26 had so angered the president. It was a conciliatory meeting, with the priest assuring Marcos that he was "praying for my success as president." And Marcos used the occasion to lecture the Jesuit leader on the Communist conspiracy, recording in his diary:

> But he did not seem to understand that communism as practiced differs from ideological communism; that communism has often discarded doctrine to attain its sole objective and that is power, so that communism may take the side of almost any popular movement to attain its ends; it could be . . . the nationalist movement, or the [striking] jeepney drivers . . . or the teachers for higher salaries.

In the end, Marcos remained deeply suspicious of the church leader and others like him, noting: "I have my misgivings. He is a do-gooder, naive and wooly minded. . . . Communism feeds on such well-meaning but naive men who know nothing of *realpolitik*."

But Father Ortiz, one of the most prominent religious leaders in a nation that was more than 80 percent Roman Catholic, pressed social justice issues. Marcos saw it as a warning he could not ignore. The night following their March 7 meeting he wrote:

> As the number of Father Ortizes increase in our society, I must acceler-ate the various programs of reform and social justice . . . attend to the media and the intellectuals to keep them on the side of liberal democ-racy, strengthen the military (I have ordered . . . a total of 4,700 new automatic rifles); but more than this, I must keep in mind the lesson learned from the history of communism — that is the timely and judi-cious use of authority and power when the communists are not yet organized enough to mount a guerrilla type massive attack which alone can save our republic from these communists and anarchists.
>
> Now that I have diagnosed the ailment, if the demonstrations be-

come violent this month, I will suspend the privilege of the writ of habeas corpus.

But significant violence did not follow. And the immediate threat of revolution appeared to have passed in the spring of 1970. If an external threat was easing, Marcos still remained a man fearful of treachery from within, a man whose diary shows that he saw potential enemies everywhere, even among his closest aides. Nor was his mind eased by an after-dinner movie screened in the state dining room one Sunday, the film *Julius Caesar* with Marlon Brando as Marc Antony. Marcos noted:

> Superb acting, but it reminded me of the conspiracy going on now against me by all the envious men who have failed. Remind me to have my guards around me always. I have often wondered why Caesar had no protection when he was assassinated.

Meanwhile, cement reinforcement of the palace gymnasium was completed, and Marcos was assured it could withstand "any possible mortar or grenade attack." And the president was getting accustomed to wearing his newest bulletproof vest. It weighed thirteen pounds and was, he found, "a little lumpy" under his tailored barong. But it "protects from the most penetrating rifle fire."

He had his new bunker. He had his new body armor. He had his armed guards. In the security area, Ferdinand Marcos had almost everything — except a feeling of security.

CHAPTER FIVE
Divine Whispers

As the chartered Alitalia DC-8 taxied slowly toward its gate at Manila International Airport on a Friday morning in November 1970, an exuberant crowd of five thousand waved tiny yellow and white flags, chanted *"Viva el Papa!"* and pressed against police security lines reinforced with wooden barricades. All across Manila, from hundreds of steeples and towers, church bells pealed. On the tarmac, heading the delegation of dignitaries to greet the plane, waited a decidedly nervous Ferdinand Marcos with his wife and family.

For several days the president had been working on his speech of greeting. Writing and rewriting. He agonized over tone and content, over nuance and number of words, a singularly uncommon display of anxiety over a speech of any kind, least of all a ceremonial greeting. And he was anxious about other speeches that would follow: an official welcome at the palace and, in three days, a farewell. In one of his fretting entries about those speeches in his diary, Marcos noted: "I have to cut them down and tone them to simplicity and less pretension and ostentation."

Seldom, if ever, had a speech meant so much to the president. But seldom, if ever, had any visitor meant so much. Ferdinand Marcos was about to have his moment in the limelight with a world leader of unparalleled popularity, sharing television screen and front-page photograph with a man of power and influence not simply in some distant alien capital but in the very cities and barrios that elect presidents of the Philippines.

The door of the jetliner finally opened. Ten-year-old Irene Marcos, in butterfly sleeves and a long white *terno*, scampered up the portable stairs with a bouquet of flowers. A frail man draped in a great red cape emerged — Pope Paul VI, looking tired and pale, but smiling. His arms raised in greeting to the crowd. He accepted the Marcos child's bouquet with a gentle pat on her head. The Holy Father had come to Manila.

For devout Filipinos, the moment inspired spiritual ecstasy. For the political Filipino, for President Marcos, it was a moment of triumph, the end of months of top-level negotiations, diplomatic missions, presidential entreaties and persistence. For years, Ferdinand Marcos had dreamed of standing before his predominantly Catholic nation alongside the Vicar of Jesus Christ.

At first sight of the pope, the crowd roared and surged forward. Police lines sagged. Wooden barricades collapsed. The jubilant throng rushed squealing onto the tarmac, pushing close to the knot of dignitaries beneath the DC-8. Carried along by the human flood was a hawk-nosed man in a priest's cassock, Benjamin Mendoza y Amor Flores of Bolivia. He clutched a golden crucifix and mingled with priests from Malaysia, Korea, and Vietnam as Paul VI carefully descended the jetway stairs toward them. Like Ferdinand Marcos, Benjamin Mendoza long had dreamed of being close to Pope Paul.

Already it had been a long trip for the pope, with brief stops in Tehran and Dacca. Manila was to be his first extended visit on a thirty-thousand-mile tour of Asia and the Pacific. There were concerns on the eve of his Rome departure that the seventy-three-year-old pontiff was ailing and might suffer from the grueling travel schedule. But on the Manila tarmac he seemed buoyed by the eager reception. The pope greeted Ferdinand and Imelda at the foot of the steps, then — with the beaming president at his side and Mrs. Marcos close behind — he moved slowly down a receiving line of cardinals and bishops and other church leaders, each reaching to kiss his ring and kneeling in reverence along the crowded path to a planeside bank of microphones. All across the Philippines, from Forbes Park mansions to the slum shanties of Tondo and rural nipa-thatched huts, television sets displayed the scene. Marcos, first at the pontiff's left elbow, then moving around to his right, was constantly in or near the camera's frame — the hovering, delighted host. In the crowd, Benjamin Mendoza moved slowly to intercept the pope's path. Finally, the thirty-five-year-old Bolivian and the venerable bishop of Rome were about to meet. But, like Marcos, Mendoza was a bit nervous. He fingered an object concealed beneath his golden crucifix. And he waited.

Marcos had been hoping to arrange a papal visit to Manila since his first term. In the spring of 1969, Imelda had underscored the president's invitation during a private audience with the pope. She had traveled to Rome for the elevation of Monsignor Julio Rosales of Cebu to the College of Cardinals. Padre Juling, as Imelda had known him when he was her childhood priest in Leyte, became the nation's second cardinal. Imelda turned her Rome trip into a publicity bonanza. In a series of public ceremonies preceding her private Vatican audience, Mrs. Marcos attracted sensational international press attention wearing the colorful national dress of the Philippines — the scoop-necked, butterfly-sleeved *terno*. At the formal investiture of Cardinal Rosales in the Colegium Urbanum on the Via Janicolense, women in the audience wore traditional high-necked, long-sleeved black dresses — except the statuesque Imelda Marcos, who entered in a saffron *terno*. Every camera lens focused on her image. And for every other occasion there was another *terno*: emerald green or pink or white with black accents. Tourists followed her. Locals addressed her as "Your Majesty." She was tall. She was beautiful. She was news. She was getting more press attention than the new cardinal. In the midst of the 1969 presidential election campaign, it was the next best thing to a papal visit.

Later, in the aftermath of the *First Quarter Storm*, efforts to arrange a papal visit accelerated. At that time, Marcos felt the Philippine church was becoming altogether too critical. He came to harbor suspicions of a Jesuit-Communist conspiracy against him, a plot he seemed to base on little more than the fact that Jesuits and Communists both criticized the president's social and economic policies. And he seemed influenced by questionable intelligence reports. In one such report, priests and nuns were accused of inciting labor strife among jeepney drivers and fomenting unrest in the Tondo slums. Marcos wrote:

> Some nuns have even coerced the jeepney drivers, threatening bodily harm. . . . A little unbelievable, but [the sources] swear it is true as now the priests and nuns are using goons. Where has our pious church come to!

The president's notion that priests and nuns were hiring thugs to force the poor to rise up in protest says much about his abiding distrust of the Church, a powerful if lethargic institution in 1970 that was beyond his political control. Ferdinand Marcos, the political genius who left nothing to chance, trusted no one who was beyond his control.

In the midst of 1970 student riots, Marcos launched secret investigations into the conduct of activist priests, leaked reports to friendly media that some clerics were Communist revolutionaries, and pressed contacts with the Vatican to arrange a papal visit — an event he could use to blunt local Church criticism. In May the Vatican announced Paul VI would visit Manila in the fall.

The mingling of politics and religion has a long tradition in the Philippines. And it had been a potent mix in the Marcos political experience from his youth. Young Ferdinand's father, Mariano, was an early follower of the revolutionary Ilocano bishop Gregorio Aglipay, a Filipino nationalist who in the 1890s had fought to replace Spanish friars with Filipino priests. During the Philippines insurrection against Spain in 1898, General Emilio Aguinaldo appointed Aglipay "Spiritual Head of the Nation Under Arms" with the title of military vicar. A year later the priest was leading a guerrilla band against the American forces who replaced the Spaniards. Aglipay broke with the Vatican formally in 1902 to form the Iglesia Filipina Independiente, more commonly called the Aglipayan Church. Although it followed Roman Catholic forms of worship, it was strongly influenced in the early years by Unitarian doctrine. It also was aggressively political.

Bishop Aglipay, a native of Marcos's hometown of Batac, established the Republican party and ran for president in 1935 against Manuel Quezon, who became first president of the commonwealth.

When the cleric lost, so did Mariano Marcos, Aglipay's congressional candidate in Ilocos. It was the election defeat that ended in the assassination of Julio Nalundasan and propelled young Ferdinand to public prominence — convicted of the killing.

Beyond politics and religion, Aglipay also was a supernatural influence in Ferdinand's life. According to legend perpetrated by official biographers of the president, the bishop rewarded young Marcos for his family's long loyalty by giving him a talisman imbued with magical powers, what Filipinos call *anting-anting*. His was a sliver of petrified medicinal wood that supposedly gave him the power to disappear and appear at will, an *anting-anting* with power even over death, a charm he credited with saving his life during World War II.

The president also considered the number 7 a powerful force in his life. In November 1964, he won the Nacionalista presidential nomination over party rival Emmanuel Palaez with 777 votes, an outcome Marcos regarded as a sign. His luxurious presidential yacht, the 2,200-ton *Ang Pangulo*, Marcos renamed *The 777*. And he signed the most important presidential documents on dates divisible by seven.

At times Marcos consulted mystics, soothsayers, astrologers, and faith healers. A month before the papal visit, an Indian fortune teller called on the palace, forecasting peace and prosperity for the nation. For the president, the seer predicted "greatness and health" and a long life at least to the age of eighty-five. But Marcos worried:

> I hope the media does not pick that up and blow it up into a story that I am consulting astrologers and horoscopists before I make decisions for government.

Marcos also was influenced by Imelda's superstitions. She shunned the palace bedroom of former president Ramon Magsaysay, for example, because he had died in a plane crash during his term. And the First Lady was so convinced that plane crashes occurred in clusters that she would "put her foot down" and insist that the president restrict his travel to boats or cars after a plane crash anywhere in the Philippines. Imelda also had the palace analyzed by a mystic, who recommended various alterations to repel evil or otherwise harmful spirits. Over the years she replaced three massive crystal chandeliers in the reception hall with a numerically significant seven smaller versions. She installed numerous mirrors and ordered architectural and interior design changes featuring patterns of seven triangles, for example. And, with a nod to more traditional religions, she assembled for the palace chapel a collection of icons and sacred artifacts representing every major religion of the world. Imelda was a devout Catholic, but in matters spiritual — much like Ferdinand in matters political — she would leave nothing to chance.

Marcos considered himself a devout Catholic. Indeed, he regarded himself as being on the most intimate of terms with the Almighty. He made it an annual habit to attend a Jesuit-sponsored religious retreat in the mountain resort town of Baguio during Holy Week each spring. In 1970, Marcos traveled to Baguio with some misgivings because of his political conflicts with activist Jesuits, but he was accompanied by Colonel Ver and other close aides and cronies.

Such retreats proved to be more than a spiritual balm for the beleaguered president. It was there each year that his own messianic self-image seemed to blossom, where Marcos came to see himself ever more clearly as an instrument of God — not in a metaphysical sense, but literally. His voice spoke the words of God; his hands did the work of God; his dreams were visions from God. He revealed his growing sense of divine purpose when, during the 1970 retreat, he wrote in his diary:

> And I am strengthened as I hear the Lord say: Fear not. I am with you. You shall not fail. For you bear my words in your mouth and my courage in your heart.

The spring religious sessions also provided what the president called a "renewal of my conversations with my Maker." Over the next two years, those would be portentous conversations. Marcos would come to heed what he perceived to be divine whispers, God's call for him to save the Philippines — from greed, corruption, and the communist threat.

It was one thing for Marcos to believe he was God's chosen leader for the Philippines, but it was quite another to convince his countrymen, especially as his personal and political popularity plummeted. The beleaguered president needed a boost of prestige. To that end, the pope's visit held great promise.

Marcos set out to exploit every possible advantage. The pope would stay at Malacanang, of course. Philippine hospitality required it. By late spring Imelda already was planning special renovations. The Holy Father's very presence in the palace would be a blessing of enormous political significance.

But papal representatives declined the offer. Pope Paul, they informed the palace in June, would stay with the Vatican's diplomatic envoy to Manila. Disappointed but undeterred, Marcos continued to negotiate.

President Richard Nixon had tried to say no to a similar offer of hospitality in the summer of 1969. He and his wife, Patricia, had insisted on staying in the Intercontinental Hotel's presidential suite, much to the chagrin of Ferdinand and Imelda. The Nixons were to stay less than twenty-four hours in Manila, on their way home from a mid-Pacific greeting of the *Apollo 11* astronauts on their return from Neil Armstrong's historic first small step on the moon. The Nixons wanted a place to rest. But Marcos was running for reelection. Imelda finally issued an ultimatum, according to writer Raymond Bonner in *Waltzing with a Dictator:* "Either Nixon stayed at Malacanang, or he didn't come to the Philippines." The Nixons stayed at the palace.

Pope Paul VI was not so easy to persuade. All summer long negotiations continued. Finally, as a concession to the persistent Marcos, Vatican representatives said the pope was willing to "go through a symbolic acceptance" of presidential hospitality at the palace. Paul would call on the palace. Possibly even rest briefly at the palace. That would have to do.

Then, another disappointment. The pope declined to ride in the president's car from Manila International Airport. The president and the pope would not be seen together on the motorcade route into the city. There were "some manifestations of offense" by palace insiders over that rejection, Marcos noted in his diary, possibly referring even to his own pique. But the president tried to console himself. He wrote:

> [E]ven in the United States the pope refused to go to Washington and [instead] received Pres. Johnson in his suite in the Waldorf Astoria [in New York] for only 10 minutes. And we should not be petty about it. He is the Vicar of Christ.

Marcos threw himself into his speech-writing. By November all of Manila was preparing for the pope's arrival. Potholes along the motorcade route were getting new asphalt. Expensive archways were being constructed. Grass, trees and parkways were getting manicures and buildings were getting fresh coats of paint. Even a vicious typhoon that flooded the city and reversed many of the cosmetic improvements did little to dampen enthusiasm for the impending visit.

There was another storm building in a poor corner of Manila. Benjamin Mendoza, a tormented artist, wrestled with demons of poverty and anonymity as he, too, prepared for the pope's arrival. He laid out his dark gray priest's cassock, his golden crucifix, and, finally, a ten-inch Moro dagger.

Mendoza, the brooding son of a Bolivian seamstress, had wandered the globe — Argentina, the United States, Japan, Communist China — lonely, frustrated, and usually broke. At times he painted simple, traditional Bolivian scenes, or animals such as cats and horses. Other times he created haunting, surreal images of Jesus Christ in a gaudy, grotesque, even angry style. He had told a Filipino journalist: "I am a painter still unable to express with all the necessary power what lies dormant in the dark recesses of my soul and brush."

Mendoza did not talk with God. "There is no God," he said. But he accepted a messianic mission, of sorts: to "save the people from hypocrisy and superstition . . . to make people everywhere realize reality." To that end, the pope's visit held great promise.

On the tarmac at Manila International Airport, Pope Paul VI eased his way slowly through a sea of priestly raiment and tailored barongs beneath the wing of his jetliner as an eager crowd pressed forward. With President Marcos close by his side, the pope paused to greet Stephen Cardinal Kim of South Korea. Mendoza shouldered his way closer. Cardinal Kim dropped to his knee and kissed the pontiff's ring. Mendoza dropped his crucifix and lunged forward with his ten-inch knife.

The blade intended for the frail man in the red cape instead caught Kim's arm, slicing through his robe, drawing blood. Pope Paul froze, then instinctively recoiled from the assault. There was such a crowd around the pope, the violence so confined and its resolution so swift, that few outside the immediate vicinity of the attack had any idea the first papal assassination attempt in centuries had just occurred.

Mendoza's lunging assault failed. Cardinal Kim's minor wound

was the only casualty. Miraculously, it seemed, Pope Paul was unharmed. But how? Ferdinand Marcos was sure he had the answer,
opening his diary entry that night with:

> This has been an eventful day. I probably saved the life of Pope Paul VI
> this morning, five to ten minutes after his arrival. . . .

Not surprisingly, accounts of the incident varied. According to the
New York Times, Malaysia's bishop, Anthony Dennis Galvin, two-
hundred-pound son of an Irish policeman, intercepted Mendoza and
helped subdue him. Most of the foreign press carried similar versions.
The most widely published picture, taken by a United Press International photographer, appears to show that papal secretary Monsignor
Pasquale Macchi had immediately stepped between Paul VI and the
dagger and grappled with the much larger assailant. Other news photos
and television film footage did not show the incident clearly enough to
reconstruct how the pope was spared. But Ferdinand Marcos declared
in his diary that it was he who "parried the hand of Mendoza" and
delivered a life-saving karate blow to the would-be assassin's arm.

> My karate chop had dislodged the dagger from his hand and the Pope
> whom I pushed (twice) lost his balance backward into the arms of
> Imelda who was right behind, who held him up, otherwise he would
> have fallen to the ground.

Marcos the hero, the savior of the Vicar of Christ. Such tributes
could not be better timed. For the president and his budding messianic complex, this was a sign from heaven of his special place in God's
grand scheme. Proof for the whole world to see, even if it was missed
by the *New York Times*. It gave the president a palpable thrill to con-
template his own bold and daring act. He wrote:

> I feel that I have been an instrument of God in saving the life of
> the Pope.
>   When the assassination attempt was made, my mind and body func-
> tioned automatically. Of course there was no time for rationalization
> and deliberation, but I felt myself move as if guided by an Unseen
> Hand. As I write this my hair stands on end as I realize what this means.

What it apparently meant to Marcos was that God had entered his
body and assumed control of his actions. But more significant was its

tacit endorsement, certainly in the president's mind, of Marcos's growing conviction that he was divinely chosen to lead his country. In his diary he reveled in details of the confrontation with would-be assassin Mendoza:

> There was no hesitation in my movements. It was as if there was a script I was following which I had been made to memorize long, long ago and which I merely executed — the role and action coming naturally as to a well-rehearsed actor.
>
> And there was no feeling of anger or fear or any other emotion on my part.
>
> It was as if I was just an instrument — unfeeling, unthinking and unhesitating.

If Marcos had been cool and flawless in following God's script on the tarmac, he was only human at the microphones. Pope Paul insisted on keeping his schedule and proceeded to the microphones moments after the attack to accept what the *New York Times* simply described as "a lengthy welcoming address by President Marcos." The pope "seemed calm," according to the press account. The nervous Marcos, however, introduced his guest as "Pope Pius" instead of Paul. Explained Marcos in his diary: "This was the only slip I made in what listeners called an impressive welcome speech."

Palace aides promptly credited Marcos with saving the pope. He had "parried the thrust" of Mendoza's dagger. He had seen the knife tip sticking out from beneath the crucifix because he routinely looked at the hands of people in a crowd, part of his security training. He had pushed the Holy Father to safety in the arms of Imelda. When the story met immediate and widespread skepticism among journalists, however, Marcos appeared with his right hand bandaged, explaining that his karate chop had aggravated an old wrist sprain. He wrote: "It was worth the pain. What a tragedy it would have been if Mendoza had succeeded in killing the Pope!"

And for the next several days Marcos pored over every newspaper and magazine account of the assassination attempt. For a political leader with substantial disdain for the press, Marcos was obsessed with journalistic acceptance of his claim to saving the pope. Friends in the United States and Europe cabled reports to Malacanang on how it was being covered by the foreign press and television networks. Like the producer of a Broadway show, Marcos waited with great eager-ness, as he would many times throughout his career, for the reviews of his work published more than seven thousand miles away in the *New York Times*. When correspondent Henry Kamm acknowledged in a carefully qualified reference that "sources close to Mr. Marcos" contin-ued to credit the president with saving the pontiff from harm, Marcos promptly entered the *Times* account into his diary — but without the disclaimer.

Interrogation of Mendoza by Philippine authorities centered on two questions: what was his motive, and who parried the thrust of his dagger? Given the president's preoccupation with the Communist menace it cannot be surprising that police asked their prisoner: "Do you believe in Karl Marx?" Mendoza, who said repeatedly that he had acted alone to save the people from superstition, to prove that the pope was simply human, dismissed questions suggesting some Com-munist link. "My concept is a little broader than that of Marx," he scoffed. As to how the assassination was stymied, Mendoza finally signed a statement for Filipino police saying that it was President Marcos. Mendoza even used the president's verb to describe how Marcos had "parried" his knife thrusts twice. Though most journalists remained skeptical and debate continued for weeks between pro- and anti-Marcos commentators in the Manila press, Marcos felt vindi-cated. He had the *New York Times* and now Mendoza's affidavit saying he had saved the pope. Bongbong called from school in London to say he was proud of his father. The call cheered Marcos, who, in his diary, noted that the boy's response to his father's daring was: " 'Runs in the family,' he bragged."

In the months to follow, the president would sense again and again that he was a tool of his Maker, simply doing the will of God as he parried the thrust of Communist subversion and struck repeated blows for reform of Philippine institutions and society. He showed no signs of doubt that God controlled his personal and political destinies, coming to accept that his will and God's will were one. And how could critics question Ferdinand Marcos when he was acting as an agent of God? To Marcos, it all came clear after the pope's visit. Hav-ing saved Paul VI, his next mission was to save the Philippines.

Not long after the Alitalia DC-8 carried Pope Paul on to Western Samoa and Australia, Marcos was reminded of his days as a guerrilla fighter during World War II. In his diary he reported getting a lump in his throat on recalling his own willingness back in those days to give up comfort and even his life for his country. Now, faced with civil and economic strife and a still-vague Communist threat, Marcos felt another calling:

> . . . I must risk comfort, the future, love, family and even life and honor itself for a people and country the strength of which [is] being eroded slowly but systematically by their ill-wishers.
>
> But I must be just as cool, deliberate but bold and daring as we were during those dark days of the war.
>
> There [is] no other course. God [has] made it so.

Between the encouragement of divine whispers and the constant influence of his mammoth ambition, Ferdinand Marcos became an eager messiah. Ultimately, however, it would be a demon that defined and drove his mission: the demon paranoia.

CHAPTER SIX
Sex, Lies, and Audio Tapes

On the movie screen the action was fast. Machine guns bursting. Japanese soldiers and Filipino guerrillas dying violently in frame after frame — typical action footage in a World War II adventure film. But from the audience watching in deep shadows came the sounds of a woman crying. On the screen a woman appeared, her light brown hair flowing over her shoulders and spilling down across her breasts. *Stop!* The film flickered to a halt, the projected image of the actress frozen on the screen. In the audience the tearful woman moved closer, her shadow cast on the screen like a partial eclipse. For several long moments the woman studied the actress's frozen image: the big eyes, the thin Western nose, the full lips, the soft smile, the round breasts. Finally, bursting into sobs again, she could only wave the projectionist on. The movie resumed. It was *Maharlika*, the story of Ferdinand Marcos, war hero. But on this day at Malacanang, it was the story of Ferdinand Marcos, unfaithful husband. The only audience was his aggrieved wife, sitting through six hours of screenings and rescreenings in the privacy of the Music Room, Imelda's palace office. She studied only one performer: the American actress Dovie Beams.

On the screen Dovie played "Evelyn," Ferdinand's wartime girl-friend. But in the fashionable Manila enclave of Greenhills Dovie had played Ferdinand's real-life mistress, a role that erupted in public scandal on the eve of Pope Paul's arrival.

Ferdinand knew the scandal was coming, knew it was going to be embarrassing, probably even knew that he would have to make amends privately with Imelda. But in early November 1970 he also was confident that he could deny his way out of any serious trouble — just as he had in the past. Still, few Lotharios had encountered so disquieting a prospect as that facing Marcos: a spurned lover stepping before lights, cameras, and microphones to hold a press conference about their once secret affair. In his diary Marcos lamented: "And we are impotent to do anything as this woman wants publicity. If we file a libel . . . case, she will just thrive in it."

"This woman," as Marcos often referred to her in his diary, was privately demanding still unpaid compensation for her screen role. She also was trying to meet with Marcos. He refused. The president's commissioner of immigration had tried to have Dovie deported in October on a trumped-up visa violation, but that only renewed gossip-column interest. While that was an irritation, the prospect of a scheduled press conference had to be distressing.

Marcos decided on a counterattack to contain the damage — political and domestic. Accuse her of extortion. Shift the blame. Attack the media. Express contempt for malicious gossip. And deny, deny, deny. It would be the word of a foreign B-movie actress against that of the president of the republic. What Marcos failed to anticipate, however, was the tape recorder she had hidden under their bed to capture the president's own unguarded words and songs and tender moans of love.

What no one else could have anticipated was how the so-called lovey Dovie scandal would affect the course of Philippine history, transforming a humiliated Imelda Marcos into a more independent and powerful partner of her president husband. Any lingering vestiges of that once shy, reluctant politician's wife were gone forever, with profound consequences for the nation.

"She got harder and harder," recalled Imelda's priest in an interview with Katherine Ellison, author of *Imelda*. "Her personality couldn't seem to handle it: She had held on to this fairytale vision of romance, this life-long dream of hers, and now it seemed she had decided to trade in that dream for another." That other dream, as Ellison and historians have noted, was power.

For Ferdinand Marcos, the Dovie Beams disclosures and the pressures he felt in their aftermath — coming as they did amid his plunging popularity and the mounting civil turmoil — only aggravated his anxieties. He developed stomach pains and feared he was getting an ulcer. Meanwhile, the unabating criticisms in press and Congress seemed more sinister. His paranoia flared. Behind Dovie he saw the shadows of conspirators out to destroy him: the wealthy oligarchs, Ninoy Aquino, American intelligence agents.

Somehow, Marcos the exposed adulterous husband came to see his dilemma as the product not of his own indiscretions but of a conspiracy by his rivals and enemies. It was a convenient delusion. In fact, the story of Dovie Beams exposed a host of presidential lies and delusions — so many that he could not keep the fictions straight. According to his first diary reference to Dovie, Marcos said he had met her only once. Later, he noted it may have been twice. Then, he listed three specific occasions when he saw her. From page to page his stories changed. Ferdinand Marcos lied to himself. It was a familiar pattern throughout the diary.

Earlier in 1970, for example, at the height of student rioting and press denunciations of administration policies, the president had called in three prominent Manila businessmen to request their help in retaliating against his most persistent newspaper critics. Two of the men were major film distributors, controlling most of Manila's movie theaters, and the other was Manila's leading liquor distributor. All were major newspaper advertisers. On February 20 Marcos wrote:

> I asked [them] to withdraw advertisements from the *Manila Times* which was openly supporting revolution and the communist cause. They agreed to do so.

Barely a month later Marcos met in the palace with a number of leading journalists, including publisher Chino Roces of the *Manila Times*. At one point Roces "pointedly asked" if the president was not trying to pressure the media by asking advertisers to drop their accounts. He denied it. Ignoring what he had written in February, an indignant Marcos rewrote history shortly before midnight on Friday, March 21:

I had nothing whatsoever to do in suggesting the cut of advertisement although I did say that if [ads were pulled], it would be a legitimate act against a paper that was becoming uncontrollably leftist.

But one of the most extensive and revealing concentrations of diary delusions was spawned by the story of Dovie and the president, the man she called "Fred."

Dovie Beams had been in Manila only a few hours when she was brought to a big house in the Greenhills section of Manila for a cocktail reception in December 1968. The film investors were to meet her. Potenciano "Nanoy" Ilusorio, who had selected Dovie from a casting catalogue, introduced her to the others only by their first names or nicknames. There were Dado, Manuel, and Norrie, for example. Last to arrive was a man who commanded instant respect and deference from the others, a man who sat at the head of the table when food was served, a man introduced as Fred.

According to the actress's detailed account of that evening, presented in the book *Marcos' Lovey Dovie* by Filipino newsman Hermie Rotea, the men asked about her commitments to other film projects, about her contractual obligations to studios, and about her personal life. What kind of men did she date? She ruled out lawyers, doctors, and ministers. She talked about movies, about art, about politics. She sang "I Want to Be Bad." Later that night, when they were alone for a moment, Fred told her she had "the best-looking legs I have ever seen." But he confided: "I don't think you are going to like the work that I do." She thought he must be a lawyer. "I have something to do with the legal profession — I am the president of the Philippines." Ferdinand Marcos kissed her on the back of the neck, declared "I'm in love with you," and then left.

They met again the next evening at the same house. It was located only a short distance from the Wack Wack Country Club where Marcos and Ilusorio frequently golfed. Again, Fred and Dovie talked. But if the conversation became more intimate, the physical contact did not. At least, not for another day.

As Dovie later told author Rotea, her first sexual encounter with Marcos occurred the night of December 28, 1968, at the presidential mansion in Baguio, a resort town in the cool, pine-covered mountains north of Manila. It is regarded as the summer capital of the Philippines. It also is the site of the Philippine Military Academy and the president's annual Holy Week retreat; Imelda liked to go there for skin treatments.

The presidential residence in Baguio is called the Mansion House. With the assistance of Colonel Fabian Ver, the palace security chief, Dovie said she was smuggled through a gauntlet of sentries patrolling the residence. Marcos greeted her on the ground floor and escorted her upstairs. They passed through one door that Marcos locked behind them. Then a second and a third. They were alone in the presidential bedroom suite, a room furnished in white French provincial furniture with two double beds side by side. Marcos told Dovie that he was impotent with his wife and that they had been sexually estranged for some time. And there, behind three sets of locked doors, the affair began.

"Dovie Beams, she could paint. She could talk about history, politics, the arts, philosophy. . . . That's what I think attracted Marcos to her," recalled Ilusorio in an interview. She had a body and a brain.

Dovie grew up in Tennessee, played the church organ in Nashville, taught piano lessons, and dreamed of Hollywood. After divorcing husband Edward Boehms in 1962, she moved to Beverly Hills to pursue those dreams — with limited success. It was for Hollywood that she changed the spelling of her name. She landed bit parts in television programs such as *Name of the Game*, worked some shows in Las Vegas, appeared in Los Angeles–area stage productions, and had roles in such movies as *Wild Wheels*. Then Ilusorio called with the *Maharlika* film offer and she was off to Manila.

Production of *Maharlika* was much slower starting than was the romance. Shooting did not begin until May 1969. Dovie, meanwhile, moved into the Greenhills house, where Marcos was a regular caller. He told her he wanted to have a baby with her. Another son. In fact, having a second son seemed to be an obsession with Marcos in his marriage as well. Even his children knew about it.

In the spring of 1969, while Dovie said Ferdinand was trying to persuade her to have his illegitimate son in Greenhills, Imelda and her daughters, Imee and Irene, were in Rome, discussing the question of a baby with Pope Paul VI. Near the end of their Vatican audience, wrote a palace biographer, Imee broached the subject, asking the pope for a special blessing. "You have blessed us all, Holy Father, but please bless Mommy especially so she will have another baby boy."

The diary also describes various family conversations about the subject. On May 2, 1970 — a few months after Dovie had moved out of the Greenhills house and returned to California — Marcos wrote about a discussion in bed aboard the presidential yacht with Imelda about "all the things she and I had been through together since we were married." Imelda was worried about Bongbong going away to school in England.

> When I laughingly asked her what she would do if he brought home a child with an English mother, she said seriously and intensely — "Keep the child but not the mother." She thought that we would then have a child to play with. I jokingly asked why she felt that way about her son but not about her husband.

Imelda's subsequent response, as Marcos recorded it months before the Dovie scandal broke, reveals another dimension of his obsession with having another son:

> She said, I love you so much I would be willing to allow you to have a child by another woman if you want it . . . so much, but I have to be there and you must do so not because of love for the woman. Of course, we both laughed the thought off with unanimous assurances of love.

But the matter came up again nearly three months later when the Marcos family was together one playful morning in the presidential bedroom at Malacanang. The children gave their parents instructions on French kissing and how to recognize a telltale hickey. In his July 24, 1970, entry Marcos wrote:

> The children were all kidding us that if there should be another child, they would all be [jealous]. I suggested in jest that their mother was willing for me to have children by other women and they said, "Unthinkable." Although they were laughing, I knew they were serious.
>
> I told them, too, that if Mommy should ever leave us, I would never marry again.
>
> Bongbong said in bravado, "Why do you want any other sons when I am worth a thousand sons." And I hope he will be.

And even as the presidential sex scandal was blossoming — only five days before Dovie's bombshell press conference — Imelda was undergoing gynecological examinations to determine if she could conceive again. On November 6, 1970, Marcos noted:

> [W]e would like to have another child. And [the doctors] are very optimistic that she is quite ready for it. There seems to be no reason why we should not have another child — a boy I hope.

Why Imelda never had another child is not clear. Some writers have speculated that she was unwilling to have more children, but the diary seems to contradict that view. Over the next two years, according to the diary, the couple engaged in what Ferdinand occasionally called "Our Project," a continuing effort to conceive another child. It would be a source of continuing disappointment and frustration.

According to Rotea's book, Dovie Beams was not eager at first to have a secret offspring of the president. Unbeknownst to Marcos, for several months she continued taking birth control pills while the president apparently was under the impression she was trying to get pregnant. As Rotea described it, when Marcos one day discovered a supply of contraceptive pills in the Greenhills house, he threw them out and angrily confronted Dovie. In later months, Dovie's attitude changed. At least she told Marcos in tape-recorded conversations that she wanted to have his baby and was willing to keep it a secret. Marcos, in turn, kept track of her fertility cycles, reciting them months into the future during another meeting recorded on Dovie's hidden tape machine. Meanwhile, on their bed headboard in Greenhills they kept a picture of an American-Filipino baby, a big-eyed child that Dovie said looked like the baby they might have together.

Maharlika would begin shooting in May 1969, with American actors Paul Burke (playing Marcos) and Farley Granger. But before work began, Dovie invited her mother and preteen daughter, Dena, to Manila. With Imelda still in Rome, Marcos entertained Dovie and her family at Malacanang. Afterward, Dena referred to Marcos as "Daddy Fred."

Marcos courted trouble with the Beams affair from the outset, but sometimes the risks were even more brazen and audacious. In late April 1969, Marcos addressed the Philippine film industry's Famas Awards ceremonies, local equivalent of the Oscars, and was so openly ogling Dovie as she sat in the front row with Farley Granger that Manila journalists noticed. And in May, Marcos insisted that Dovie attend Bataan Day ceremonies where he would speak at the site of the infamous World War II death march. Dovie wore a dress selected, she said, by Marcos. They agreed on a series of hand signals to communicate secretly in front of the crowd (a hand to the cheek meant "I love you"). It was on Bataan that Dovie first saw Imelda in person — and vice versa.

Although *Maharlika* was intended for release in advance of the 1969 presidential elections, it was clear by late summer that such a production schedule was impossible. Filming was completed, but dubbing and editing would take considerable time. In September, Dovie returned to Hollywood for postproduction work. Marcos earlier had given her a souvenir to keep her company during his increasingly long campaign absences — an audio tape on which he sang a Spanish love song and *"Pamulinawen,"* his favorite Ilocano folk song, supposedly recorded in their Greenhills bed. Then, on the eve of her September departure for the United States, Marcos arrived with a Polaroid camera. He wanted his own set of souvenirs: a series of nude snapshots of Dovie Beams. And there was one additional souvenir. An odd request. Marcos wanted a lock of Dovie's pubic hair. She resisted, then agreed if Marcos would make the same sacrifice. She said they exchanged snips.

It turned out that the movie was in serious trouble. Ilusorio and the investors, including Marcos, were reluctant to pour more money into the project at a time when so much was being spent on the campaign. The Philippine Central Bank was churning out pesos almost as fast as Ferdinand and Imelda could give them away in bulging envelopes to local officials — often for unspecified local "development projects." The movie offered little if any propaganda value, especially since it was so late coming out. Dovie was not paid. Postproduction funds were delayed. Finally, Ilusorio took the raw footage from Hollywood back to Manila and hired a prominent local film studio to cut it.

Louie Nepomuceno, whose father founded the Philippines' oldest movie studio, said he first declined the job. But told it was a project linked to President Marcos, he was shown documents and margin notes on a copy of the screenplay in the familiar handwriting of the president. "We had no alternative but to accept the task of finishing the film," said Nepomuceno during a 1989 interview videotaped by the Manila-based Asian Television Corporation.

In November Marcos won reelection by a landslide two million votes, out of eleven million cast. But critics attributed those numbers to payoffs and intimidation, to the three Gs: "goons, guns, and gold." In fact, Marcos had spent more than $50 million, the most costly campaign in Philippine history. And campaign violence was so extensive that the press dubbed it "the bloodiest election" in Philippine history. Nor did Marcos denials of fraud and intimidation satisfy students and opposition leaders. Street demonstrations first flared in late 1969. Instead of enjoying his mandate, Marcos found himself the object of political and personal attack, hanged in effigy, scorned in placards and editorials, jeered and taunted. Dovie told Rotea that she noticed his attitude change — from a happy man in September to a withdrawn and increasingly hostile man by year's end. Of course, those also could have been symptoms of a failing romance.

In January 1970, just a few days before Marcos was to deliver his State of the Nation address that would precede days of deadly rioting, the president and Dovie agreed to cool their relationship for a time. People were watching, Marcos said. Imelda, in Veterans Hospital at the time to have a cyst removed from her breast, was suspicious, too. Ferdinand abruptly moved his personal belongings from the Greenhills house, but not before Dovie got one more souvenir of her own — another secret tape recording of a lovemaking session with Marcos on January 22.

According to Rotea's published transcript of that session, the rendezvous was interrupted by Colonel Ver, who arrived with urgent news about a demonstration. "They're attacking and bombing. Here I am fucking around," Marcos said, apparently rushing to get dressed. "I think I'll wear this. I'll look like I just came from golf."

That night in his diary Marcos made no hint of his Dovie meeting. He did, however, mention the demonstration. A plainclothes palace security agent had been spotted taking photographs of the demonstrators, who promptly set upon and "mauled [him for] no reason except that he was allegedly infiltrating." Marcos hoped that the attack would gain some public sympathy for authorities. He wrote:

> The demonstrators (some ten of them) are still there with their mike shouting unprintable and vicious imprecations at me, Meldy and everybody. You can hear them in all rooms of the palace except our bedroom and the study.

The tumultuous and deadly *First Quarter Storm* was blowing across Manila's political landscape. By the end of January 1970, Ferdinand Marcos was under siege physically and politically. He also was a man apparently in some personal turmoil over his romantic conflicts. Perhaps all of those factors contributed to the president's decision to disappear into weeks of seclusion after the student riots outside congress and Malacanang.

Dovie was gone before the rioting broke out. But what was to be a two- or three-month hiatus stretched to seven months. Clearly, the affair was over. But Dovie still had not been paid — at least, not enough. She returned to Manila late that summer, ostensibly to work on a travelogue about the Philippines. It also seems likely she had hopes of salvaging her relationship with Marcos. At the very least, she intended to press for money she said was owed her. A rough cut of *Maharlika*, possibly a pirated version, already had appeared at a theater in Guam. And it was being advertised in Manila — until Imelda got hold of it.

"I was told that the film would be banned from the Philippines and all over the world," Louie Nepomuceno said, recalling the six-hour meeting with Mrs. Marcos at Malacanang during which he screened *Maharlika* for her alone. He remembered that several times during his lengthy visit in Imelda's Music Room office President Marcos passed through. It was an awkward time for the studio owner. "She was sad. She was crying and obviously upset over the whole affair," Nepomuceno recalled. But Marcos "was mostly in a joking mood. There seemed to have been some estrangement between him and the First Lady and I suppose he was taking advantage of my presence to kid around a little bit . . . to break the ice with the First Lady, who appeared to be not on speaking terms with the president, at least at that moment."

Imelda's determination to ban the movie was a major disappointment to Nepomuceno, who held distribution rights to *Maharlika*. In fact, when he first heard sensational news accounts linking one of its stars romantically to the president, his first reaction was: "Jackpot!" It sounded like the kind of publicity even pesos could not buy. "Of course, we had not thought further on to consider the fact that the film had to be banned."

From August to November, 1970, Dovie waged a bold campaign of her own, privately insisting that she be paid approximately $100,000, which she said was owed her, or she was prepared to embarrass the president. The investors, partners in the production company called USV Arts, paid her $10,000, then refused to pay more. Dovie was warned that she might be harmed. The battles raged in private meetings and exchanges of private correspondence until October when Dovie's bikini-clad figure filled the cover of the *Philippines Free Press*, the legs Marcos so admired now adorning every newsstand in Manila.

The otherwise serious Manila news journal made a habit of spicing its pages, and often its full-color cover, with rather modest cheesecake photos. For the first cover of October 1970, publisher Teddy Locsin had dispatched a photographer to the swimming pools of hotels along Roxas Boulevard in search of free modeling talent. By incredible coincidence, he would later insist, the *Free Press* photographer found Dovie. The cover headline near her knee read:

> Dovie Beams —
> A Lovely Argument
> For "Special Relations"

On the morning that the Dovie cover appeared, Locsin's wife got a call at home from Malacanang. Imelda was irate. They had been friends once, the Locsins and Marcos. During the first round of student riots in January, the president had offered the Locsins safe haven in the palace if anarchy spread. And Marcos repeatedly had tried to persuade their son, Teddy Boy, to come work in the palace press office. But, now — the Dovie cover. How dare they publish a picture of the president's mistress! This was news to the Locsins. Sensational news.

Reporters hounded Dovie. Is it true? Officially, she stuck to the story she was involved with a man named Fred, but speculation about Fred's true identity became a favorite media game. Suddenly, the efforts to deport the actress mounted. The American embassy found itself embroiled in the spat — an almost comic escapade but for the ominous rumblings. Embassy officials warned Dovie to leave the country before some zealous loyalists tried something violent to protect the president. It was no idle warning. According to an account in Ellison's *Imelda*, a band of sympathetic palace security guards offered to "take care of the girl" for the First Lady.

Ferdinand's first diary reference to Dovie appeared on October 19,

1970, the day that the deportation story hit the Manila newspapers. In an entry nearly a page long, Marcos denied that he knew her, writing:

> Many ladies have claimed the dubious honor of being my girl friends. But the most obnoxious is a Dovie Boehms [*sic*], the leading lady in *Maharlika*, a film supposedly based on the war exploits of Lawni, alias Ferdinand Marcos. I met her or she was introduced to me during the Famas Festival last year. . . .
>
> She approached Imelda in the tourism conference and program at [the] Hilton . . . and proudly announced that she knew her (Imelda's) husband. Imelda properly ignored her. But over TV and in interviews with newspapermen, she insinuates that she has been my *inamorata!* And I have not even seen her on this trip of [hers]. The only time I saw her was during the casual introduction last year. How the media can indeed swallow a story that appeals to the morbid curiosity of men!!

It was Marcos attacking the media. Marcos denying everything. Whether or not the tactic was playing well among supporters or the public at large, it apparently was not persuasive in the palace. Imelda was desperately unhappy. On October 31, 1970, the president joined his wife and daughters at a seaside residence in Paranaque, where Marcos raved about how invigorating the atmosphere by the sea was. But he also felt compelled to note that Imelda had been "in a very depressed mood in the past several days." He offered no explanation but wrote: "[She] only came alive when she showed me the corner of the garden where she had . . . prepared for a tea or [breakfast] nook. Cozy and refreshing area for a gathering of friends."

Imelda's unhappiness persisted. Two days later the family traveled to Baguio for a lengthy stay at the Mansion House. The election of delegates to the constitutional convention — the "ConCon," as Filipinos dubbed it — was scheduled for November 10, and Marcos intended to stay in the mountains until election day, fly to Batac to cast his vote, then return to Malacanang. The president immediately turned to golf, a favorite form of exercise and sport. Over the next several days Marcos mostly kept his diary informed about his daily scores on the John Hay Golf Course. But hints about Imelda's attitude also emerged. On November 5, 1970, he noted: "Imelda is out of sorts because of the extortion activities of the Boehms woman."

Finally, there seemed to be a thaw in their chilly relationship in the aftermath of Imelda's gynecological exams. On Friday, doctors had said they were confident she could have another baby. And on Saturday, November 7, Marcos wrote:

> Imelda is in high spirits and full of tenderness. This stay in Baguio has turned into a second honeymoon with reminiscences of our days of courtship and a favorite chapel . . . and how she refused to live with me as man and wife until after the religious ceremony in Manila on May 1st 1954.

They would not last long, those high spirits. Dovie announced her press conference soon after. The renewed scandal was a serious distraction for Marcos at a critical juncture in his political future. The pending election of constitutional convention delegates held the key to his hopes of succeeding himself.

Marcos flew to Batac on November 10 to cast his vote for friendly delegates. But that day he devoted most of his diary to Dovie. He wrote:

> I am being blackmailed by a Dovie Boehms who has called a press conference . . . and [says] she was my mistress. A damned lie! Some time ago she threatened that if she was not paid a big sum of money, she would scandalize me and spread all forms of lies about me.
>
> A diabolical plot. But what a well prepared one it is. . . . I have asked the editors to check the story and not use it.

Feeling frustrated and vulnerable, Marcos again was seeing conspiracies behind his troubles. Dovie must have a political patron, someone using her to embarrass the president, someone urging her to attack. Marcos considered a number of suspects.

> [W]e must investigate if there is some other person behind the plot. Some quarters suggest the CIA or the American embassy. . . . Again it may be my political opponents who are encouraging this or have planted her.

He looked for every possible explanation except the most likely: a woman scorned. When Dovie pulled out her tape recorder for a battery of Manila journalists on November 11, 1970, she may as well have been launching a torpedo into the president's stubborn defense. His languorous and slightly off-key rendition of the Ilocano folk song drowned out a thousand denials. His hoarse, recorded pleas for oral sex mocked a thousand more. Further denials seemed pointless, but Marcos had other plans.

Dovie Beams, meanwhile, hurried from the hotel press conference to Manila International Airport escorted by U.S. consul Lawrence Harris, her Filipina secretary, and a maid. Before she boarded Philippine Airlines flight 396 to Hong Kong, someone slipped a flowered lei around her neck, a tribute to Philippine hospitality. Standing by to witness her departure was a waiting-room crowd of Marcos appointees, some suspected Malacanang spies, and many news reporters. As she ascended the jetway steps with Consul Harris, photographers snapped her final wave to the Philippines. She was smiling.

Aboard the plane, however, Dovie discovered her seat assignment had been changed. She was not sitting with her secretary as planned. Beside her was a Filipino man. He introduced himself: Delfin Fred Cueto. Fred? He claimed they had met before. At the Hilton Hotel. Dovie was sure she had never seen the man. To Rotea she later recalled there was "something creepy" about the man.

Delfin Cueto was a thug and the reputed half brother of Ferdinand Marcos. He operated a protection racket in Makati and supposedly hired out as a hitman. Two summers later he would die in a shootout at the Intercontinental Hotel, gunned down by bodyguards of the Makati mayor. Some writers have speculated that he was dispatched to Hong Kong on November 11 by Imelda or her loyalists to kill Dovie. It is also possible that Marcos planted him on the flight in what turned out to be a feeble attempt to create another alibi. In fact, the next day Marcos wrote:

> There is an indication that the Fred whom she talks about is Federico Delfin Cueto. He is also known for having been introducing himself as Pres. Marcos. And he may have done so to Boehms.
>
> He is in Hongkong in the same Ambassador Hotel in which the Boehms woman is staying.

Marcos called in Ambassador Henry Byroade and James Rafferty from the U.S. embassy to "find out what the participation of the American government is in the Boehms blackmail conspiracy." They assured Marcos that Consul Harris had accompanied Dovie to the airport only to guarantee her departure. They seemed to be telling the truth, Marcos acknowledged after their meeting on November 12.

Then he changed his mind. The new Marcos defense was to blame the CIA.

Word spread from Malacanang that Dovie Beams was an American agent. The story galled Ambassador Byroade. Whether or not anyone else was buying the notion, Imelda seemed to subscribe. In fact, she may have originated the idea. It was an excuse. And both Ferdinand and Imelda needed an excuse.

Imelda's somewhat desperate embrace of the CIA theory apparently gave Marcos the false sense that she believed his denials. After the Dovie press conference, he recorded:

> Imelda has resolutely stood by me and this has increased my admiration for her. I am sure she has doubts as to whether I have been faithful to her but she can smell blackmail and is quietly helping out — no hysterics, no crying — just determined loyalty.
>
> And she is not wrong. For I have been faithful to her. And I have not known this woman Dovie Boehms. I met her twice or thrice — all formal occasions. She was at the Famas Awards, then she was with the cast of Maharlika which was introduced to me and then she visited the palace with some other tourists. That is all.

It seems apparent from the diary that Marcos either came to believe his own fantasy about Dovie's role as a U.S. agent or he feigned such belief in his papers. In fact, he decided to punish the U.S. for its imagined role in the scandal. On Sunday, November 15, 1970, Marcos wrote:

> Lest our people feel the Americans have succeeded in coercing me with the Dovie Boehms alleged revelations of "intimate relations" with me (which are patently false) I have ordered a renegotiation of the Military Bases Agreement with the U.S.
>
> And tomorrow I will reiterate the demand for the return of Sangley Pt. by the U.S.

Meanwhile, in Hong Kong Dovie had gone into hiding, eluding Cueto and any other Philippine agents who might have been trying to find her. When she emerged a few days later, trying to board a Pan Am flight to the U.S., the Philippine consul general appeared at the airport to block her departure. An altercation was interrupted by Hong Kong police, who put her in the protective custody of MI-5, the British intelligence branch. Finally, Dovie was escorted safely to America with the help of U.S. and British agents. Hong Kong police detained Cueto and deported him to Manila.

Cueto insisted to reporters that he was Fred, that Dovie Beams was his mistress. The claim was regarded as a joke. In fact, "Fred" jokes swept Manila. During that period anyone named Fred could expect to be teased about it. One day the very proper Supreme Court Justice Fred Ruiz Castro was greeted jauntily by a colleague as "Fred" only to be corrected, emphatically: "My name is Fred Ruiz." Nor could Marcos escape it. Giving away typhoon relief materials in a remote barrio on the island of Mindoro on Christmas Day, the president and Imelda lost some of their holiday cheer when they saw signs of criticism in a crowd that they had expected to be overwhelmingly grateful and affectionate.

"We were irritated by some posters about me fooling the people and references to 'Fred,'" Marcos noted that night in his diary. He was not amused by "Fred" jokes.

Despite such surprises, Marcos continued his year-end tour of other remote regions "seldom reached by politicians" in what was, at least in part, a search for personal relief from the scandal and controversy. Even while plowing through uncomfortably heavy seas off Palawan, Marcos seemed invigorated, writing on December 26, ". . . how refreshing it feels to visit the provinces after the artificial and morbid atmosphere of Manila." But his escape was short-lived.

The Dovie scandal would linger well into 1971. Imelda's brother Kokoy Romualdez was dispatched to Los Angeles and Nashville to direct a thorough background investigation of the actress. He came up with damaging records, including a psychiatrist's deposition given in connection with her divorce case. The doctor had testified she had "schizoid traits." The psychiatrist also said in his sworn statement that he found no evidence of explosive aggressiveness but rather of "withdrawal from responsibility and the pursuit of erotic self-satisfaction through romance." In the diary, Marcos called her "a psychiatry case." Kokoy's findings and Ferdinand's nude Polaroid shots ended up featured in a ten-week series of sensational stories in the Marcos-controlled *Republic Weekly*. And given extensive public airing in that series was the critical and very personal court report of Tennessee psychiatrist Henry B. Brackin, Jr.

The attack was probably a mistake. It prompted another counterattack from Dovie. Instead of putting the case to rest, the rather vicious

Republic Weekly series exposed still more embarrassing details. From Beverly Hills, Dovie sent more tapes to Manila publications. And this time she enclosed some bonus evidence: strands of pubic hair clipped from the Philippine president's loins. "DOVIE BEAMS CLAWS BACK," trumpeted the *Graphic* news magazine as it launched its own series, based on Dovie's sensational rebuttal package from California. Marcos never forgave editors of the *Graphic*. The president's moment of vengeance would come. And he was keeping a list.

Imelda, too, was keeping a list. Palace aides loyal to the First Lady gave her constant reports on her husband. His meetings. His suspected rendezvous. He could not have been oblivious of her intense suspicion and doubt. He gave her gifts, among them a diamond rosary. He wrote her poems:

> *To Imelda my love —*
> *My soul crawls in the nightmare of my long night*
> *Yet there is darkness when you are away . . .*
> *Please return the sun into my life.*

And he made concessions, apparently under pressure from Imelda akin to blackmail, turning over control of some mining interests to the Romualdez family.

It was at the height of the scandal that Marcos also mentioned, for the first time in his diary, the possibility that Imelda might be a candidate for president. On December 18, 1970, he wrote: "More and more leaders are beginning to refer to Imelda as the next President."

A provincial congressman assured Marcos a few days later that the island of Masbate was "a hundred percent behind Imelda if [Marcos] allowed her to run." And in welcoming crowds organized by the First Lady's energetic brother and presidential advance man, Kokoy Romualdez, there was a sudden proliferation of placards touting "Imelda for President." It may have been a trial balloon, Ferdinand's way of testing the notion by generating press reaction. Marcos did not want to be a lame duck, a president without a future and therefore without political bargaining power. If he could not succeed himself, then perhaps his wife would. He could retain power in the family. But it also is possible that the burst of presidential speculation swirling around Imelda in the scandal's aftermath was part of a more limited domestic campaign — Ferdinand's efforts at reconciliation with his unhappy wife.

At no other time before in her life would Imelda have been more likely to assert her independence more forcefully than in the fall of 1970. Not only was she confident of her political strength at home — as a popular campaigner, a prominent figure in community and cultural improvement projects, and the force behind a potent political volunteer organization that was the "Blue Ladies" — but she also had just returned from what she and the president regarded as a hugely successful international tour of Rome, London, and Washington.

She had private audiences with Pope Paul VI at the Vatican and with Richard Nixon and Henry Kissinger in the White House Oval Office. At the United Nations she was toasted by Secretary General U Thant. Queen Elizabeth interrupted her vacation in Scotland to receive the Philippine First Lady at Buckingham Palace. A London dinner at which she encountered Greek tycoon Aristotle Onassis and his wife, the former Jacqueline Kennedy, prompted an apparently playful call home to Ferdinand. On September 10, 1970, the president wrote:

[A]s the Londoners have said, "Jackie is not a shade of the First Lady of Asia." Imelda says Onassis, who looks like a dried prune, was trying to catch her eye. Senile flirt!! But she says he is ugly as Hades.

Throughout the month-long world tour, Imelda's enthusiastic telephone reports to her husband generated regular diary entries — the most intriguing written after Imelda's thirty-minute meeting in the Oval Office. Imelda said she advocated more financial and military aid and raised the specter of the Communist menace. Marcos was delighted. On September 23 he wrote:

Imelda has practically shocked Pres. Nixon and Kissinger into doing something for the Philippines by informing them in candid words that the Philippines will be lost to the U.S. if she does not help. So now the White House is in a state of agitation looking for a crash program to help the country.

She told me this over long distance at 5:30 PM and she is due to meet with the Senate and House leaders today.

Kissinger keeps saying that she is a very articulate and talented as well as keen sighted woman. . . .

[She] casually informed them that if we cannot get any help from the U.S. then we would go to Moscow and Peking. And he (Pres.

Nixon) will be known in history as the man who lost the Philippines and Asia.

Clearly, Imelda was soaring. She was negotiating with the Federal Reserve Bank for stabilization loans, with the State Department for rural electrification and population-control funding and with well-connected lobbying firms to represent the Philippines in Washington. Philippine monetary officials were scurrying up and down the East Coast trying to keep up with her. She impressed her American hosts. The Federal Reserve Board chairman, Arthur F. Burns, in autographing a book for Mrs. Marcos, called her "the most beautiful, talented and eloquent woman" he had met. Marcos himself was so impressed with her efforts that on September 27 he concluded: "[S]he certainly is more effective than any ambassador we have. But we have only one Imelda."

Flattered and fawned over by the most powerful and important men in the world, Imelda returned home to a profound disappointment: her arrival back in Manila coincided precisely with publication of the *Free Press* cover photograph of Dovie in her bikini. But there was yet no hint of the anger and anguish to follow when Marcos welcomed her return the night of October 2, 1970. According to his diary entry:

> Although we had announced that she did not wish to be met at the airport, there was a big welcoming crowd including the diplomatic crowd.
>
> She has grown thinner and slimmer. She says she is 126 pounds. And of course lovelier.
>
> And still as energetic and lively as ever. She does have the stamina of a paratrooper.
>
> Now the Palace will be happy again —

But his vision of the "happy palace" was only illusion, soon to be displaced by the bitter reality of scandal.

CHAPTER SEVEN
New Year's Delusions

Congressman Floro "Floring" Crisologo of Ilocos Sur was not too rich or too powerful to be a devoutly religious man. Indeed, as he made his way to St. Paul's Cathedral to celebrate mass on Sunday, October 18, 1970, he had much for which to be thankful: a wife who, as the provincial governor, was his partner in life and politics; a devoted son who zealously managed his local political affairs; lucrative business interests in tobacco, the dominant local industry; an effective franchise on regional smuggling operations; an army of loyalists with better weapons than the constabulary to protect those interests; and a lifelong alliance with the president of the Philippines. With few exceptions, it could be said, life was good to the warlord of Ilocos Sur. And such good fortune deserved prayers of thanksgiving. At least once a week it brought Crisologo to his knees before God and man in the three-hundred-year-old church adjoining Plaza Burgos in the heart of Vigan, the provincial capital.

On this Sunday, the sixty-year-old warlord arrived for the afternoon mass with his private secretary and the usual entourage of armed bodyguards, most of whom remained discreetly outside the house of worship. The church was, after all, a sanctuary — one place, even in this most violent of Philippine provinces, where the people could escape the guns and private armies that terrorized the region.

Under the political and economic stewardship of the Crisologo family, Ilocos Sur had acquired a well-earned reputation comparable to the worst of America's lawless Old West towns. Vigan was the Dodge City of Luzon. It was said that the leading cause of death in the murder capital of the nation was "lead poisoning." In fact, by the fall of 1970 Ilocos Sur was in a state of virtual war. A bloody feud raged between Crisologo and a rival member of his own family — nephew Luis "Chavit" Singson, who had run unsuccessfully to oust Crisologo from Congress in the same 1969 campaign that had reelected Ferdinand Marcos. Crisologo was a Marcos Nacionalista, Singson a Liberal.

The campaign did not end with the voting. Ballots simply gave way to bullets. The congressman's son, Vincent "Bingbong" Crisologo, and his men looted, shot up, and then turned flamethrowers on two barrios that had voted for Singson. Like two gangs, both sides took shots at each other. Prominent citizens were assassinated in their own homes. The law was enforced only by what the press called "a goonstabulary," the hired guns of the rival warlords.

It was not surprising that, even a year after his reelection, Crisologo would go nowhere without his bodyguards. President Marcos had tried to intervene, ordering both factions to make peace or have their private armies forcibly disarmed. It was a futile gesture. While Crisologo was an ally of Marcos in the Congress, he had made it clear that in Ilocos Sur "*I* am the king." Marcos was not pleased, noting one night in his diary: "[H]ow unreasonable Crisologo has become."

The "king" of Ilocos Sur entered the huge arched doorway to the yellow stone cathedral on October 18 with his private secretary and one bodyguard. Stepping from sunlight into the dim, cavernous sanctuary, Crisologo needed a moment for his eyes to adjust. He followed the voice of the priest, striding down the long, familiar aisle past flickering candles, past row after row of wooden pews, past pillars displaying the portraits of saints, past hundreds of worshippers to the front row, his traditional bench. His secretary took the pew behind him; his guard stood along the wall a few paces away. The priest called the congregation to pray. The chamber echoed with the rustle of creaking benches and shuffling shoes as worshippers dropped to their knees.

Crisologo clutched his rosary and slipped to his knees, his head bowed over the prayer railing.

At that moment, in a church full of bowed heads, a single gunshot exploded. Crisologo slumped to the floor, a hole in his head, his blank eyes staring at the high ceiling of peeling blue paint. Immediately, a man stooped over the prone form, extending a hand toward Crisologo's heart. A second shot erupted. Crisologo no longer had a heart.

There were two gunmen. Some said they were strangers. The priest thought he recognized one as a local policeman. They slipped out a side door, through lines of horse-drawn taxis and pedicabs where barefoot, sleepy drivers waited for fares after the conclusion of mass. The assassins were last seen crossing Plaza Burgos and disappearing into the labyrinth of Vigan's narrow lanes. They were never caught. No one was ever charged.

Marcos got news of Crisologo's death during his stay at the seaside residence in Paranaque. It was the same weekend when Imelda's early depression over the Dovie Beams scandal had started to become a burden to the president. Marcos dispatched his most trusted aide, Defense Secretary Juan Ponce Enrile, to lead the Vigan inquiry. That night Marcos wrote of Crisologo:

> There goes a friend whom I warned against injustice and repression about a year ago. For he and his men were held accountable for the burning of Barrio Ora in Bantay and for various killings in Ilocos Sur — whether justly or not.
>
> What I fear is the retaliation that will follow. The wife, Carmeling Crisologo, is a courageous and hard woman who will now probably go after the faction of Chavit Singson . . . who is of course suspected of masterminding the killing. . . .
>
> We must also look into the possibility that this is the work of the Huks. Although I personally do not believe so.

In fact, years later, Tibo Mijares would write that members of the Malacanang presidential security command under Colonel Ver were behind the assassination. According to the former Marcos aide, the shooting in St. Paul's church neatly resolved a troublesome dispute over control of tobacco-smuggling revenue between Crisologo and Ver, who acted for Marcos. Crisologo had been threatening to expose the scheme, Mijares said.

There were no such references in the diary. Instead, Marcos paid notably reserved tributes to his longtime friend and political ally, writing: "The truth is I will miss Floring. He was one of the more pleasant leaders we had. And his personal habits and attitudes were not abrasive."

The killing was big news in Manila, but the violence was not unique. Murders, assassinations, even massacres were unfortunate facts of life in the provinces, a practice engaged in by rival warlords, insurgents, vigilantes, and uniformed members of the Philippine military. Three months before Crisologo fell, the *Free Press* had carried a lengthy article on "Massacre — Philippine Style: Under Marcos's 'Liberal Democracy,'" predicting that the Marcos administration could "go down in our history as the bloodiest ever." Much of the violence was related to government-ordered Huk suppression, constabulary units or paramilitary Barrio Self-Defense Units gunning down unarmed farmers and local officials regarded by military intelligence as "Huk sympathizers." During election seasons, the violence was more likely related to voter intimidation. Campaigns with fewer than two dozen deaths were seriously regarded as "peaceful." In a country where politics could be a blood sport, governors, mayors, and barrio captains were all-too-common targets of assassination, usually the victims of vendettas and local feuds.

Marcos saw opportunity in the violence — both in exploiting public weariness with it and in using or encouraging violence for his own advantage. For example, in the spring of 1970 he ordered Enrile to plant agents in different Communist camps to foment internal strife among radical groups. It seemed to work. On May 29, the president wrote in his diary:

> The policy of intriguing among the subversives so they will divide and even kill each other is paying off. Arthur Garcia [a prominent leftist] was ordered gunned down by [Commander] Dante. . . .

Regardless of who was behind the still-unsolved Crisologo killing, Marcos anticipated that public revulsion over the brutality could generate sympathy for the besieged president and his allies. Furthermore, he could use the example of such lawlessness possibly to justify severe government action.

In his diary, Marcos noted that Enrile had warned him the Crisologo attack could be "the beginning of the implementation of the plan to liquidate my political leaders and then me." The president expressed some alarm over reports that student activists greeted news of Crisologo's death with the cheer, "Crisologo is dead. Now the revolution starts." Marcos was grateful for Enrile's warning and wrote: "So I assured him that I am taking proper precautions and I have prepared an order of martial law which I will sign if an attempt against my life is made."

But what was particularly telling about the Marcos diary reaction to Crisologo's killing was the apparent ease with which he continuously shifted blame to suit his political agenda. The president's first diary entry blamed the local feud. Then he considered blaming the Huks. Later, he blamed the press, student demonstrators, and Jesuit leaders for creating the hostile environment that led to the killing.

Finally, by year's end, his paranoia fanned by a two-month siege of scandal and political criticism, Marcos shifted blame one more time — a shift that nicely fit his argument that the nation was under attack from subversives and political opportunists. On December 30, 1970, he wrote:

> It is now believed that the killing of Cong. Crisologo was an NPA [Communist New People's Army] project directed by Sen. Benigno Aquino. . . .

Nothing supported that conclusion except fear, suspicion, and the president's imagination. It was delusion, one of many apparently embraced by Ferdinand Marcos in the closing days of 1970. His diary reveals one striking example in December, embodied in his own separate and contradictory assessments of the year.

It was a year, the president candidly noted, filled with trials and crises. But things were looking better, he was happy to say, because of a recovering economy and more peaceful streets. He even minimized the insurgency threat when on December 23 he wrote:

> The [Communists] are on the run, demonstrations are tamed down to placard-carrying with an occasional Molotov cocktail. . . .
>
> After serious study, I find no reason to fear the demonstrators, [not] even the radicals and the [Huks] and NPAs. They serve the purpose of keeping our people reminded that we must reform for the better if we would keep our heads.

They may harass, but that is all they can do.

Such a view of the Philippines was remarkably optimistic for a president who was contemplating martial law or the suspension of constitutional protections to preserve peace and order. The description did not match a nation in trouble, in need of reform, in need of a savior. But within seven days, the Marcos diary entries reflected his old self. Once again he was alarmed about the risk of his own extermination. And he was darkly self-righteous, scattering blame for the nation's troubles to all corners of Philippine society, when on December 30 he wrote:

> Undoubtedly our society is sick and the government muddles on on compromises. The legislature waits to arrogate executive and even judicial powers to itself . . . arrogant and vain. The city people are more interested in gossip than in achievements. The media is sensationalist and deliberately distorts and even falsifies news in order to raise a headline. The businessmen are not interested in the plight of the common people but are obsessed with amassing wealth. The oligarchs are at their favorite pastime, to get to the levers of power. The opposition party is irresponsible and didn't care less whether what they do would prejudice the people provided it enhances their chances to return to power.
>
> All attempts at progress are deliberately blocked. Even the radicals seek nothing but power for power's sake.

That, finally, was a vision of the Philippines to fit the delusions of a would-be messiah, a vision of a country needing Ferdinand Marcos more than it needed democracy or freedom itself. And Marcos was ready. In the closing hours of 1970, the president reviewed another contingency plan for martial law, this one code named "OPLAN Bukang Liwayway." He seemed anxious, unable to enjoy traditional New Year's Eve festivities, calling them "empty ceremony" and a "waste of our precious time."

Then, alone with his diary at two-thirty in the morning, still hours away from the first sunrise of 1971, Marcos entered his last comments on the past year — and his first ominous notes on the year ahead:

> As we were gathered to await the new year . . . I wondered whether the year 1971 would usher in an authoritarian government in the Philippines.
>
> During the mass, I prayed God for strength, wisdom and guidance. For I knew I would have to make awesome decisions this year.

CHAPTER EIGHT
Dictator Dreams

Ferdinand Marcos had visions. He heard the voice of God telling him he was needed to save the Philippines, telling him to confront the enemies of the republic. He had no choice; his very life was at stake. One Saturday morning in March 1971, the president awoke to share the somewhat disturbing dream with his wife, quoting to her what God had told him.

> "This is your principal mission in life — save the country again from the Maoists, the anarchists and the radicals." This is the message that I deduce from the visions that I see asleep and awake.
>
> "Subordinate everything to this," God seems to be saying to me.
>
> "And you are the only person who can do it," He says. "Nobody else can.
>
> "So do not miss the opportunity given you, [because] if you do, it will mean not only your death but that of your wife and children and of the wives, children and friends of men of equal persuasion."

Marcos described the divine messages to Imelda as they lay in bed. Together they had endured weeks of sometimes violent street demonstrations, blistering editorials, and popular ridicule. Nude pictures of Dovie Beams were in the current edition of *Republic Weekly*. But there was no hint of any stress between them in the president's diary account. He called her "my strength and inspiration," and he wrote:

> "I have learned to love our country as you do," she said as I told her that a time had come again when I must stake my life for our country and people as I did during the war. For the risks may be great and only God knows how it will end.
>
> "If die we must to save [our country], then let us do so gladly," we agreed.

Marcos was dreaming of dictatorship. God's voice was calling him to declare martial law. What had been a flirtation with options for authoritarian rule a year before evolved into obsession through the first half of 1971. The dream occupied his sleep, his contemplations, his work, and his diary. At his annual religious retreat, Marcos concluded that martial law was "a Christian solution" to the nation's "explosive social situation." Aides like Defense Secretary Juan Ponce Enrile urged him to institute "a benevolent dictatorship."

Only Enrile knew how close Marcos had come to dictatorial rule early in 1971. Anti-Marcos sentiment was high at that time and showed no signs of abating. The president's popularity was plunging, accompanied by — if not propelled by — the ever-more-critical press that Marcos regarded as venal, vicious, and Communist-infiltrated. His feud with the family of Vice-President Fernando Lopez had taken a turn for the acrimonious with stinging revelations of rampant and unprecedented government corruption published in the Lopez-owned *Chronicle*. It was the first public disclosure of the Marcoses' long-rumored hidden wealth. Political foes discussed impeachment.

Meanwhile, the nation's economy was spiraling downward as the peso slumped and oil prices climbed. Manila was hit by a crippling transportation strike when jeepney drivers walked out and joined students demonstrating against the administration. Another street riot left three youths dead and many more injured. Prices were out of control. Economic hardship in the provinces was driving more people into crowded Manila. Slums were growing. Crime was rising.

A frustrated Marcos complained in his diary that the media were "blaming me for all the ills of the country." If things got much worse, Marcos mused in his diary, the public soon would rise up and demand martial law to restore peace and order. In the month before hearing God's voice in his dreams, Marcos wrote: "The opinion is developing that what the Philippines needs is a benevolent dictator. . . . Some day soon I must make a decision on this."

To suggest he had not already made that decision was delusory. The only question unresolved was the timing. Weeks earlier Marcos had set in motion a series of internal military changes specifically designed to enable seizure of the civil government and the media. And, then unbeknownst to his nation, he had taken another extraordinary step.

In taking that secret action, Marcos was less inspired by heavenly visions than he was frightened by temporal events. It happened on the road to Baguio.

The president was returning from his successful and ego-boosting 1970 Christmas tour of the provinces. The presidential yacht *777* had brought him and his family to San Fernando and a warm Ilocandia reception. Then the presidential motorcade headed up the twisting Naguilian Road to the summer capital where the buoyant Marcos planned a few days of golf and relaxation to conclude the holidays. But somewhere amid the hairpin turns of the mountainous road, the caravan abruptly pulled to a stop. Security men scurried to change the license plates on all the official cars. Helicopter gunships were called to provide overhead escort for the entourage.

Troubling word had been radioed to the Marcos party. A dissident young army lieutenant just hours earlier had led a raid on the armory at the Philippine Military Academy in Baguio. Lieutenant Victor Corpuz and an estimated ten Huk insurgents escaped with high-powered rifles and explosives. The group was believed to be hiding somewhere in or around Baguio, perhaps waiting for the president's arrival.

The incident inflamed the president's abiding fear of assassination. It also aroused deep-seated suspicions about the loyalty of his military. Marcos promptly issued rapid-fire orders reorganizing the military.

He ordered creation of a Special War Center, an Internal Security Agency, and a Psy-war (psychological warfare) Branch within the Department of National Defense under Enrile. It was intended that the Psy-war Branch would supervise the media and monitor the loyalty of military officers. He also directed the aide of one general to "watch" for signs of disloyalty in another general. His paranoia flourished.

Colonel Fabian Ver's mission and authority were greatly expanded. Not only would the president's devoted Ilocano aide assume command of provincial security forces, but the palace security chief also was ordered to field and train "a special team" of operatives prepared to arrest target personalities (notably, those on the president's enemies list) or to take over target areas in the event of martial law.

And various military units were realigned. The president promoted Lieutenant General Fidel Ramos, a Marcos cousin and West Point graduate, to head the 2nd Philippine Constabulary Zone. Marcos wanted his military engineering and infantry divisions brought up to full strength. Engineers were especially important, as the president intended that they be able to operate the nation's utilities and transportation companies. Finally, Marcos ordered the immediate expenditure of three million pesos to purchase machine guns.

One day in January, a few days after the Corpuz raid, a delegation of Nacionalista allies called on Malacanang to complain about the civil strife and political turmoil they feared was undermining the administration. They pressed for an immediate declaration of martial law. Recounting their advice, Marcos noted in his diary:

> "We cannot understand why you are so patient. Do not wait until we are completely debilitated and the people [are] against us. It will be too late. One swift blow and we remove the cancer from our society," they all said.
>
> I could only answer that it may be sooner than we think.

Indeed. The next day, on January 14, 1971 — a date divisible by his lucky number seven — Marcos signed a secret declaration of martial law. He gave an undated copy of the extraordinary document to Enrile, "so that if anything happens to me, he . . . can execute and implement the proclamation."

While the secret proclamation was unknown to the country, details of the president's military reorganization plans quickly leaked. The result was rumors of imminent martial law. Editorials condemned the threat, even as Marcos publicly denied the rumors. Liberal party leaders published a full-page newspaper advertisement declaring they would boycott any Congress operated under martial law, in part an effort to deprive Marcos of any claims to constitutional legitimacy. Student protesters tempered their street demonstrations so that, as the president's diary noted, "Marcos will have no reason to proclaim martial law."

But Marcos seemed especially concerned about one uncertainty. What about the Americans? Would Washington support such drastic and antidemocratic action, or would he find himself like Chiang Kai-shek, feeling abandoned by the United States? He wanted Ambassador Henry Byroade to obtain assurances from President Nixon.

After the ambassador returned from a trip to Washington, Marcos received him at the palace to hear what the American president had to say. On February 1, 1971, Marcos wrote:

> I had before this asked him to tell me frankly if the American government would support me if there was need to declare martial law to save the country from the communists. Nixon's answer was "Absolutely!"

Despite his underlying eagerness to prepare for martial law, Marcos was like a man poised on a high diving board: at once thrilled and anxious about taking the plunge. It made his stomach hurt. Early in January he noted:

> My tummy shows some hyperacidity so I take something every two or three hours. It is most probably due to the tension arising out of the plans for the proclamation of martial law.

Marcos feared getting an ulcer. Worse, he worried about developing a gastrointestinal malignancy. Indeed, even in the best of times his self-preoccupation bordered on hypochondria. For a man who seemed to regard himself as God's chosen savior of the Philippines, Marcos could be strikingly fearful over his mortality — equally afraid of assassins and disease, never quite reassured even by those visions that his divine mission might entitle him to some divine protection.

His hypochondria ranged from extreme to trivial. On one pleasure outing to Ursula Island with friends and family, the president said he felt a mosquito bite. Immediately, he ordered everyone to take two extra doses of prophylactic medicine against malaria. When he caught a summer cold, he "called a conference of doctors." When he noticed a chest pain after exercising, he called for an electrocardiogram. It turned out to be "muscular fatigue of the pectoralis" — or, too many push-ups.

Then there was the time he needed a heart exam after watching a pornographic movie. That was back in the summer of 1970. After his Saturday morning exercises, Marcos paused to view what he described as "one of those green pornographies that pass for a movie." He described what he saw and how it affected him when he wrote: "[T]he girls were completely nude, pubic hair and all, which disgusted me and actually gave me a stomach ache."

He took two doses of Gelusil, an antacid. And, as he noted in the diary, at Imelda's prompting he agreed to take an electrocardiogram —"which turned out to be excellent."

At times it seemed that Marcos noted every sore muscle, ache, pain, or twinge he endured. Once, after stubbing "the second smallest toe on my left foot," he had to be carried to mass in a wheelchair. He complained of a sore back and summoned a doctor. The diagnosis: a lumpy mattress.

When he got indigestion, he recorded how many doses of Gelusil relieved his discomfort. When he suffered from a virus, he filled a page with symptoms, a list of medications, and the description of his sponge bath. When he had diarrhea, he recorded the frequency and volume of his bowel movements. He once noted that the affliction had plagued him for so long that "my voice is falsetto." After a proctoscopy examination, he recorded the length of the insertion: twenty-three centimeters.

In the midst of his martial-law planning early in 1971, Marcos's "nagging fear" of gastrointestinal ailments flared anew with a series of upset stomachs. After one Sunday golf game in February he downed a concoction of Welch's grape juice mixed with beer and complained of stomach pains. He diagnosed his symptoms as possibly "the beginning of an ulcer." Doctors said it was minor tension-induced hyperacidity. Nonetheless, Marcos was troubled by the continuing stomachaches.

On a Saturday in March, in the palace dining room, the president watched actor Rod Steiger's performance as the ailing Napoleon Bonaparte in a film about the French emperor-general's epic battle with British General Wellington. Just as the French appeared to have won, Napoleon was stricken with severe stomach pains and temporarily retired from the field, leaving a blundering subordinate in charge. In that spring of 1971, the oft-ailing Marcos noted in his diary: "Saw the movie 'Waterloo' which depressed me as I saw Napoleon lose his last battle from a stomach ache."

He also saw Steiger's Napoleon declare: "Do you know what the throne is? The throne is an overdecorated piece of furniture. It's what's behind the throne that counts — my brains, my ambitions, my desires, my hope, my imagination, and, above all, my will!"

Notwithstanding his hypochondria, his delusions of divine calling, his paranoia about assassination or afflictions, Ferdinand Marcos coolly and carefully was constructing the framework of a dictatorship for the Philippines in the spring of 1971. He had worked out not only the military reorganization, but plans for mass arrests of opponents, nationwide censorship, and sweeping curfews. The "will of the commander," he wrote in March, must be "unlimited by any restrictions from statutes or the Bill of Rights."

But Marcos still needed an act of violence sufficiently threatening to peace and order to trigger his declaration of martial law. At a meeting with his generals on June 2, the president was assured that the people would support martial law if there was destruction of public utilities, the burning of Manila, or the bombing of government buildings. One general "suggested that the armed forces itself could bring this about." Marcos wrote that he declined the offer of self-sabotage, agreeing instead to an undefined strategy by which radicals would be "stimulated into violence."

Clearly, Marcos long had entertained some form of provocation as a tactical option. Early in 1970 he discussed with congressional allies the possibility of introducing tougher antisubversion bills as a way to "provoke violence by the communists." During a spring breakfast that year he warned Manila publishers that the Philippine military "felt that if there was going to be a military confrontation [with Communist insurgents] anyway, it should be triggered as soon as possible so that there may be less casualties." A year later, still wrestling with the temptation to take provocative action, Marcos wrote on February 1, 1971:

[I]f there is going to be an inevitable collision, then perhaps we should induce it now while the communists are weak and unorganized.

Military reorganization efforts moved ahead quickly. The contingency plans for martial law underwent repeated review, refinement, and improvement. But public criticism also was unrelenting. The president grew increasingly impatient. He considered dictatorial control inevitable when in the spring of 1971 he wrote:

> ... I go through these days with a feeling of unreality, as if it were a dream or drama of which you already know the ending.
>
> Thus we all go through the required rituals of ceremonials of our respective roles ... while I wait for the right moment when I must proclaim martial law and practically take over the government.
>
> In the meantime we must fence and hedge and dissimulate. ...
>
> So there actually is no alternative but to push the situation into its logical conclusion — the denouement of a military confrontation.

The showdown might have come then. And Marcos might have acted on his powerful temptation to seize control of the nation in the summer of 1971. Instead, he succumbed to another temptation, to a political dare from Ninoy Aquino and the Liberal party. They challenged the president to make the November off-year elections "a referendum on Ferdinand Marcos" and his administration. The races for eight Senate seats, all selected by nationwide balloting, offered the first national vote since Marcos won his disputed landslide reelection in 1969.

If Marcos believed the negative independent public opinion polls, he should have followed his father's advice — avoid any fight you are not sure to win. But the president was not persuaded. He apparently believed, as his advisers constantly assured him, that he was a popular president. He also knew how to win elections. And, finally, he had an intense desire to give Senator Ninoy Aquino his political come-uppance.

When it came to Ninoy Aquino, Ferdinand Marcos sometimes lost his sense of political and emotional balance. Ninoy provoked him like no other rival. Indeed, Aquino's popularity, his oratorical skills, his political success, all made him the president's nemesis nonpareil. Marcos referred to him in his diary as "a congenital liar" and "a Huk coddler" and "the most dangerous man" in the country who, he wrote, "makes my blood boil."

In the summer of 1971 Marcos had been provoked again, this time into an election duel with that popular nemesis. Like the president, Aquino himself would not be on the November ballot. But the young Tarlac senator was a symbol of the Liberal party — its sole winner in the previous Senate elections and a favorite for the party's presidential nomination in 1973. Marcos could not resist the challenge. And on June 28 he wrote:

> Since I have decided to turn the local elections this year into a referendum on my leadership and policies, we will have to prevent any outbreak of violence that may lead to . . . martial law before the November elections.

To answer the dare, the president's dreams of dictatorship would have to wait.

CHAPTER NINE
Democracy in Traction

On a rainless August evening in 1971, Plaza Miranda was packed with ten thousand Liberal party faithful, waiting to cheer official introductions of the party's Senate and local candidates. The traditional proclamation rally crowd looked huge in the small, church-dominated square. From the elevated reviewing stands, draped in bunting and partisan banners, dozens of the nation's leading oppositionist politicians reveled in the enthusiastic atmosphere. Despite the fact they were poorly organized and underfinanced, they were confident that 1971 would be a Liberal year and that a strong showing in November could propel the party into Malacanang in 1973. Polls showed the Liberal party senators favored over the Nacionalista slate by a margin of five to three.

The president, meanwhile, was in trouble. His approval rating was an all-time low of barely 20 percent. Anti-Marcos delegates seemed to dominate the recently convened constitutional convention [ConCon], threatening the president's hopes of a charter change extending his term beyond 1973. More polls showed public support for such an extension to be negligible, an astoundingly low 8.8 percent.

Still, Marcos remained outwardly confident. Publicly, he assured his Nacionalista party colleagues of victory. Even in his diary he privately expressed pity for the hapless Liberals and predicted they would be lucky to win 20 percent of the November ballots. Ferdinand Marcos so disliked bad news that he seemed capable of ignoring it. But the Liberals planned a rousing campaign rally that would be hard to ignore, filled with fiery rhetoric and new disclosures about alleged financial and political corruption in the administration. Plaza Miranda was ready.

Opening night of the Philippine political season began with prayers, band music, and bombastic oratory. Shortly after 9:15, the Liberal party slate was introduced. Everyone stood to sing the national anthem. It was customary at such events for the anthem to be followed by a display of fireworks, but party leaders this time had decided against having symbolic bombs bursting in air. During the previous year and a half, Manila had seen too much of the real thing, the fireworks of bullets and Molotov cocktails. Tensions remained high. There were rumors of assassination attempts by Marcos loyalists. Days earlier, in fact, party leaders were warned that fireworks could be used as a cover for such an attack.

Consequently, Senate candidate John "Sonny" Osmena was surprised and a little annoyed by the first burst of fireworks after the national anthem. He sat down shaking his head. He thought one of the local Manila candidates must not have heard about, or else ignored, the leadership's fireworks ban. The young congressman from Cebu was watching the crackling display in the dark sky when a thundering explosion shook the reviewing stand. There were screams. People scrambled away from the far side of the stage where smoke billowed. They were torn and bloodied, but Osmena had not yet moved from his chair when a second blast erupted, engulfing him in a gust of hot air and acrid, gray smoke.

"They're murdering us! They're murdering us," he choked as he jumped up to run with the fleeing crowd. He could not take a step, collapsing to the rough wood platform. His left leg spewed a fountain of blood. His last conscious thought was: "I need a tourniquet."

Senator Eva Kalaw had a clear view of the first explosion. She saw chairs tossed up into the air. She saw Senator Jovito Salonga hurled to the ground. She threw herself down on the stage, but it was too late.

Her body was riddled with shrapnel, her right leg mangled by the blast.

Plaza Miranda was in chaos. On the stage and in the crowd, lifeless and mutilated bodies were strewn through the debris. A barefoot boy selling cigarettes was dead. A *Manila Times* photographer was killed. Television stations broke into their programming for live news bulletins. One of Eva Kalaw's sons was at home celebrating the first birthday of the senator's grandson when he saw the televised bombing report.

Meanwhile, one of Eva's friends had found her on the stage. Somehow the friend, another woman, was able to carry the wounded senator down the stairs to the plaza, then up one of the narrow side streets to a waiting Jeep. On the way to Jose Reyes Memorial Hospital, Eva worried that Senator Salonga had been left on the stage. Her rescuer could not turn back.

It would be hours before the extent of the tragedy was clear: nine dead, sixty-eight others injured or maimed, all eight Liberal party Senate candidates among the wounded. Salonga was near death. He had lost an eye and much of his hearing. Also in critical condition was Sergio Osmena, Jr., Sonny's uncle and the party's last presidential contender. Shrapnel penetrated the old man's lungs. Sonny's kneecaps were shattered. And Manila mayoral candidate Ramon Bagatsing lost a leg.

When Sonny Osmena awoke in the hospital, doctors were doubtful his legs could be saved, but the young candidate was still unaware of their concern. His first conscious thought was of the campaign. "Jim — " he rasped to a friend in the emergency room, "we just won the election." Senator Gerardo "Gerry" Roxas, head of the Liberal party and the son of a former Philippine president, also was carried unconscious from Plaza Miranda. Soon after awaking, he released a statement from his hospital bed declaring that he was "holding President Marcos personally responsible for the brutal and senseless carnage" at Plaza Miranda.

That night, police investigators sifted through rubble to find the remnants of two American-type fragmentation grenades. The explosives later were traced to a Philippine military arsenal. Had Marcos loyalists in the military actually done what the president, in his diary, said they had offered to do? Had they carried out acts of sabotage to

A triumphant Marcos at a campaign appearance in 1969.

Imelda reaching out to seas of hands at a campaign appearance in 1969.

Ferdinand and Imelda Marcos with Vice-President Spiro Agnew and his wife during the 1969 inaugural ball.

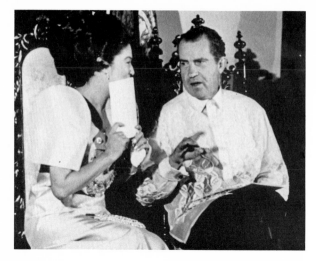

Imelda with Richard Nixon in a barong at Malacanang Palace in 1969.

Imelda singing at a 1969 campaign appearance in Cebu.

Marcos family portrait taken on election day, November 1969. Children, left to right, are Bongbong, Irene, and Imee.

Imelda at Manila airport on October 27, 1970, returning from an early foreign trip during which she met with Pope Paul VI in Rome. The Dovie Beams scandal is about to break.

Dovie Beams on the cover of the *Free Press* during the height of the scandal.

Juan Ponce Enrile, right, with armed forces chief of staff, General Romeo Espino, and Mrs. Enrile.

Benigno "Ninoy" Aquino and his wife, Corazon, on April 6, 1971.

Riot police battling students in a jeepney during rioting on the night of January 26, 1970.

Student rioters swarming over the grounds of Malacanang during a demonstration that turned violent on the night of January 30, 1970.

Anti-Marcos posters and signs that appeared all over Manila, from the 1969 election campaign into the *First Quarter Storm* of 1970.

Marcos under assault from flying debris outside Congress on January 26, 1970, after delivering his State of the Nation address. Presidential security chief Colonel Fabian Ver (in white shirt on left, with hand on car) assists Marcos into the limo.

Philippine boy injured in the Plaza Miranda bombing, August 21, 1971.

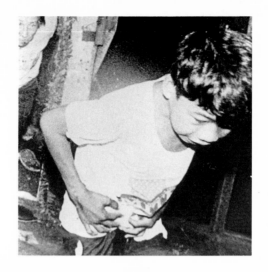

Plaza Miranda in the immediate aftermath of the bombing.

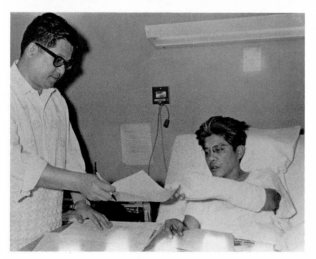

Aquino with hospitalized Liberal party president Gerry Roxas on August 27, 1971, a few days after the Plaza Miranda bombing.

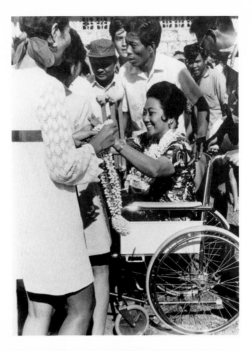

Eva Kalaw campaigning in Laguna from a wheelchair after her injury in the Plaza Miranda bombing.

A tearful Imelda with Ferdinand laying the remains of their unborn child in the Romualdez family plot on Leyte, June 19, 1972.

be blamed on the Communists? That was the immediate suspicion of one leader from the president's own party, Nacionalista Senator Jose Diokno. In a dramatic break with Marcos, the highly respected senator and former justice secretary resigned from the party and charged that "the military, or men trained by the military," committed the attack. Later Diokno would pay for such public disloyalty.

At Malacanang, Marcos immediately blamed the Maoist New People's Army (NPA). He also blamed rival Ninoy Aquino. It was Saturday night, August 21 — another date divisible by his lucky number seven. Marcos secretly signed Proclamation No. 889 suspending the writ of habeas corpus. Metrocom police were free to arrest virtually anyone without warrants and to imprison them indefinitely without bringing formal charges. Marcos targeted suspected NPA sympathizers. He assigned General Fidel Ramos to draw up the list of about thirty people to be arrested. It was an abbreviated version of the much broader list of state enemies already targeted for arrest in the event of full-scale martial law.

In his diary the next day, Marcos said the still-secret suspension of constitutional protections was ordered because the bombing "was caused or done by subversives." He also wrote:

> Sen. Aquino who was absent from the platform during the bombing (suspiciously so) is the prime suspect as the mastermind . . . of the whole dastardly plot. . . . Ninoy Aquino is the most ruthless man in the Philippines today."

Marcos made similar assertions on television and in the press, turning what had promised to be a dramatic political duel into a tense and bitter personal feud. In fact, Aquino had not been on the stage when the bombs exploded. The popular speaker was scheduled to address the rally last, to deliver the oratorical grand finale of the event. The promise of an Aquino speech always kept crowds from leaving early. So, to assure maximum impact, he was supposed to delay his appearance until sometime around 11 P.M.

The unidentified bombers struck well before Aquino arrived. Their deadly attack was just the kind of violence Marcos had been warning would justify an authoritarian response. Indeed, he wrote that on the night of the bombing Enrile, his closest adviser, had urged an "outright declaration of martial law." But Marcos took only a half-step, launching what looked more like a trial run of his untested plans for martial law.

Arrests had been going on for two days before the president finally told the nation that he already had suspended the writ of habeas corpus. More than twenty of the "target personalities," the so-called Maoists, were detained at constabulary headquarters in Camp Crame — among them a university president, a professor, leftist students, and radio-TV commentator Roger "Bomba" Arienda. Few were avowed Communists. All were rabid critics of Marcos. None was ever charged with complicity in the bombing.

The president had suspended a cherished constitutional safeguard in the name of peace and order. The press objected. The detainees objected. Top leaders of his party objected. Most notably, even the victims of the bombing objected. But Marcos waited for the Philippine people to rally around him, to endorse his stern response to the Communist menace. And while waiting, he contemplated "the loneliness of the presidency."

Meanwhile, Ninoy Aquino maintained a furious pace of public appearances, denouncing Marcos, denouncing the mass arrests, and challenging the president to file charges against him so he could prove that he was innocent and that Marcos was "the biggest liar in Philippine political life." And he thundered that "Lady Justice has worn a peek-a-boo since you came to power." Each day Aquino toured the hospitals to meet with the injured bomb victims. Images of bandaged, bedridden Liberal candidates in slings and plaster casts became a staple of television and newspaper coverage.

Only a divided Nacionalista delegation in the Philippine House of Representatives provided any encouragement for the president. Fifty of 108 congressmen called his suspension order a "bold act of statesmanship." It was a minority view. A poll of Manila residents a month later showed that only 25 percent supported suspending the writ.

Marcos also was getting signals of dissatisfaction from the United States. One of the "Blue Ladies" reported that the American ambassador made a late-evening call on her and her husband, who was already in his pajamas, suggesting that Imelda cancel plans to visit Washington in the fall. And Imelda said that Ambassador Byroade, in comments to her, had minimized as merely "circumstantial" the president's case against Aquino. The ambassador was "acting strangely,"

Marcos thought. Marcos had been troubled two months earlier when a visiting American journalist told the president about his conversations with Byroade in which the ambassador supposedly said "that I had terrible people around me and that I was not as popular as I thought and further that I was due for a disappointment in the coming local elections. . . . In a way I am sad," Marcos had written on June 23, "because I had considered Byroade as a friend. . . ."

The pressure of rejection from all sides put Marcos under great stress. He was impatient and short-tempered. A day after the opinion polls showed overwhelming public opposition to his suspension order, a disgruntled Marcos wrote:

> Today I must plan my life anew. All the old concepts must give way to the new, objective and cruel tyrannies of the present. Painful but unavoidable. And I am deeply sad.
>
> But all the more am I resolved to be strong and resilient.
>
> I am getting irritable and sensitive. And while outwardly calm, I am boiling inside me.
>
> And my problem is I take it out [on] Imelda, my poor wife. I do not know how she can tolerate my boorishness these days.

During that period he had described Imelda as frustrated, depressed, and "in a crying jag," which, he said, "shatters my morale."

His morale also was troubled by the media, broadly skeptical of the president's claims that an existing Communist rebellion justified drastic actions. Headlines in the *Manila Times* derided the president's "fictitious insurrection." And Marcos complained that "columnists and commentators keep repeating that the military has foisted a big fraud on me with intelligence reports of the communist conspiracy." Marcos brooded that "communists are still succeeding in distorting news."

Even a group of senators from the president's own party joined with Aquino in September to issue a report minimizing the threat of revolution. They said banditry and common criminals posed a greater menace than Communist rebels. Finally, some of the nation's top military officers also expressed misgivings about suspension of the writ. Marcos conceded that he felt "nagged and bothered" by the lack of support.

He found solace in delusions of his personal popularity, again predicting a landslide Senate victory over the Liberals in November.

He found inspiration in a religious service at the palace. As he had during previous religious retreats, Marcos reported a close encounter with God when he wrote:

> I could feel I was in communication with my Creator. The sermon on being alone was apropos. And as I prayed I felt tears springing to my eyes from the joy of communication. I was on the verge, I believe, of one of those mystic seizures where the spirit lifts up from the body.

But, for the practical politician in Marcos, solace and inspiration were not enough. Nor could he wait for public opinion to recover. That was hopeless because the media, he determined, were partners of the Communists in subverting the republic. Indeed, in a September observation that would echo ominously into the future, Marcos wrote:

> The suspension has taught us some very clear lessons. One of them is that the greater weapon of subversion now is apparently the media.
> The media terrorizes [*sic*] the people and the public officials into inaction against communism. . . . Many of our people are beginning to stop from acting to combat communism because of the adverse reaction of the media [to suspension of the writ].

So, having lost his case in the court of public opinion, Marcos turned to a court supposedly sheltered from partisan politics and media influence, a court, more importantly, to which he had appointed most of the judges who would hear his case — the Philippine Supreme Court.

Not since Ferdinand Marcos was a young man convicted of murder had so much of his future rested on a single ruling of the Supreme Court. If the justices determined that his suspension of the writ of habeas corpus had been unconstitutional, Marcos would be left with neither popular nor legal mandate for his actions. Moreover, he feared such a setback would undermine his authority with some already reluctant military officers. Clearly, it would undermine his ability to impose the more drastic measure of martial law under similar circumstances. If he wanted to retain unhampered authority to do so, Marcos simply could not afford to lose in the Supreme Court. He needed every ally he could rally.

By the fall of 1971, Marcos was the patron of many political careers — low-level civil servants, high-ranking bureaucrats, local politicians, congressmen, cabinet members, military officers. Literally thousands of men and women felt they owed their political lives and status directly to the man in Malacanang. Some were so grateful they erected shrines to him in their homes. Some, like a group of Ilocano congressmen, pledged him loyalty "even to the extent of suicide." Many referred to him almost reverently as *Apo* (godfather).

While he enjoyed such fawning respect, Marcos reacted badly to anything he perceived as disloyalty. When the president's appointee to the Commission on Elections (Comelec) publicly criticized him for excessive campaign spending in 1971, Marcos scrawled: "What an arrogant ingrate he has turned out to be." When Senator Eva Kalaw bolted the Nacionalista party to run as a Liberal, taunting Imelda in the process to run on the opposing slate, Marcos called her "a petty fishwife" and wrote: "[S]he owes her political career to Imelda and me . . . [but] she has never been grateful for it."

And when the first rumors reached Malacanang that one of the president's Supreme Court appointees might vote against his position, Marcos concluded the jurist was influenced by friendship with wounded Senator Sergio Osmena. In his diary Marcos huffed: "And to think that I appointed him justice because he would be scholarly and fair!" In fact, six justices on the eleven-member Supreme Court panel owed their appointments to the president. And with so much at stake, Marcos was prepared to call due those debts.

On September 1, the court began hearing arguments challenging the president's right to suspend the writ of habeas corpus. It had been less than two weeks since the order went into effect, but already public pressure to lift the suspension was almost overwhelming. Detainees in Camp Crame had turned their cells into soapboxes, speaking out in media interviews and written communiqués. In the streets of Manila, demonstrators marched to support them. Liberal party candidates made freedom for the detainees a centerpiece of their election campaigns. With each passing day the detainees seemed to gain stature as popular heroes at the expense of the administration. Nonetheless, in his diary Marcos vowed not to lift the suspension before the November election.

The president turned to two fellow Ilocanos to help secure the crucial Supreme Court victory. One was a public ally: Solicitor General

Felix Q. Antonio, a native of Laoag, who would direct the administration's case. He was a former lower court judge and, by good fortune, a relative by marriage to one of the justices, the Marcos-appointed Claudio Teehankee.

The other ally never was revealed outside the pages of the diary and a discreet circle of close aides. He was a confidential adviser who relayed regular details of the secret deliberations of the court. The spy for the president was, in fact, one of the justices: Fred Ruiz Castro, another native of Laoag and the senior Marcos appointee on the bench.

At the time, Castro had designs on a prominent cabinet position. When it was announced that Defense Secretary Enrile was stepping down to run for a Nacionalista senate seat in the November elections, Castro sent word to Marcos through a senate intermediary that he was available for Enrile's vacant office. No political appointment was forthcoming, but those contacts opened a back channel for intrigues with Malacanang.

Marcos, meanwhile, worried about the court's leanings. He considered Chief Justice Roberto Concepcion and Jose B. L. Reyes to be staunch civil rights advocates. The two elders of the bench were highly respected and independent jurists whose leadership could sway others on the court. Marcos regarded Justice Arsenio P. Dizon an outright foe because he was related to the family of Ninoy Aquino. Justice Calixto Zaldivar was suspect because he asked worrisome questions during the opening hearings. Justice Enrique M. Fernando, one of the Marcos jurists, was "inscrutable" but seemingly leaning against the president. Castro, too, was a question mark and had told the intermediary that he intended to "vote his conscience." Marcos wondered if that should be considered a threat. At best, the president thought he could expect a favorable vote of 8–3. But even a decision in his favor could be seen as a setback if the court was badly divided. Tense and irritable in the early days of September, Marcos was eager to shore up support in the court.

The key intermediary was loyalist Senator Jose J. Roy. Through his intervention, Fred Ruiz Castro came to dine with the president on Thursday night, September 16. It was an extraordinary session, far outside the norms of judicial decorum and wholly disdainful of any notions or principles of the separation of powers. Others on the court were neither invited nor informed. During their private meeting, Marcos showed raw intelligence data to the justice, underscoring his claims that the nation was under attack by insurgents and that Ninoy Aquino backed the NPA. For his part, the jurist reported on the leanings of his colleagues. He described highlights of a likely majority opinion. And he offered Marcos a suggestion: lift the suspension in some regions of the country and Castro believed he could persuade the court to uphold the president's proclamation *unanimously.*

The promise of a possible 11–0 Supreme Court decision had enormous appeal to the president. His vow to wait until November was set aside. Marcos would travel to Cebu and announce that he was lifting the suspension in the Visayas region on Saturday, "so that it will hit the Sunday papers." He would do the same later in Mindanao and other provinces, including the Ilocandia region of northern Luzon. It was a calculated political move intended first to influence the court, but also expected to ease public criticism. And it was the beginning of a close but clandestine relationship between the president and the associate justice.

Marcos left nothing to chance. There were additional private contacts between Malacanang and the court. Marcos, as well as Imelda, also conferred with Justices Teehankee and Antonio P. Barredo. But none was as crucial as Castro, who not only kept the president informed but also lobbied his colleagues with intelligence data provided exclusively to him by the palace.

The president and his justice spy met at night, mostly — and not in the palace, but at Pangarap, a house across the Pasig River in a more remote section of the Malacanang compound. When Chief Justice Concepcion made an emotional plea for his colleagues to investigate more fully the president's claim of subversion, Castro promptly told the president that the chief justice feared the court might lose public confidence without a thorough judicial review. Marcos groused that "even the honorable justices want to be popular! What a grave disappointment." The justices were confronted daily with anti-Marcos demonstrators picketing the court. Castro warned the president that jurists were "only human" and were bound to be influenced by public opinion and the media. Marcos wrote he was "disturbed by the statement." The court insisted on getting a military intelligence briefing laying out the evidence of rebellion and threats to the national security that Marcos alleged. Castro rushed to Pangarap to counsel Marcos on what data would appeal best to his fellow judges. He also recommended that Marcos put his military chief of staff through "a dry run," to practice his briefing before facing the court. And finally, the night before the crucial intelligence briefing to the full Supreme Court, Castro himself secretly presided over the administration's last midnight practice session at Pangarap. Through it all, Castro's confidence had encouraged Marcos. On October 1, 1971, the president wrote:

> He [Castro] assured me there is nothing to fear from the Supreme Court. That even if the case would not be decided unanimously that it would be decided with an overwhelming majority. . . . He said this would strengthen my hand.

While the court was being lobbied from the inside by Justice Castro, there were acts of violence in the city that skeptics openly suggested were crude attempts to impress the court. A bomb badly damaged pipes of the water and sewer utility. Other bombs went off in the gardens of Senator Roy and another loyalist senator. No one was hurt in any attack. Marcos said Communist subversives were responsible. Liberal Senate candidate Ramon Mitra, Jr., blamed military psychological warfare teams. Noting how carefully timed and executed the explosions were — no one was even bruised — Mitra quipped: "[They] should at least have seen to it that a dog or puppy got hurt in their bombing operations of the gardens . . . to give some plausibility to their ruse."

Deliberations dragged on. Marcos was growing impatient. He worried that the mere fact of the court's review might be a bad precedent. Marcos resented being second-guessed by politicians, the press, or the Supreme Court, but there were other, more practical, reasons to worry. What if in the future his military officers waited to execute a controversial order until the Supreme Court had a chance to rule? In his diary Marcos pondered:

> The doctrine of review is dangerous as it will undermine the habit of obedience inbred in the military. For every soldier may entertain doubts as to the legality of the order suspending the privilege of the writ or even of martial law — and thus cause a delay which would be fatal to the security of the state.

Nonetheless, the judicial process inched forward. Finally, it was clear there would be no ruling before the November elections. If the process seemed slow to Marcos, it had to seem positively paralytic to those in detention cells at Camp Crame. Frustration grew as prisoners who had been branded subversives could not even mount defenses because they still had not been charged with any crimes. All the media attention had, at least, improved their daily routines. The meals were better. "Bomba" Arienda had been allowed to have a radio and his typewriter. Dr. Nemesio Prudente, president of the Philippine College of Commerce, was able to set up a portable television in his cell. But the numbing boredom was taking its toll and there was no end in sight. For Arienda, the cell began to close in during his forty-eighth day. He screamed. He kicked his bunk. He pounded on the steel bars that confined him to a dingy six-by-five-foot space. He cursed. He called on his guards to kill him. He raged at the resignation of his fellow prisoners. His bellows echoed through the cellblock: "Why don't they charge us with something?"

In the fall of 1971, the fledgling New People's Army was still small. Independent intelligence sources considered it poorly armed, poorly organized, and poorly financed. In fact, the Communist threat to the Philippines existed primarily in the rhetoric and politics of Ferdinand Marcos.

Even as his intelligence agents churned out top-secret reports of questionable veracity to support the president's warnings, his top military advisers were on record minimizing the menace. Two months before the Plaza Miranda bombing, General Eduardo Garcia of the constabulary told an American newspaper, "Insurgency and subversion are not serious problems of the government now. . . . Notwithstanding the occurrence at times of some crimes against persons or property which usually result from unemployment and economic difficulties and from which no country can claim immunity, the inhabitants of the Philippines sleep soundly in their homes, move freely and safely throughout the country and initiate enterprises on which they place their hopes for better life. It can safely be stated that peace and order in the Philippines can stand favorable comparison with other countries in the world."

Privately, chief of staff General Manuel Yan and army chief General Rafael Ileto also minimized the threat. Marcos wondered about their loyalty. Ileto's son was a radical, he noted. And Yan would have to be replaced soon. He already had ordered the staff of General Romeo Espino beefed up so as "to watch over the movements of Gen. Yan."

The United States, meanwhile, was very skeptical and let Marcos know that it did not share his alarm. In October, Marcos was informed that the CIA regarded the NPA as "small and vulnerable," confined to the isolated rural province of Isabela in northeastern Luzon. The CIA report also blamed Marcos for allowing the insurgency "to establish itself with little or no opposition from the government." Indeed, Marcos had noted in his diary more than a year earlier that he intended to "allow them to gather strength but no such strength that we cannot overcome them." The CIA further minimized the durability of the NPA. Marcos quoted the U.S. intelligence report on October 11, 1971, when he wrote:

> "At present, the insurgency is being run practically out of the hip pockets of Sison, Dante and perhaps a few [Communist] party leaders. If they are in some way removed from the scene, the NPA could degenerate into just another non-ideological outlaw band that could more easily be contained or eliminated."

While continuing to press the Nixon administration to provide more military aid to help him fight communism, Marcos took no issue with the CIA's confidential report. In fact, it was consistent with some of his own diary entries. Back in January of 1971, when the shock of Lieutenant Corpuz's defection prompted Marcos secretly to sign a standby declaration of martial law, the president wrote that all the demonstrators, rioters, activists, radicals, Huks, and NPA combined "do not now constitute a serious threat to our society." Furthermore, he added: "Even if the government were to help them mount a rebellion, they would still be nothing but harassing groups incapable of taking over government."

But such a "sober judgment," as he called it, clearly contradicted the case Marcos himself was trying to make before the Supreme Court. So, he did not repeat it to Justice Castro or to the jurist's colleagues. Nor was it compatible with the case he was trying to salvage in the court of public opinion: the case for a savior to rescue an imperiled nation.

A verdict on that latter case would be rendered by Philippine voters on November 8.

Marcos entered the final days of the 1971 Senate campaign on the defensive — defending his suspension of constitutional protections, defending his military against allegations that its agents committed the Plaza Miranda bombing, defending his continued detention of prisoners who still had not been charged (and never would be) with complicity in the bombing that precipitated their arrests. Media criticism was incessant. Ninoy Aquino, a surrogate campaigner for the gravely injured Salonga, was flouting threats that he might be arrested in the bomb inquiry and drawing big crowds all over the country. So, too, were the Liberal candidates who were able to hobble along the campaign trail on their crutches or in wheelchairs. Marcos countered with the proven weapons of past campaigns: money, media, and Imelda.

The Nacionalista Party Directorate had convened in July to select its slate of candidates. Marcos was sure then of a sweeping victory, and he noted with apparent delight that his party colleagues "felt pity for the Liberals." Marcos did, indeed, hold a formidable advantage. He controlled the release of funds for local public works projects, and as the first order of business in the 1971 campaign season, Marcos opened the peso floodgates. On July 28 he wrote:

> Spent the afternoon handing out public works releases — P200,000 for each congressman, P100,000 for each governor, P20,000 for each municipality, P2,000 for each barrio, P50,000 for each province, P50,000 for each small city, and P100,000 for each big city. [Note: At the time, 1,000 pesos was about $150.]

Then came the bomb blasts in Plaza Miranda. The campaign changed dramatically, but not the tenacious optimism of Ferdinand Marcos. In September, when the Liberals were unable to field mayoral and gubernatorial candidates for scores of cities and provinces, Marcos saw a landslide Nacionalista victory and predicted that his Liberal rivals would "cry 'fraud' and give all kinds of excuses for their defeat."

First signs that the president's optimism might be premature crept into the diary in October, when Marcos acknowledged the need for funding "a special operation in Iloilo," home province of the Lopez family. In a terse reference Marcos noted that the Senate team was "doing badly." The flow of pesos increased. "I attended to politicians asking for funds all morning and afternoon up to 4 p.m.," he wrote on the last Friday in October.

Marcos tried to dominate the airways with paid advertisements and appearances on news and talk shows. Late in the campaign he was a guest for more than two hours on Channel 7's interview program "What the People Want to Know." He noted in his diary that night that the people wanted to know about "my wealth, dictatorial tendencies, the First Lady's political ambitions, bankruptcy of the government, the political campaign, prices." It should have been a warning. Instead, to protect his delusions, Marcos chose to notice only the more promising signs — like Imelda's performance on the stump. On November 4 he enthused:

> Imelda's rallies are a roaring success. . . . She is an experienced trooper. She will probably tilt the balance . . . for the Nacionalista candidates. And if she ever runs for public office, she will swamp any opponent.

For the final seventy-two hours of the campaign, Manila had the look and sound of a carnival. Parades. Demonstrations. Honking motorcades crawling through clogged streets. Dueling loudspeakers. Marcos kept his Nacionalista party appeals on the airways, buying up radio and television time on Sunday evening for a seven-hour talkathon. His diary entries exuded confidence. He watched the Liberal party's last pre-election extravaganza on television and wrote it "was dull — all speeches. I have directed that ours be fast-paced. . . ." Apparently it was, as Marcos seemed proud to note: "Instead of the dull speeches . . . we had dances and skits and songs."

Marcos skipped his regular golf game on Monday, election day, to campaign to the last moment. As one Filipino commentator would remark later: "He campaigned as if his whole political life and fortune depended on it." Certainly his ego and prestige were heavily invested in the outcome.

Voting trends were obvious from the moment the first ballots were counted. This time Marcos could not avoid the unpleasant truth as distressing reports poured in throughout Monday night. At 2:00 A.M.

he retired to his diary with the stunning news: "The initial reports of the voting indicate a possible debacle. . . ."

The Liberals were going to win six of the eight seats in a landslide of historic proportions. The trumpeted referendum on the Marcos administration was a disaster for the president. In an election that also had become a bitter contest between Ferdinand Marcos and Ninoy Aquino, it was the whiz kid from Tarlac savoring the victory press conference. Galled and shaken by the results, Marcos's first instinct was to assign blame. In Nixonian fashion, he blamed the press for kicking him around:

> For two years now we have been the subject of criticism, bitter and vicious, by all the newspapers and other media. False news as well as slanted reporting was a consistent pattern of the last two years. And we had no way of answering. Our efforts to do so were late and ineffectual. . . .
>
> Then came the rice shortage, the increase of prices and Plaza Miranda with its bombing. And the concocted stories of corruption. . . .
>
> [The results] may also indicate that the activists and subversives have obtained the support of the affluent as well as the lower classes. So we must now fear for a growing strength of the subversives that will be shown in various ways in the future. They may now become overgrasping and force a showdown of force or slowly peck at the strength of the government, and then cause it to waste away in indecisive battles of attrition.
>
> For one thing, we must now prepare for the violence in action of the communists who will be encouraged, and [the] continued spite of the political opposition and the oligarchs who have tasted first blood.

To Ferdinand Marcos the lesson of defeat was not that the public had repudiated his administration or his policies but, rather, that the threat of violence and subversion was greater than ever.

Publicly, Marcos reacted with grace and equanimity, appealing for unity in the national interest at a press conference two days later. In his diary account of that meeting with reporters on November 10, Marcos wrote: "The elections I cited as an example of the capability of democracy to solve our problems without violence and as an achievement of the people. . . ."

But by the following weekend his private thoughts bore little resemblance to those measured public statements. On Sunday afternoon, while waiting to embark on a cruise with World Bank President Robert McNamara, a brooding Marcos wrote:

> For the last several days I have been overwhelmed by a sense of frustration because of the implications of the senatorial elections. . . .
>
> [T]he results indicate that the people still do not have the wisdom and the discrimination required for a truly democratic republic. For, the demagogues and the simpletons were elected instead of the highly qualified.
>
> So, the consequences may be dangerous. I now fear for our Republic.

CHAPTER TEN
A Glimpse of the Rubicon

Public rejection of Ferdinand Marcos and his handpicked slate of Senate candidates was sweeping. Liberal Jovito Salonga, who campaigned from his hospital bed with the help of surrogate Ninoy Aquino, topped the field with 4.3 million votes. His nearest Nacionalista rival trailed him by more than 600,000. Salonga even won in Ilocos Norte, the president's "Solid North." The Liberals carried Imelda's home province of Leyte by a margin of 5–3. And two members of the Marcos cabinet, Defense Secretary Juan Ponce Enrile and Labor Secretary Blas Ople, finished far behind, well out of contention. Nacionalistas barely salvaged two of the eight seats. In short, the Marcos political machine was devastated. Not since Julio Nalundasan buried the political aspirations of the president's father in 1935 had Ferdinand been so embarrassed in defeat — or so deeply resentful.

For the next several days he watched, bitter and helpless, as Aquino and other Liberal leaders appeared "all over town, through all the media and the coffee shops and gatherings, pontificating on their victory." His ire flared when Aquino suggested that while he knew the president was not fond of him, he was sure Marcos respected him because Marcos "sees in me himself in his younger days." To which Marcos scrawled: "Presumptuous!"

He listened for whispers and unguarded comments that might foreshadow dangerous plots or schemes. At the Manila Golf Club, Senator Jose Diokno was heard to tell a small group that "the best way in which Marcos can help the country is for him to commit suicide or be killed." A friend named Ricky told Marcos it sounded like a macabre joke. But not to Marcos. He wrote: "[P]oor Ricky does not know that Diokno DOES REALLY want me dead." Someone else overheard Ining Lopez at a luncheon table say that after Marcos left office in 1973 he "should not be allowed to go scot-free, but should be prosecuted." Lopez's *Chronicle* was the leading media voice accusing the administration of corruption. In his diary Marcos speculated that his rivals intended to punish him "by imprisonment or worse." With apparent apprehension, Marcos considered his future, his life beyond Malacanang, his possible jeopardy as a powerless ex-president. And he worried: "These are dangerous men. Small boys with power. Not only for our own good, but for the good of the country, they must never be entrusted with power."

He fretted, too, about his allies. Marcos wondered again whether the CIA might sanction efforts to replace him before the 1973 elections. A friend warned him to be watchful in case the Americans were "setting me up like a Ngo Dinh Diem for liquidation as an oppressive tyrant by an armed forces supported coup d'état. . . ."

And as Marcos felt more vulnerable personally, he seemed to express more concern about the nation's future. He had apparently come to believe that if he was in peril, so was his country. "I am convinced that the communists will try and take over the government before 1973 . . . ," he wrote about a week after the election debacle. He predicted an increase in urban guerrilla activity in January and outright revolution in the streets of Manila by the next summer. Peace and order and economic stability all seemed beyond reach, he concluded on December 5, 1971 — unless the president "is a dictator for at least a short period."

Philippine democracy had put Ferdinand Marcos in the presidential palace. The Philippine constitution made him the nation's official defender of its democratic institutions. But the stunning election failure confronted him with a dilemma: he no longer trusted democracy.

In truth, Marcos never was entirely comfortable with the brawling, freewheeling style of democracy practiced in the Philippines. He called the independent and critical press "unreliable as a participant in the democratic dialogue." And his intolerance of criticism made him, at best, a grudging champion of free speech and an unfettered news media.

He did pay it lip service in his public speeches, telling a group of journalists one day in January 1971, for example: "I believe democracy will outlast and survive all other ideologies. . . . Democracy will be able to protect itself. It carries within it the seed of self preservation. For it is vital and can withstand any test and crisis. . . . We should encourage the full and free ventilation of ideas no matter how hurting they may be to the man in power." Ironically, two days earlier, while preparing to secretly sign the standby declaration of martial law, Marcos had called the media "a serious threat to security." And on that day, January 4, 1971, he had privately told Defense Secretary Enrile what must be done with the media if or when martial law was imposed: "We have to take them over immediately."

Marcos had tried his best to control press criticism through a combination of courtship and bribery. He invited editors and reporters to Malacanang to dine, to talk, to trade gossip. He loaned books from his private library to journalist Teddy Boy Locsin and offered him an administration job when Locsin's father became critical of Marcos policies in the influential *Free Press*. Sometimes he paid stipends, dispensed gifts, offered bribes. Reporters traveled free of charge, and even got spending money, on trips abroad with Imelda. To encourage favorable coverage, Marcos seemed willing to try almost anything. Back in 1970, during the late stages of the violent *First Quarter Storm*, he gave one critical columnist an ambassadorship. On April 24, 1970, Marcos wrote:

> J. V. Cruz, the *Manila Times* columnist and one of my most ardent supporters, has suddenly turned against me and suggests that "something has snapped somewhere," and I have become "hysterical" and "govern by intimidation."
>
> This is probably because I have not appointed him ambassador to Bonn, Germany.

Two months later, the Marcos diary entry for June 20 noted that the president had just returned that night from a dinner "for J. V. Cruz, new ambassador of the Philippines to West Germany."

Finally, in the aftermath of the 1971 elections, Marcos created his own newspaper, the *Daily Express*. Its nominal owner would be Roberto "Bobby" Benedicto, one of the president's closest friends and a former law school classmate. But it was Ferdinand's newspaper. A week after the November election loss that he blamed on a "vicious media," Marcos personally approved selection of the paper's original staff personnel. Marcos had decided to start his own partisan newspaper sometime earlier. In September, amid constant criticism of his suspension of the writ of habeas corpus, Marcos had written:

> I can see that most of my troubles stem from the media. . . . So I am decided to continue with the project to put up a metropolitan newspaper. . . . It is unbelievable that the government cannot disseminate its side of every controversy.

All through 1971, as the president's personal and political popularity plunged, Marcos blamed the media, the "empire within the Republic," he called them. The public was too easily swayed by his critics, the president had decided when that spring he wrote: "The [Lopez-owned] ABS-CBN TV and radio networks are blanketing the whole country with vicious lies and distorted propaganda. But Imelda feels that it is becoming effective in turning some of the people against us."

By the spring of 1971, Marcos not only was considering martial law, but he was reconsidering his general philosophical commitment to democratic principles. The press was not his only bane. Political foes spoke their minds on the floor of Congress. Students and labor leaders criticized the president with chants and placards in the streets. Freedom of expression had become a license to attack Ferdinand Marcos in every manner and medium. He was beginning to doubt the lesson he said he learned from the example of Mexico, that "the best defense against communism is a good democratic government." On March 20, 1971, he wrote:

> But the politicians keep on blocking good government — specially the senate. And the media will not allow the good that is being done to be known by the people. They distort and falsify news to increase circulation. They headline nothing but crime. The demonstrators and riots stop production and economic activity.
>
> So before we can have a good government, or before the people are convinced that we are setting up a good government, the three factors

must be solved — the media, the politicians and the demonstrators. And there is possibly no way of solving these questions except by a take-over of the government. . . .

Democracy, according to the Marcos diagnosis, could benefit from a dose of authoritarian control. Certainly, he felt, some media restraint was in order. He blamed journalists for most of the nation's ills. When crime rates jumped and tourism dropped in Manila, he accused the press of reporting too many stories about crime. Media criticism and the Communist insurgency were as one: harmful to the nation. He expressed alarm in May 1971 that "the media and the communists are slowly getting a foothold" even in rural areas beyond Manila. He suggested that his military wished to attack the media as well as the insurgents. If the press kept up its "vituperation and vicious fault-finding," Marcos wrote, he might not be able to control the military's urge to punish the press for its malice and ill will. "I must counsel the military against any rash action," he told himself in another May entry.

One evening aboard the presidential yacht, en route to Corregidor for ceremonies commemorating those who died defending "The Rock" from vastly superior Japanese forces in World War II, Marcos found himself thinking about his current domestic troubles. Like the defenders of Corregidor, he felt besieged and threatened. He mused:

> What would the dead counsel us today? The libel, the slander, the slanted news and the fabricated story are all weapons in the arsenal of communism. And they are being used and employed by political upstarts who seek power. . . .
>
> So there is a partnership of the cheap politician, the vicious newspaper and media crowd, the communists and the permissive society seeking to destroy our democratic institutions.
>
> But the dead counsel patience and fortitude. If they could pay the ultimate price, we can pay less.

From the beginning of 1971, when Marcos was flirting with martial law, he seemed to blame the media for driving him to the brink of dictatorship. In fact, just before signing the standby martial law order early in January, Marcos had raged about the media when he wrote:

> From the vantage point of future plans I cannot but feel a little self-righteous as I witness the spectacle of petty men tearing to pieces the source of their liberty. . . . And when I watch the supposedly patriotic

men, in their selfish and egoistic ways, wreck our republic, I almost lose my objectivity and dispassionate attitude as anger boils within me and eggs me to immediately put in effect the plan to establish martial law.

Marcos took the press attacks personally. Indeed, some of them *were* personal, accusing the president and Imelda of extravagance and corruption. During a three-month period early in 1971, the *Chronicle* ran a daily editorial cartoon linking the First Family to secret owner-ship of Manila companies and extensive real estate, the largest collec-tion of diamonds and precious gems in Southeast Asia, and wardrobes filled with imported European gowns, each worth more than what twenty average Filipino families earned in a year. The president, in turn, regarded some press moguls in similarly personal terms — as his mortal enemies. Notable among them was Chino Roces of the *Manila Times*. Nonetheless, a top Marcos aide had suggested naming Roces to Enrile's vacant secretary of defense post as a way to "change the atti-tude of the media to give us much needed popular support." Whether the independent Roces would have entertained such an offer is irrele-vant because Marcos flatly rejected any notion of making the offer. Enrile would get his old job back after the election. Besides, Marcos thoroughly distrusted Roces, politically and personally. In a 1970 di-ary entry Marcos noted:

> His son . . . is reported to have said that if he has a chance he will shoot me. However, he should be happy that I am not the ill-tempered, egois-tic and arrogant dictator he wants to picture me in his papers.
>
> Someday he will be thankful that I have helped preserve our free-doms — including the freedom of the press which he always clung to as a license for abuse and distortion.

Two things were clear from the 1971 election debacle: first, Marcos faced a leadership crisis that seemed to doom prospects for popular backing of a term extension; second, he could no longer sustain the unpopular suspension of constitutional rights.

A week after election day, most of the remaining detainees at Camp Crame were released. After eighty-three days, "Bomba" Arienda was freed, something of a public hero but also a much angrier man. He bolted from jail cell to podium to denounce in radical rhetoric the president and America's presence in the Philippines. He was cheered by student throngs at antigovernment rallies. "The military stockade enabled me to learn more about the tentacles of U.S. reactionary forces," Arienda told the crowds. "Now I am more than ever ready to pursue this struggle to liberate our beloved country from foreign control." He urged students to abandon their books and "go to the countryside" to wage revolution.

The president's suspension of the writ of habeas corpus seemed to be a thorough political failure. Indeed, it had only succeeded in driving new converts into the opposition — not only the traditional Liberal party, but the radical opposition as well. It seemed Marcos could look nowhere on the political landscape for relief. His last hope lay with the eleven Supreme Court justices still deliberating the constitutionality of his suspension order.

In every practical sense the suspension already had been lifted nationwide. Within a week of the election, Marcos had ordered all arrests without warrants to stop. The only detainees still in custody had been brought up, finally, on formal subversion charges which, the press and opposition noted, had nothing to do with the Plaza Miranda bombing. Still, Marcos wanted a Supreme Court ruling in his favor, a finding that he had acted within the rules of the constitution. Poor election results only heightened the political stakes.

In another round of secret lobbying sessions with members of the court, Marcos was reassured by Justice Antonio Barredo that he would support the president's position. In fact, the fifty-nine-year-old jurist said he held the minority view that the Supreme Court had no jurisdiction to limit or even to question the president's order. Barredo was a loyal appointee. In fact, the associate justice had been one of the first appointments to the new Marcos Administration when he was named solicitor general in January 1966. Two years later, Marcos named him to the Supreme Court bench. And in December 1971, it was Barredo, during one of those private meetings with his political patron, who relayed the final reassuring message: The court not only was going to uphold the president, but would do so with a unanimous opinion.

Marcos was euphoric. The decision was announced on Saturday, December 11, 1971. Marcos declared it "a red letter day." He called it the "biggest legal victory" of his administration. The unanimous vote had, he said, "electrified everyone . . . [and] heartened all the men in the Armed Forces and the civil government." Much of the country, unaware of the secret presidential lobbying campaign inside the court, was surprised by the ruling, but most paid it little attention. The matter seemed academic. The writ of habeas corpus was restored. The president, at best, had won a technical victory. His rivals were content that the decision could hardly compensate Marcos for the political fiasco he had orchestrated. Indeed, the somewhat puzzling high spirits at Malacanang finally were dismissed as exaggerated optimism, as little more than political cheerleading in the face of one demoralizing setback after another.

But Marcos had his precedent: a Supreme Court ruling that acknowledged the existence of "a sizeable group of men who have publicly risen in arms to overthrow the government." And, on page 31 of the opinion, the court conceded to the president constitutional powers to call up the armed forces, to suspend the writ of habeas corpus, and to declare martial law "in the case of invasion, insurrection or rebellion or imminent danger thereof." Others might see that as a belated technical victory. Marcos saw it as a license to use dictatorial powers.

In his diary, the president made absolutely clear how he interpreted the December 11 Supreme Court decision: "This merely means I can place the Philippines or any part thereof under martial law."

After weeks of gloom, Malacanang was festive again. It even affected the president's golf game. He shot an eagle on the first hole Sunday morning. Aides, advisers, and friends flocked to the palace to hail the president's victory. After his Sunday afternoon nap, Marcos was roused by a group of generals and friends of Imelda who "all trooped into the bedroom for light hearted congratulations." Marcos was bursting with pride over his role in swaying the court. But he had to be careful. His pride had to be contained. Word of his lobbying efforts could undermine the decision. He confided only in his diary, boasting of his role and ignoring his abuse of democratic processes when he wrote:

[T]he decision to suspend [the writ] was mine. The justification before the Supreme Court was prepared by me. And the resolution to sustain it even against the demonstrations and seemingly popular clamor to lift it, was mine.

I had pointedly told my critics: "You will be glad that there was one man who stood against the mob to protect the Republic. I would rather protect and save the Republic than be popular."

The president's euphoria was short-lived. The Supreme Court decision did not temper public criticism. The decision did not reverse the new Liberal influence in the Senate. Nor did it improve the economy or reduce crime or improve Marcos's standings in opinion polls. Later in December, his paranoia flared again. Associates warned him of wholesale disloyalty among his aides and allies. He was told that press secretary Kit Tatad was sympathetic to student radicals and keeping in touch with them; that the governor-elect of Ilocos Sur had entered a secret alliance with the NPA; that General Ileto should not be trusted because his son, a Cornell University doctoral candidate, was a radical; that another colonel was secretly training NPA recruits.

Marcos was especially sensitive to hints of disloyalty in the military. However, that was one segment of the Philippine public from which the president continued to receive broad and reliable support. He had invested much time and expense to curry its favor. He made promotions. He financed new and better arms. He improved living conditions. The annual military budget had soared under the president, increasing by more than five hundred percent. Furthermore, for the first thirteen months of his first presidential term Marcos had retained for himself the portfolio of secretary of defense, helping him to establish his own direct links with military personnel. By late 1971, the young officer corps wore the Marcos stamp. Also, Marcos had filled the lower ranks with so many loyal Ilocanos that congressional leaders from other regions complained. The "Ilocanization" of the Philippine military even prompted legislation requiring more proportional recruitment.

Still, the president did have some doubts about the personal loyalties of older generals such as chief of staff Yan and army boss Ileto. Both men seemed cautious about any plan to use the military to enforce martial law. Marcos required more positive support from such top officers. Yan was replaced by General Romeo Espino, a Marcos favorite. He gave the president books about Hitler. Espino was told that early in the new year he would be named chief of staff. At the same time, Ileto would be removed from command of the army and made deputy to Espino.

While firming up support at the top, Marcos also paid special attention to the troops. His public rhetoric glorified their mission. He pledged them his comradeship. He never missed an opportunity to review the troops, striding before rows of rigid soldiers even in pouring rains. Speaking at a December 21, 1971, ceremony honoring the thirty-sixth anniversary of the Philippine armed forces, Marcos again praised the military as the saviors and protectors of the republic against "the evil forces that seek to destroy it by violence." He assured the troops that he felt the same "affection that must be felt by every right thinking Filipino for you." And that night, in his diary, Marcos wrote:

> The officers and men are in high spirits, but of course such newspapers like the Daily Mirror are promoting discontent in the military. . . .
> I believe that we have been able to keep the loyalty of the AFP [Armed Forces of the Philippines] — with a few exceptions. We will be needing this loyalty to flag and country in the next two years. I expect violence to erupt in a year."

In the final hours of 1971, Marcos reflected on the state of his nation. Deadly local feuds continued to terrorize Ilocos Sur and other rural areas. Manila slums continued to grow and fester with crime. The Philippine economy continued to deteriorate. Production was down. Foreign investment was down. U.S. officials had served notice that foreign aid cuts were likely. Tighter U.S. import quotas threatened to curtail vital Philippine sugar exports to its biggest customer. Complaints and warnings poured in from representatives of the steel, copper, cement, and lumber industries, some on the verge of closing down plants. "I have a feeling all is not well with the economy," the president acknowledged.

At 2:00 A.M. on Christmas Eve, surveying his reeling economy and the civil unrest of the day, Marcos saw nothing but disorder. He wrote: "Peace and order is at its worst. There is cynicism and frustration." What was a president to do?

He read "the book of Bailey on Presidential Greatness," a book examining the qualities of chief executives recognized by history as great leaders. It kept him awake deep into a December night. Its message appealed to his ego, to his sense of destiny. As he reflected on his reading: "Greatness is judged by the manner a President overcomes the obstacles presented to him. The bigger the crisis, the bigger the President."

A few lines later, still on the same page, Marcos contemplated how to deal with the obstacles he saw before him when he wrote: "The formal suggestions for martial law and the setting up of a dictatorship is certainly increasing."

Finally, relaxing in Baguio at Christmas, Marcos read an article about Julius Caesar. Marcos saw parallels between ancient Rome and modern Manila — both torn with civil strife. Rome was sinking into anarchy as Caesar waited beyond the Rubicon River for the government to regain control. Finally, a reluctant Caesar brought his army across the river to restore order by assuming dictatorial control. And Marcos quoted historian Theodore H. White, regarding Caesar's decision: "If men cannot agree on how to rule themselves, someone else must rule them."

From his mountain retreat in Baguio, Marcos had glimpsed the Rubicon. He declared the article "strikingly apropos to our situation!" He saw violent antigovernment demonstrations as a sign that the Philippines, like Rome, was slipping into anarchy. He saw the election results as a sign that the Philippines, like Rome, could not decide who should rule.

And on the night after Christmas of 1971, Marcos of the Philippines considered the rhetorical question: *Who waits beyond our Rubicon?*

CHAPTER ELEVEN
The Constitution Con

The dinner guests at Malacanang Palace had finished their meals, but the president had not yet excused them. Some had to be tiring of sitting on the high-back wooden chairs that encircled a massive table dominating the state dining room. The furniture was made by inmates of the national penitentiary, and a long evening session on the hard chairs could be punishing. But the party was not over. No one moved. The president still was joking and telling stories. He talked about politics and his critics and the constitutional convention, ConCon as everyone called it. He hoped his guests would help defeat efforts by those who would undermine or strip away any powers of the president.

As he spoke, the waiters still scurried about, stopping at each place-setting. But now, instead of food, they were serving gifts. It was the president's way of entertaining important guests. And on the evening of January 6, 1972, few Filipinos were more important to Ferdinand Marcos than these guests. During the day they were rewriting the constitution and considering charter changes that could alter the power of the presidency and change his political future. The guests receiving presidential gifts were ConCon delegates. Dinner was a lobbying session with about thirty delegates from the central island region of the Visayas.

Eduardo Quintero, a soft-spoken seventy-two-year-old delegate from Imelda's home province of Leyte, had been a guest at Malacanang in previous administrations. He was a former Philippine ambassador to Japan. But this dinner was turning out to be, for him, an unusual palace experience. He reached to examine his gift. A small box. Everyone around the long table had a similar box. He opened his. Inside was a Ronson cigarette lighter. He glanced at his neighbors. Everyone had received the same cigarette lighter.

Still, the waiters scurried. They were circling the table again, making more stops at each place-setting, serving another round of gifts — this one a wallet. Quintero examined his more closely. It was stamped with the message: "Greetings, President and Mrs. Marcos, December 25, 1970." A murmur rose from the table. Finally, someone called out to Marcos: "Mr. President, why is this 1970?" Marcos shrugged and said it would simply appear that the delegates had received the wallet more than a year earlier. Quintero opened his wallet. Inside was a crisp one-peso note, a symbol of luck.

Again, the waiters circled. Another small box was delivered to each guest. Inside was another freshly minted one-peso note, for luck. Finally, the waiters disappeared.

Marcos adjourned. The ConCon delegates pushed back their chairs and filed down the wide stairway to the palace entrance hall. They were straggling out onto the grounds when someone said: "The envelopes are ready. They will be distributed in a couple of days." Everyone paused. Quintero glanced around the milling crowd suddenly struck by what he sensed as "a sepulchral silence." Now, everyone present knew that everyone else present knew about "the envelopes."

When Quintero received his envelopes, they always were filled with cash. Crisp pesos. Usually ten fifty-peso notes. Sometimes more. The morning after the Malacanang dinner, Quintero's envelope would hold one thousand pesos — twenty fifty-peso notes. Always they were distributed discreetly. He received them in the hotel suite or at the home of fellow delegates. He found them at his mailbox just off the convention floor, or in his desk drawer or slipped under a stack of papers atop his desk. He was handed one while on his way to the men's room. Sometimes he was told they came "from the First Lady."

Ferdinand and Imelda Marcos were taking no chances with the whim and caprice of democracy. Control of the convention was too important. The president could not afford to lose ConCon the way he lost the Senate elections. And it was possible. Marcos knew he was in trouble even before the opening gavel. An invitation for him to speak during opening day ceremonies turned into an angry controversy. Many of the three hundred twenty delegates wanted the convention to have nothing to do with the president or with any other partisan political leader. Their rather impractical hope was for "a nonpolitical convention." Marcos and his political machine represented everything the idealists feared. The vote was close, close enough that some regarded it as a repudiation of the president, but Marcos finally was asked to address the delegates on opening day, June 1, 1971.

The convention's inaugural ceremonies at the stately old Manila Hotel attracted eight thousand protesters, who denounced it as an assembly controlled by political agents, U.S. interests, and the ruling class. There were demonstrations inside, as well. When Marcos stepped to the podium in the hotel's Fiesta Pavilion, about twenty delegates walked out in protest. Then, in an eight-minute speech that he later described in his diary as "inspired" and "profound," Marcos told delegates that "the greatest act of freedom is the writing of a constitution. We test the democratic principle that democracy is self-rejuvenating, self-recuperating, self-healing. . . . Society can be revolutionized by constitutional means — not by destroying democratic processes, but by strengthening them. . . . The writing of a constitution is the coming all at once together of the past, the present and the future in one great single movement, in one upheaval and in one cry."

Democracy had one flaw. The president's advisers earlier had completed a head count that identified no more than one hundred loyalists among the delegates, barely 30 percent of the convention vote. Marcos expressed worry that radicals might buy off some of his loyal delegates. He launched his own modest envelope campaign.

From the beginning of deliberations and debate, the ConCon delegates were divided over their options. Some of the pro-Marcos faction proposed to eliminate term limits but to keep the presidential form of government; some proposed to extend the presidential term to six years; some proposed a more drastic move, to institute a parliamentary form of government. The strong anti-Marcos bloc supported no changes that might keep Marcos in office any longer than December 1973. In fact, one hundred six delegates won seats in the convention by vowing to keep the presidential system of government and to bar Marcos from reelection.

To Marcos, the parliamentary option offered both security and an escape from the term limits. He could run for a seat in parliament from Ilocos Norte with the assurance of winning easily. Assuming his Nacionalista party retained majority control of Parliament, as it did the Congress, Marcos could expect to be named prime minister. Malacanang would remain his without risking a national election battle against Ninoy Aquino or anyone else. The hostile Manila press would have only limited influence in his home province. He signaled his supporters to unite behind the parliamentary system.

Marcos did have one other option. If ConCon retained the presidential system, and kept the restrictive term limits as well, he could back Imelda for a run at the presidency in 1973. Imelda seemed to like the idea. In fact, she encouraged speculation, saying she would run "if the people want." But that was not the president's first choice. Journalists joked about the prospects of Ferdinand as First Gentleman, playing the role of consort to the president. Columnists snickered about what Marcos would do with his ego. Clearly, to Marcos the Imelda option was a last resort — but he was not ruling it out, despite his repeated public denials. Soon after the convention went to work in the summer of 1971, Marcos wrote:

> If the Cons. Con. adopts the parliamentary system of government, this will settle the whole question. . . . Otherwise, Imelda will probably have to run in 1973 so that my reform program can go on for the next several years.

It was a telling entry, making clear what was implicit both in his political strategies and in other diary observations: the Marcos goal was to remain in power "for the next several years." He saw himself standing alone between violent insurrection and peace, between a possible military coup and civilian democracy. The Communists "will not mount a rebellion . . . while I am still president," he wrote a few months later. But if the next president "does not have the confidence or trust of the military, the military may take over the government." In short, Marcos had to remain in Malacanang for the good of the nation.

But on the floor of the constitutional convention one obstacle stood between Marcos and all of his options and ambitions. One issue threatened to make moot any victory won on all other charter revisions. One vote menaced the rest of his political future — and Imelda's, and even Bongbong's. It was Resolution Number 3167, what came to be called the "Ban-Marcos Proposal." It not only barred any president's reelection after two consecutive terms, but it included antidynasty language barring a spouse or other members of the immediate First Family from succeeding to the office.

Resolution 3167 was introduced on September 16, 1971, a day after the Manila papers had published stories showing the president's popularity at an all-time low. He was being blamed for the Plaza Miranda bombing. His suspension of habeas corpus had generated universal condemnation. Already suffering pangs of insecurity, Marcos received word that twenty-two delegates were sponsoring the resolution that amounted to a political death sentence for him and for his family. Worse, a majority of delegates had declared support for the measure. Then had come the embarrassing Liberal election sweep in the Senate races. And what had started as a somewhat modest envelope campaign became, thereafter, a major economic enterprise. From Malacanang, the pesos simply flowed. Hundreds of thousands of pesos each month. To paraphrase the president: The writing of the constitution turned out to be the coming all at once together of one great campaign of bribery.

Assigned to run "Operation ConCon" for the president was his chief assistant, executive secretary Guillermo "Gimo" de Vega. He organized a small core of loyal delegates to act as floor leaders, principal among them Gilberto "Bibit" Duavit and Venancio "Ven" Yaneza. Fortunately for history, the president's ConCon cabal filed detailed records and reports that Marcos saved with his diary.

In those documents, what appeared to be routine monthly payoffs were called monthly "messages." One peso equaled one "message." A budget sheet for the first week of February 1972 showed, for example, that the total "MESSAGES DUE" were 797,000 — something close to $130,000. The sheet, bearing Duavit's initials, also showed that about two hundred delegates — a substantial majority of the convention — were receiving those Malacanang "messages." That month, individual delegates on the presidential dole each found envelopes crammed with four thousand "messages" (about $650), an extra two thousand "messages" each for the delegates on key committees.

Special outlays to sway avowed anti-Marcos delegates were referred to as "gifts" or "grants" or "units." In one instance, floor leader Yaneza sent a memorandum to the president's assistant marked "URGENT." The memo detailed apparent progress in lobbying three delegates who had previously declared support for a "Ban-Marcos Resolution." Yaneza needed substantial funds to seal the deals. He wrote: "We intimated a gift to them." He recommended payments of ten thousand pesos each (about $1,600). And he noted: one delegate who agreed to switch votes "is hard up and almost asking for it"; another delegate who agreed simply to abstain "needs it to support his vices"; and the third delegate who agreed to abstain, unless or until another "no" vote was required, "is virtually captive in view of his gambling losses." The document was sent along to Marcos with de Vega's added handwritten note: "Sir: I recommend the [10,000 peso] grant — Gimo."

Not all the payoffs were monetary. One delegate on the important Suffrage and Electoral Reform Committee was facing a family crisis early in 1972. His son was charged with murder and awaited trial in a Quezon City court. The trial judge, by de Vega's description, was "Kokoy's man" — an appointee with close ties to Imelda's brother Kokoy Romualdez. In a February 12 memo, de Vega told the president that the delegate "may likely abstain from the ban issue. However, the family is expecting our help in the murder case. . . ."

Throughout the president's private ConCon papers, Marcos backers are referred to as "all the boys." Opponents are called "Marcos haters" — or simply, "the haters." Clearly, it paid either to be one of "the boys" or to be flexible. The constitution business was turning out to be quite a profit center. And Marcos was regaining some of his lost confidence in democracy.

But what if all the payola and influence peddling failed? What if, in the end, public opinion rather than pesos swayed more votes? Polls showed that 80 percent of the country opposed a third Marcos term. An Imelda presidency was equally unpopular. Marcos might dismiss such overwhelming opinion, but what about the delegates? When the crucial convention voting finally began, Marcos might have to explain another political embarrassment. How could he rationalize a stunning loss in the ConCon? He would have to blame it on the Communists.

Already, Marcos had begun sowing seeds of that alibi. In the fall of 1971 he had sent word to President Nixon that the Philippines was in danger, that ConCon was being subverted by the Communists. His messenger was Imelda.

She began her foreign mission with a call on the shah of Iran, as a guest for the 2,500-year celebration of the Persian Empire. In the desert near Persepolis, site of the ancient capital of Persia, Imelda, Imee, and Christina Ford — then wife of Henry Ford II — shared one of the $120,000, air-conditioned tents set up to accommodate perhaps the grandest party of the modern age. Imelda, herself a consummate hostess, took note.

From the gala in the desert, Imelda moved on to the presidential suite at the Madison Hotel in Washington. This was a business trip. Her mission, according to her husband's diary entry on the night that she left Manila, October 9, 1971, was "to see President Nixon to reconfirm Nixon's assurance that they would not intervene on any internal matter which may lead to martial law. (Ambassador Byroade had said they would support me, stating further that this assurance came from Pres. Nixon.) I do not want any Ngo Dinh Diem plots by the CIA."

In Washington, she first summoned Richard Usher, a State Department official who knew Imelda from his days as a political officer in the Manila embassy. According to writer Raymond Bonner's account of their meeting in her hotel suite, Imelda crowded close to Usher on a small sofa and, in a sultry whine, said: "Dick, you're not taking care of your baby. The Philippines is your baby, and you're not taking care of your baby." She told him the Communists were in control of ConCon. Later, she dined and talked with U.S. senators, telling them the same thing. Suddenly, State Department officials were getting inquiries from senators demanding to know what they intended to do, as Bonner reported, "about the communists who were trying to write the new Philippine constitution."

Finally, Imelda carried the message to the White House. According to writer Stanley Karnow's account of her twenty-minute meeting with the president, Imelda told Nixon that she and her husband were determined to stay in office until the Communists were "licked" and that she would replace Marcos if he retired. Nixon said little in response, but he directed a National Security Council aide to check out with the State Department her worries of Communist tampering in the constitutional convention.

At the time, the State Department's Bureau of Intelligence and Research [INR] was conducting its own analysis of ConCon. As reported by Bonner, one INR officer's initial private response to Imelda's claims of Communist influence was simply, "Oh crap!" But in a more measured response to the White House inquiry, she reported: "The people who control that convention are spelled M-A-R-C-O-S." The officer said ConCon was dominated by vested and decidedly conservative interests, whether for or against Marcos. And a secret INR report further concluded that Marcos could expect to control the bulk of the delegates "through the traditional tactics of manipulation, coercion, concession and bribery."

The "Red Menace" ploy might have seemed poorly timed in a capital preparing to send its president on a historic mission to Beijing. Few — certainly not the CIA or State Department — gave any weight to the Marcos contention that the People's Republic of China was exporting revolution to the Philippines. Marcos had been making that claim since at least 1970 in a bid for increased U.S. military aid. By the end of 1971, with the flowering of Sino-American detente, the Marcos tune was especially off-key.

But Imelda had planted a seed. If Marcos was humiliated by developments in ConCon, their warnings of Communist subversion were, at least, on the record. And if Marcos felt compelled to preempt the constitutional process by seizing military control of the government, it would be to save his nation from that same Communist subversion.

It seemed that Marcos, the master strategist, had a plan for any eventuality. One thing he had not anticipated, however, was the honesty of a weary old man.

Eduardo Quintero was not a brave man when it came to risking his frail and aged frame on airplane travel. A life of international travel in the Philippine foreign service had not cured his fear of flying. So, when he commuted between Manila and his home province on the island of Leyte, the old man preferred getting no higher than sea level. He traveled by interisland ferries.

In mid-May 1972, Quintero was called away from the constitutional convention, where he was a delegate, to the bedside of his dying brother, Vicente, in their Leyte hometown of Tacloban. He hurried from the session hall to the North Harbor to board the passenger ferry *m/v Sweet Grace*. Then he waited. The ship did not sail. He waited through a long, sultry Manila afternoon. The overloaded ship sat low in the water, still tied to the dock. It was a day behind schedule already and apparently going nowhere anytime soon. The operators of the *Sweet Grace* were unwilling to pay port authorities sufficient pesos to get a sailing permit. Quintero knew the situation: both sides were negotiating a bribe and the passengers were the bargaining chips.

When the ship's captain could not predict a sailing time, Quintero finally stomped from his stifling cabin and returned to the air-conditioned ConCon chambers. Bribery was a pervasive and crippling ailment of business and government. Someone had to say something. Quintero knew something about bribery, about how it afflicted what the president called "the greatest act of freedom . . . the writing of a constitution."

Quintero stood on the convention floor, seeking recognition from the presiding officer. Finally, he had the floor. He said he wanted to get something "off his chest in the interest of truth." And he went on to tell a story — of dinners at the palace . . . of his envelopes filled with cash, eighteen of them with a total of 11,500 pesos . . . of his understanding that the funds were intended to influence his vote on the "Ban-Marcos Proposal." Within moments his rambling speech had brought silence to the session hall. His oratory was without bombast or rhetoric. He said that many delegates received pesos and other Malacanang gifts. After the January 6 palace dinner, he said, some had joked: "Suppose we open our Ronson lighters in the session hall at the same time so that they will know who are the *tutas* [the Marcos lap dogs]." But Quintero identified no other delegates who received bribes. His goal was not to embarrass any individuals.

The old man said he had kept a careful record of his payments. Indeed, he had saved each envelope and its crispy peso contents, noting where and when he received it, and from whom. Again, he named no names. The "givers" were only agents of others, he explained. Finally, clutching the eighteen envelopes with their 11,500 pesos, Quintero stepped toward the presiding officer, former Philippine President Diosdado Macapagal, as he concluded:

"Mr. President, allow me to leave this money in the hands of the convention secretariat so it is safely kept for disposition depending upon the decision of the proper authority. . . ."

Abruptly, his speech ended. No flourish. No gesture to the gallery. After a pause, the hall erupted with a thunderous ovation. Reporters rushed to the convention floor. General pandemonium forced Macapagal to gavel the session closed. Quintero slipped away to resume his sad journey. During the delegate's speech his brother had died.

It was Friday, May 19, 1972.

The Marcos boys huddled to assess the damage. Early returns looked bad for Malacanang. Marcos complained that the press and opposition had "jumped on us and crucified us." A few days after the scandal broke he wrote: "[A]t the first impact of the news the Palace was blamed for everything!"

Time did not reduce the impact. As the scandal mushroomed, Quintero was called back from Leyte to testify before a convention investigative panel, specifically to name names. Who provided the pesos? A navy cutter was sent to pick him up in Tacloban. Quintero was in poor health, and he arrived on the Manila docks suffering from high blood pressure. He nearly stumbled as he walked the gangplank to the pier. After stopping at a nearby church to pray, the ailing delegate went straight to the San Juan de Dios Hospital where he would remain through the summer. An investigative subcommittee of Con-Con convened at his bedside. Finally, he named names: a dozen other delegates and the wife of a Leyte congressman had delivered the envelopes. They were the agents. But in the case of envelopes number one, seven, twelve, and thirteen, Quintero testified, he was told specifically that the money came from Imelda Marcos. The news rumbled through the island nation like an earthquake.

Now the president's blood pressure soared. He exploded in a rare public display of temper, accusing Quintero of false and vicious statements, of having tried to solicit bribes from Malacanang, and of being an immoral man who had affairs with young girls.

He called the delegate's disclosures a "dastardly act to malign my family." He charged, without evidence and without regard for the breathtaking hypocrisy of his claim, that Quintero "had in the past approached me and the First Lady for money because of his alleged serious financial difficulties. He had been denied. . . . On one occasion, he came to me and asked me if any money was coming from me for the convention delegates. I told him point-blank there was none and that I was disappointed that such a question should come from a convention delegate."

Imelda did not participate in the angry counterattack waged by Marcos in the Manila press. For reasons that would soon become clear, she was in seclusion.

Meanwhile, the attacks on Quintero were about to escalate. In his diary on May 30, 1972, Marcos called the delegate "a tool of the political opposition" and vowed in private, as he had vowed openly to reporters: "I will not rest until I have unmasked this pretender, his co-conspirators and accomplices."

The next evening a five-member team of the National Bureau of Investigation (NBI) raided Quintero's modest Manila home. They arrived at 5:10 carrying two black suitcases. Quintero's daughter and other members of the household were locked in one bedroom while the raiding team searched the residence. An hour later, news reporters were called to the Mayon Street home to witness the NBI's "discovery" — 379,320 pesos (about $60,000) found in a bedroom drawer. Quintero's daughter shouted at the police agents: "There is no money in that drawer!" And her father, from his hospital bed, declared it was planted.

But Marcos expressed delight over the news accounts. That night in his diary he wrote: "The lucky discovery of the 'loot' of Quintero is a boon to the ConCon and the individual delegates pointed to as the givers [of bribes]. But more than that, it is poetic justice."

The media immediately condemned police for planting the money. Senate leaders, including some Nacionalista members, threatened for a time to investigate the police. Badly shaken by the accusation, Quintero said, "I never saw so much money in my home. If I have any money in the house, it would not be more than a hundred pesos."

Two days later, on June 2, the NBI filed criminal bribery charges against Quintero. The man who had returned his eighteen envelopes and exposed the Malacanang scheme to compromise the constitutional convention now faced arrest. The hero was the accused. But public opinion polls showed 80 percent of the country believed Quintero, not Marcos. The Civil Liberties Union called the charges, "coming closely as they did on the heels of a presidential vow of personal vengeance, . . . a blatant display of naked power which has no place in a civilized society." On the walls of Manila, pro-Quintero graffiti appeared overnight. On automobile windshields, messages scrawled in lipstick declared: "Mabuhay [long live] Quintero!"

Again, Marcos was feeling the pressure. His ego suffered as Quintero emerged a national hero at the president's expense. His hold on ConCon suddenly appeared to be in doubt. Public criticism of the administration was angrier than ever. He felt vulnerable both politically and personally. In the midst of the scandal, his paranoia flaring anew, Marcos wrote:

> I am now convinced that even if we retire peacefully, we will be hunted and killed by the communists or the political opposition.

It was a delusion born of little more than the sizzling rhetoric of his critics. Without doubt, that criticism revealed a threat to his political future. But Ferdinand Marcos, hopelessly tangled in a now-exposed web of deceits and intrigues, interpreted the verbal and editorial assaults on his leadership as threats to his life. Indeed, in the late spring of 1972 he blamed them for a death in the family.

CHAPTER TWELVE
A Death in the Family

Imelda Marcos had been feeling desperately ill in the spring of 1972, afflicted by bouts of nausea, abdominal spasms, and pelvic pain. She was sleepless and agitated. But the symptoms most worrisome to doctors and her husband were the bleeding and the abnormal hormone counts. This was no common case of "morning sickness." Doctors had ordered her to bed in late April, almost from the moment she registered positive on a pregnancy test.

In fact, like ailing ConCon delegate Eduardo Quintero, she was bedridden on May 30, the morning that Quintero gave sensational sworn testimony from his hospital bed naming Imelda as a source of those peso-stuffed envelopes. On that day, the First Lady was confined to her stateroom aboard the docked presidential yacht, attended around the clock by a medical team that included a Swiss physician. Sedatives eased her pain. Progesterone injections were tried, to save her failing pregnancy.

The president, distressed at the prospect of losing the baby, prayed and pondered the inevitable question: Why? He could have blamed the laws of nature. Imelda was nearly forty-three years old, an age when the risk of miscarriage is very high. He could have blamed Imelda's health. She was run-down and exhausted when she became pregnant, days after returning from a controversial three-week tour of Spain, London, and Moscow. Instead, he would blame Quintero. He would blame the media. And he would blame the Filipino people — "our sick society" — for tolerating and being swayed by "vicious" anti-Marcos critics. They would be held responsible for the stress endangering the life of his unborn child.

Within hours of the damaging Quintero testimony, Malacanang leaked word to the press that Imelda, a helpless and innocent target of accusations, was very sick. And it was Quintero's fault. The story was circulated in time to share the next morning's front pages, otherwise devoted exclusively to the Quintero testimony. In the *Chronicle*, the headline read:

FIRST LADY'S
PREGNANCY
PERILLED

According to the story, an unidentified government official "blamed the deterioration of her health on the increasing innuendoes unflattering to the President and Mrs. Marcos in connection with the payola scandal in the Constitutional Convention and the ban-Marcos proposal." The story also said that although Imelda had been isolated aboard the yacht, she had followed press and television coverage of the controversy, which "had upset her." Finally, the story concluded, one reason she had canceled all engagements and shunned public exposure during the previous two months was "to avoid getting into any unpleasant discussions while in the sensitive period of her pregnancy."

But it was a story neglecting to mention that the pregnancy had actually been in jeopardy from the very beginning, well before there had been so much as a whiff of the scandal. Claims that Marcos critics were to blame for driving the president's wife to the brink of a miscarriage were either deluded or part of a calculated and rather cynical campaign of disinformation. In the end, however, the news of Imelda's health crisis did succeed in deflecting the fury over the bribery scandal. And of all the examples of Marcos's skill at turning adversity to advantage, his deft exploitation of Imelda's troubled pregnancy must rank among the most remarkable.

The year had begun with Marcos working on a campaign to extract more military aid out of Washington. Imelda had played a key role. The president had been very disappointed the previous autumn when an order of military transport planes from the United States was blocked because of foreign aid cutbacks. The Vietnam war had all but removed the Philippines from any priority list for direct military aid. A few days after Ambassador Byroade told Marcos there would be no transport planes, the president wrote that it was time to start looking for a new ally, possibly Australia, New Zealand, or Japan.

By January his desire for American military supplies took him to "some unknown persons" in the international black market. A cabinet undersecretary supposedly had arranged a $50 million deal for surplus war items. The only catch was a kickback requirement. The government would have to shell out about $200,000 in bribes. In his diary Marcos conceded: "A little underhanded. But if this is the only way we can protect our country, we will close our eyes to the questionable methods used to procure the defense items."

Meanwhile, Marcos was lobbying the embassy and visiting American political leaders for more support. His concern was not invasion, he explained, but insurgencies. He wanted a military better able to control domestic threats. He told conservative Senator James Buckley of New York that while Nixon's February visit to Beijing might reduce world tensions, it was not likely to solve "our primary problem — that of internal subversion." In fact, Marcos argued, "detente may release resources of Red China for communists in countries like the Philippines." Several weeks earlier he had urged U.S. Treasury Secretary John Connally to carry a message warning the White House that the Communist threat to the Philippines was real.

Finally, Marcos set out to improve relations with the Soviet Union, a move he thought might pressure Washington. He acknowledged in his diary that the friendly gesture toward America's cold war rival might be "interpreted as some kind of veiled threat" to the United States. In fact, the ploy seemed to be an outgrowth of ideas exchanged after a 1970 Malacanang dinner with Burmese leader Ne Win. As Marcos related in his diary: "I asked him what his policy was as to military and economic aid from the Western countries and the communist world. . . . And we discussed this frankly. He pits the two powers against each other." Perhaps the Philippines could do the same.

Marcos sometimes seemed resentful of his own country's modest role on the world stage, referring to the Philippines early in 1972 as "a small frog in the big lake croaking to the tune of the big frogs." But he saw in the First Lady's mission to Moscow a chance to make the big frogs croak to his tune. "The U.S. will probably now agree to help us strengthen our defenses," he wrote on March 15, the same day that he recorded Imelda's Moscow arrival. Of her first telephone report home he also wrote:

> She was cautious but optimistic. She had seen the Bolshoi Ballet (Swan Lake) last night. She is being treated very well. She says most of the women she has met are stout as barrels.

A day later Imelda conferred with Premier Aleksei Kosygin. She said he expressed willingness to extend various kinds of aid. Clearly, Marcos was delighted. He noted after her next telephone call that the Soviet premier had met with Imelda for two hours and twenty minutes, although he normally afforded heads of state no more than fifteen-minute sessions. And Marcos added:

> Kosygin found her charming, beautiful and talented as she talked to him about our problems. He commented that she was very much in love with her country as she had come all the way to a cold country (it was 10 below zero) to represent her country. . . .
> She finds the bone-chilling cold most uncomfortable. And . . . the food is not appetizing except the caviar.

Back home, Imelda's Moscow trip generated mostly controversy — complaints about its cost, criticism of the First Lady's diplomatic qualifications, and suspicion that it was intended to further her anticipated candidacy for president a year hence. As columnist Ernesto Granada noted on March 19 in the *Chronicle:* "The sober and fundamental fact Malacanang still has to realize is that no amount of gimmickry on the part of the First Lady will salvage her and the rest of the First Family from their current and extreme unpopularity." The columnist also called her Soviet trip "an exercise in silly diplomacy."

Granada was writing his way into a prominent place on the president's enemies list.

Imelda returned home to the editorial brickbats just in time to accompany her husband on their annual spring religious retreat to Baguio. Marcos observed that she was down to 135 pounds, having lost ten on the trip. She was suffering from jet lag and nosebleeds. And she seemed especially bothered by the restlessness of their three children, who wanted to be back in Manila with their friends. The president, too, was distracted. His popular support continued to dwindle even as it seemed it could decline no further. He was confronted with two options: either he succeeded in beating down the "Ban-Marcos Proposals" and getting a parliamentary form of government approved by the constitutional convention, or he must impose martial law, seizing dictatorial control of the government. The latter option had tempted him often since the riots of 1970. Still he hesitated, waiting for violence to justify stern measures, waiting to be sure of his military's absolute loyalty, waiting for signals from Washington that it would not interfere, waiting to revise again and again his martial-law contingency plans. But he was beginning to wonder if his patience was not really indecision, if he was acting wisely or cowardly. It was a dilemma he planned to reflect upon prayerfully in the Baguio mountains.

He wanted a divine signal, a sign from God. On March 28, he wrote: "So I talk to God in my retreat asking for guidance knowing that he sees me as I am — a man with strengths and weaknesses. I keep no secret from him as he has seen me in my nakedness."

There was no question what Marcos wanted to hear. He titled a rambling account of his meditations: "Spiritual Exercises on the Specific Problem of Martial Law." And on those pages Marcos compared freedom with a diet of meat. Sometimes, he mused, meat may not be good for one's health. And he wrote:

> So I conclude that freedom is not always good. There may be periods in a country's life when it is like meat. For the time being it must be curtailed or denied.

Finally, Ferdinand heard the voice of God. It was as if God had read the president's mind and told him what he wanted most to hear — that Philippine society was sick and that the best cure was a Marcos dictatorship. Describing the divine message, Marcos wrote:

> I asked the Lord for a sign. And he has given it. In the meditation this morning, the following thoughts were brought out.
>
> "My job is too heavy. But your will and not mine be done."
>
> The permissiveness of society must be balanced with authoritativeness. . . . Is it for the glory of God that there be authoritativeness? Yes, for we return order where there is chaos. . . .
>
> And the permissiveness of our society has spawned the many evils that will wreck our Republic. It must now be balanced with authoritativeness — and that is martial law. However, I put as a condition the occurrence of massive terrorism which would alarm the people as well as the authorities.
>
> And the discussion on authoritativeness to balance permissiveness came incidentally in answer to some inquiry as to the problem of parents over teen-aged children. The [priest] spoke of the problem. . . .
>
> But that this should even be talked about when not in the subject of the meditation — This is the sign that I have asked of God.

As the Marcos family celebrated Easter Sunday in Baguio, the president was filled with new hope and confidence. Now, in his mind, both God and the Supreme Court had blessed martial law. Nonetheless, Marcos still wanted the constitutional convention to approve a parliamentary system. If or when he declared martial law, the president did not want it said that he became a dictator simply to retain power.

It turned out that the spring trip to Baguio apparently had produced one additional blessing. Still unbeknownst to Ferdinand and Imelda as they flew back to Malacanang on April 3, the First Lady had become pregnant.

Ferdinand Marcos still wanted another son. Years of inconclusive medical tests had been unable to explain why the couple had been unable to conceive again. Then it happened. Doctors said the baby was due in December.

In the pages of his diary, Marcos exhibited little exuberance at the news. By contrast, he had seemed almost obsessed at times during the previous two years with what he called "our project" to have another child. But this pregnancy was in trouble immediately, which might explain his initial reserve. On April 23, after nausea forced Imelda to leave a dinner party on the presidential yacht, Marcos simply noted: "We are keeping Imelda company as she keeps to bed on the advice of the doctor." Despite her condition, she was not even allowed to leave the boat for a more stable bed ashore.

At first, the pregnancy was kept secret from the public. In early May, however, observant reporters noted that the First Lady missed a traditional public appearance. At Corregidor she stayed aboard the *Ang Pangulo* while Marcos spoke at the annual ceremonies marking the island's capture by Japanese forces. As a gossip item in the *Chronicle* noted: "She is known not to miss any opportunity to be in the focus of the camera during official functions." Imelda's pregnancy was subsequently confirmed, prompting *Chronicle* columnist Granada to speculate, with some sarcasm, about how an infant Marcos might help Imelda's anticipated campaign for the presidency.

In his May 10 column, Granada wrote:

> Until the news broke out, the First Lady was dismissed as a losing if persistent presidential candidate because every publicity she got was of negative result. . . . But as a prospective mother before the [1973] campaign and as a new mother during the actual campaign, Imelda will be . . . unassailable — for any attack on her will be an attack on motherhood.
>
> The harassed Filipinos find it difficult to admire anything in the Marcoses, but even the most critical of them must admit that in the case of Imelda's baby, never have the First Couple timed anything so perfectly.

But Granada and the rest of the Philippines were unaware of difficulties that already threatened the pregnancy. On Saturday, May 13, Marcos met with Imelda's doctors, who relayed distressing news. Tests showed that the count of a crucial hormone secreted by the placenta was declining, an alarming trend that signaled the likely demise of the fetus. That night the president wrote: "Imelda is still feeling well although the doctors are now more pessimistic. . . . But we are praying that the pregnancy will be normal and everything will be well."

In fact, still a week away from delegate Quintero's first surprising revelations about Malacanang bribery, Imelda's pregnancy already was doomed. During the next week Imelda suffered attacks of pain, sometimes severe. She was anxious, restless, unable to sleep. She kept the president awake one night until after three in the morning.

It was then that the payola controversy erupted. The Marcos administration was under attack from the moment Quintero got his thunderous ovation on May 19. But even at that point, the elderly whistle-blower had not specifically mentioned the First Lady — or anyone else who had actually handed over his eighteen peso-stuffed envelopes. Nor had Quintero yet named Imelda on Friday, May 26, when the First Lady's pregnancy encountered another crisis. Shortly before midnight that night, Marcos wrote: "Imelda is in pain. [The doctors] seem to think that Imelda will not be able to hold the pregnancy and may have a miscarriage. She has just been given a mild sedation [*sic*]. I probably need one too."

A few days later, on Tuesday, May 30, Quintero's bedside testimony finally linked Imelda to the bribery envelopes. And Malacanang leaked word that Imelda's pregnancy was in trouble. While that story also reported that efforts had been made to shelter the First Lady from stressful news accounts, Marcos had never made such references in his diary. In fact, he wrote after the Quintero testimony that Imelda was "insistent on issuing her own statement and even going to the convention to confront Quintero." The president said he would not permit Imelda to debate "these demagogues," advising her instead to prepare a written statement in response.

At about midnight Wednesday, the next night, Imelda's condition worsened. She was bleeding. Doctors gave her another dose of progesterone. They also administered Librium, a tranquilizer prescribed for acute anxiety. The president wrote: "We still hope to save the baby." The next morning she suffered painful cramping. She was sedated.

Imelda was asleep when it ended. She experienced a spontaneous abortion at about 3:30 Thursday afternoon. Marcos described the moment in his diary that evening: "Without her noticing it, she expelled the placenta and the baby when she was heavily sedated." Not until he broke the news to his wife some hours after the miscarriage did Imelda learn that her brief pregnancy was over. She was distraught. Marcos wrote that "she . . . has been crying her eyes out" over the pain, her sense of loss, and feelings of inadequacy.

But Marcos did not release news of the miscarriage that day. Nor did he issue an official announcement the next day, Friday, June 2. That was the day Quintero formally was charged with bribery by the National Bureau of Investigation, the same government investigators who apparently had planted suitcases of currency in the old man's home.

Meanwhile, in his diary Marcos tried out his lines about the "sick society" for the first time. On Friday night the president wrote:

> I have shed no tears for my unborn child, but I have vowed that I shall cure this sick and ailing society that has brought about the anguish of my wife which caused the abortion. For the media has [*sic*] been vicious — it has condemned for a crime not charged, foisted gossip as truth and disregarded the rights of fair and impartial trial.
>
> And this sick man [Quintero] who has committed perjury, libel and bribery has done me at least one favor. He has opened my eyes to this illness of our society that may yet destroy it. And my duty and mission is now to cure that illness.

On Saturday, June 3, Imelda was transported to the Makati Medical Center, where doctors performed a D&C (dilatation and curettage), a routine procedure following a miscarriage to be certain that no fetal tissue remained in the uterus. A visibly stricken Imelda, eyes closed, on a stretcher, entered the hospital at 7:00 A.M., accompanied by her grim-faced husband. News photographers waiting at the entrance captured the pictures that topped the Sunday papers. Like his decision the previous November to time the lifting of his suspension of the writ of habeas corpus to get it into the Sunday papers, Marcos's delay in announcing the miscarriage also guaranteed that the sympathetic story would get maximum play in the nation's most widely read newspapers. Palace press secretary Kit Tatad issued a terse statement saying that the miscarriage had occurred early that Saturday morning — a day and a half after it had actually happened.

Rumors soon flared, perhaps originating from medical aides who participated in the procedure, that there was little evidence of a miscarriage that morning. Indeed, so much skepticism arose surrounding the veracity of Imelda's pregnancy that serious doubts would persist for twenty years. Historians and journalists have speculated since whether the highly publicized event could have been a charade — what Filipinos call a *palabas,* or contrived spectacle — intended to engender public sympathy. Even some members of the palace staff at the time were convinced it was a fraud. The diary makes a rather convincing case that there was, indeed, a pregnancy and a miscarriage. But it also makes clear that there was considerable contrived detail in the official announcements and in the assignment of blame. And the sad and otherwise profoundly personal loss was openly exploited for its political value.

The day that Imelda entered the hospital, a grave and resentful Marcos told reporters: "We have just lost a baby which we had hoped would be a boy." And he declared publicly what he had already confided to his diary, that the blame belonged to a "sick society" — which he vowed to reform in "the short time" that he had left. It sounded like a threat. Later that night Marcos wrote in his diary: "I hope the public does not give all kinds of meaning to this statement. But I am bitter and angry!"

For days, Imelda's condition remained prominent news. Reports tracked her recovery and discussed her depression. While the bribery scandal did not evaporate, the stories of Imelda's personal suffering softened its impact. Finally, late in June — nearly three weeks after the miscarriage — the Marcoses carried their two-inch fetus to Leyte for a twilight funeral. Marcos told a group of well-wishers and reporters at Toclaban that he and his wife had come on a sorrowful journey "to intern [*sic*] our unborn child with whom so many dreams had died." Later, in his diary, the president described the graveside mass: "Most picturesque and sad. Imelda was crying all the time."

Press coverage of the unusual rites was a mix of sympathy and scorn. The *Chronicle,* for example, under the leadership of recently appointed editor Amando "Doro" Doronila, observed on its opinion page that most sentimental Filipinos felt deeply for the grieving First Couple, but added:

> [W]e cannot help feeling a deeper compassion for thousands of Filipino mothers and fathers whose offspring had been aborted because of poverty, inadequate diet, hard work and their inability to benefit from the minimum of medical care.
>
> These thousands, who are turned back from overcrowded hospitals, have no Swiss doctors to diagnose their pregnancy . . . no yacht to repair into for comfort, no companion in times of stress except poverty.
>
> These are people who are victims of a "sick" society, who suffer in

silence. No photographers take pictures . . . of their sadness, and of their bitterness about life.

Editor Doronila may have secured his place on the president's enemies list. However, Marcos was out of town when the article appeared, cruising through the southern provinces. From the interring ceremonies on Leyte, the president and First Lady had set out for a series of meetings with military commanders in the south, as well as various public appearances that looked very much like political rallies.

Marcos was particularly eager to visit Mindanao, where violent conflict between Muslims and Christians was growing worse. Before leaving Manila he had met with a group of Muslim political leaders from central Mindanao who had "pledged loyalty to me — 'even if you declare yourself dictator.' "

At Cagayan de Oro in northern Mindanao, Marcos met with constabulary officers and area mayors to discuss regional security issues and to golf. Imelda toured the marketplace where, he wrote, she "was mobbed by thousands of people who kept asking her to run for president. She attracted more spontaneous attention than we did."

In Zamboanga City, at the western rim of the Moro Gulf, Marcos and Imelda met with the local Catholic leaders who warned that fighting between Muslims and Christians had created a virtual state of revolution in the region. The priest told them that "democratic ways will not solve the violence. So martial law may be necessary. . . . [T]his has impressed Imelda and me." To Marcos, it was another sign.

And in Cebu, a group of municipal mayors introduced a good-natured resolution in honor of their Malacanang visitors: "Resolved that since no one can lead the country in this troubled time but Pres. Marcos, Imelda is directed to run for President in 1973!!" Sailing home the next day, Marcos wrote: "I am glad that we took the trip."

The trip that started with a funeral had buoyed the president's spirits. He even seemed to enjoy the company of reporters from the Malacanang press corps who were along for the cruise. Recounting one session with the journalists, Marcos wrote:

> They asked me that now that I am retiring if I knew of anybody who could lead the country in these troubled times. I told them that we have to develop a leader in a year and a half.

I told them that what I feared most was when I had retired, the armed forces may be pushed to the wall and for their own individual survival they might take over the country.

And he discussed some of his options. He could "run out of the country or stay and help stave off the revolution." But it was, he assured them, an easy choice. "I do not intend to run away after I had been given the honor of serving as president of the Republic!!"

Ferdinand Marcos had no intention of leaving the Philippines. Indeed, he had no intention of leaving Malacanang.

CHAPTER THIRTEEN
Summer Storms

He had his own problems — trying to stabilize a staggering economy, cope with rampant crime, achieve a politically favorable constitution, resurrect his flagging popularity — but early in 1972 Ferdinand Marcos had an idea how to solve someone else's problems. President Nixon's. The United States, as he saw it, was in serious trouble with drugs, crime, antiwar riots, and a greedy, what's-in-it-for-me society. The Marcos answer for America: dictatorship.

During a February cruise aboard the presidential yacht with a visiting writer-photographer team from *Town & Country Magazine*, Marcos stayed up until well past midnight, as he recounted in his diary, talking about what could be done to save the United States.

> My answer was, at what point of anarchy would a Julius Caesar take over the [Washington] government as a dictator. Although, I added, it may be difficult to control the U.S. from one central point as it has too many centers of power. . . . And [I] wondered whether America is not showing the same symptoms the Roman Empire showed before its fall.

The president also pondered aloud the research of academicians who he said "are now studying . . . whether the old concepts of democracy and freedom are still valid, or whether dictatorship or authoritarianism is not demanded for survival."

One day in April the president cautioned his top business development adviser against resigning from the Board of Investment because his help would be needed if Marcos became dictator. The president wrote:

> I told him that I expect disorder which may end up with the communists trying to grab power by violence or legal means. The Armed Forces would not allow this. So they would, in turn, take over the government and may call on me . . . to set up a dictatorship. . . . And I would need all the good men to run government.

At that time, Marcos was reading another book about Napoleon Bonaparte, paying special attention to his "ascension to dictatorship." In his diary, Marcos singled out a passage from the book by Georges Lefebvre that said Napoleon rose to power "because an internal necessity fated that country to dictatorship." There were parallels between Napoleon's France around 1800 and Marcos's Philippines in 1972 — crime, violence, economic troubles, political turmoil, power struggles. In Paris, a devastating bomb blast that killed and injured many victims prompted Napoleon to order sweeping arrests of his political foes. He blamed the carnage on his enemies despite evidence to the contrary. In the summer of 1972, a series of bomb blasts in metropolitan Manila caused extensive damage to buildings and public nerves. Marcos blamed them on Communist subversives despite no evidence or, in other cases, evidence to the contrary.

Throughout his stormy second term, Marcos had been telling the public, the media, his generals, and his diary that he would declare martial law only if provoked by acts of violent subversion, by overt acts of terror, massive sabotage, and attempted assassination. In a 1970 speech to the Lions Club he had specifically warned against sabotage of water, power, sewer, and telephone lines as well as schools, markets, and Congress.

Frequently in his diary Marcos had predicted such violence was about to happen. He even predicted general dates — the summer of 1970, for example, and January of 1971. But his had been a poor crystal ball. Dates came and went without destruction. The Communists simply were waiting for him to retire before launching their assault against a less experienced and more vulnerable chief executive, he would explain. The only time he seemed to get it right was when he predicted the violence that occurred at Plaza Miranda in the summer of 1971. But in that instance his own military agents were blamed, not the Communists. Still, Marcos ventured one more prediction: he expected fighting in the streets of Manila by summer of 1972. Again, he seemed to get it right.

The wave of 1972 bombings began late in June, increased in July, and became almost routine occurrences through August and into September. The targets might have sounded familiar to members of the Lions Club — the Nawasa water mains, a power station, the Philippine Long Distance Telephone Co. exchange, Manila City Hall, government offices shared by the constitutional convention in Quezon City, the Congress Building, the Department of Foreign Affairs, the Department of Social Welfare, banks, the sugar institute.

Most attacks came late at night, as if intended to minimize chances of human casualties. Some were grenades tossed from cars and jeepneys. Some were hidden plastic explosives with sophisticated timing devices. Occasionally they were duds, but not on the night that Maria Paz Sampana went shopping.

The twenty-six-year-old dry goods shop owner from Malolos, just north of Manila, had come to the city on Tuesday night, September 5, to buy stock for her shelves. In the crowded shopping district that surrounds Plaza Miranda, she made her way down narrow lanes clogged by sidewalk vendors to the popular department store of Chinese businessman Jose Lau. The sign said "Joe's Department Store." At 8:30 she still was browsing among the glass display cases on the ground floor when the bomb blast erupted.

A savage explosion blew glass and shoppers in all directions — a young schoolteacher, a teenage boy from Tarlac, and forty others. Many were rushed to the same hospitals where maimed and injured Liberal party Senate candidates were treated after the Plaza Miranda bombing a year before. It was too late for Maria Sampana. The wave of bombings had claimed its first life.

"Bomb Scare Grips City," declared a *Chronicle* headline as Manila papers reviewed a week of multiple bombing incidents that had begun the previous Tuesday night, August 29. That first night there were two postmidnight blasts, one at an office building near the Manila police headquarters and the other, fifteen minutes later, hitting an armored car in front of the Philippine Banking Corporation. The next morning an unexploded twelve-pound bomb in an attaché case was discovered in a ground floor office of the Department of Foreign Affairs. Defense Secretary Enrile in public statements blamed the series of bombings on the Communists. Marcos said the attacks followed the "terroristic pattern" of a Communist plan to spread chaos in Greater Manila.

But student leftists blamed "fascist elements" and called the bombing at Joe's an attempted massacre that was "calculated to create an atmosphere of simulated disorder." Senator Ramon Mitra, one of the victims of Plaza Miranda, declared the bombings the work of the armed forces "to condition the people to martial law." And columnist Granada scoffed at how predictable it was for the palace to blame Communists for every criminal act in the country, writing on September 10 that soon "Secretary Enrile may even claim that the [illegal] gambling casinos . . . are really fund-raising units of the New People's Army."

All that skepticism seemed to be rewarded when Manila police arrested a constabulary sergeant in connection with the death of Maria Sampana. The sergeant, who by one account was overcome by guilt and actually surrendered himself, had been assigned to the firearms and explosives section at constabulary headquarters, Camp Crame. He had been off duty on a thirty-day furlough that spanned the period of the bombing upsurge.

Marcos took no note of such developments in his diary or in public statements. His blame never shifted. He attributed a rash of prominent kidnappings for ransom to the NPA and speculated in writing that Communist insurgents "may have raised their funds in this manner." When a carload of heavily armed thieves engaged in a shootout with Manila police on his birthday, Marcos declared the street thugs to be NPA soldiers. Two more bombings damaged Meralco facilities and caused widespread power blackouts. Marcos wrote: "So there is hysteria in Manila . . . because of the bombings, kidnapings and now the [police shootout with] the NPA."

Months earlier Marcos, who always was conscious of his physical condition, launched a regimen of exercise and diet intended to bring him to the very peak of fitness. His simple diet sometimes consisted of little more than sardines and vegetables. He drank water and fruit juices. He was particularly interested in a recently introduced Ukrainian vegetable "guaranteed to stop the aging process and to lower blood pressure." He lifted weights, jogged, played a form of handball, and golfed. He was like a fighter in training for The Big Bout. In the pre-dawn hours of Monday, September 11, 1972, Marcos wrote:

> It is now my birthday. I am 55. And I feel more physically and mentally robust than in the past decade. And have acquired valuable experience to boot. Energy and wisdom — the philosopher's heaven.

The day before, as had become customary in his presidency, Marcos celebrated his birthday a bit early with the military at Camp Aguinaldo. He described the event fondly: "Parade and Review — in the rain. I trooped the line in a raincoat and hat. Felt good." Then, recounting elements of his speech to the armed forces audience, Marcos wrote: "The history of our people shows this, The Philippines was the land of freedom. So I come to bear witness to the renewal of your pledge to that freedom. And I am proud to be counted as another soldier who also says — For freedom, Battle to the Death."

Marcos had a keen sense of drama. But he also had strong instincts about risk. Privately, he worried about what sort of surprises he might encounter as he drew ever closer to declaring martial law. In August, even before the rate of bombings had surged, Marcos took his children aside to warn them about the future and to counsel them. Describing his talks with Bongbong and Irene he wrote:

> I told [them] the situation in which we are — the fact that we are now fighting for survival; that whether I retire or not our family is in danger of liquidation from either the communists or our political enemies; that if I retire I would be forced to fight for our lives because the communists are growing stronger and would be much stronger without me as President; rather than fight a defensive or losing battle later, I would rather fight now by taking over the government by a proclamation of Martial Law; but that such a proclamation would succeed if the people are with us and the people will be with us if the new government is a reform government and we are all exemplars of the new society; so they, the children, must so conduct themselves that they will not antagonize the people.

It was Friday, August 11, 1972. The "New Society," Marcos's vision of a Philippines reformed under his disciplinary care, was still unborn. And publicly, the president was still denying any intentions to seize authoritarian control.

But Marcos was always more candid with his children than with anyone else — including himself. His diary entries never seemed more honest, nor his sentiments more genuine, than when he wrote about his children.

Back in January 1971, only hours after secretly signing the standby declaration of martial law, Marcos had called a family council of sorts — addressing the children, Imelda, and her brother, Kokoy Romualdez, on the eve of Bongbong's departure for Worth Abbey School in England. Marcos discussed the possibility that Imee, Irene, and their mother might join Bongbong if violence erupted in Manila. And, solemnly, he advised them that "whether I am there beside them or not, they (the children) should value education and get a doctorate degree because even if we should lose our fortune and position here in the Philippines, then they could make their own way in this world; that if for any reason we should be separated and I should not be able to guide them after normalcy returns to the world or [to] the Philippines . . . they should return to the Philippines where their roots are; that I would prefer their marrying Filipinos."

Marcos the father worried about their grades, especially Bongbong's. "He is too carefree and lazy. . . . [He] must get character. I have told him that since we have enemies, he will have to fight the battles I fought in the past . . . ," Marcos wrote in June 1972.

He worried about their career interests, especially Imee's. "We have some problems with Imee who insists on an acting career apparently," he noted earlier in 1972. She wished to accept the lead role in a Manila stage production of *The Diary of Anne Frank*. Wrote Marcos: "Imelda objects because she thinks actresses are looked down upon in the Philippines. And that group is supposed to take pot."

And he worried about their happiness and their eating habits, especially little Irene's. The youngest of the children to go off to British boarding school wrote that she cried herself to sleep with hunger and homesickness. "Irene has lost nine pounds and she has pains in the stomach," he wrote in May 1971. Marcos telephoned the headmistress at Hastings to be sure his eleven-year-old daughter got her milk and biscuits before bed.

Examples of Marcos sensitivity toward his children are scattered throughout the diary. Among the papers filed with his journal was a conciliatory letter to Imee, written on September 21, 1971, apparently following an emotional outburst between daughter and parents. Marcos wrote, in part:

> My sweet adorable scrambled-brained eldest daughter who claims the temperament of a *prima dona* and the objectivity of an Oxford Don, you have just written one of the most touching letters in the history of the generation gap. We read it while we were having dinner and I am afraid the soup received some lachrymal dilution. But this dire confession must never be revealed to our critical public until twenty years after my demise!
>
> . . . [Y]ou have just shown us up as a little infantile. But I do not know of a more enchanting way of being unmasked nor by a more charming person! (Cheers)
>
> You must forgive the old their rigid and set ways. And we must understand the ways of the young. . . .
>
> We love you always,
> Your dad —

Threats to the safety of his family caused Marcos considerable anxiety and anger. Early in 1971, the American embassy warned him of intelligence information about a possible plot by Middle Eastern kidnapers to seize Bongbong in England. Two months later his own intelligence sources reported a radical student group had "seriously proposed and discussed to kidnap the First Lady . . . and then tie her to a post naked." In his diary, Marcos fumed: "This shows the viciousness of the enemies we are fighting. First the kidnaping of Bongbong, now Imelda. And these are the evil men whom some of the intellectuals . . . are supporting. So are the media people giving them all-out aid."

While bombings and threats of bombings increased in Manila, the most devastating violence was committed by Mother Nature. The typhoon season came early and with historic ferocity. One storm after another slashed across Luzon and islands to the south, scattering death and misery in their paths. Between the typhoons with their destructive winds came weeks of persistent rain and floods that turned central Luzon into a sea. It was a national disaster of then-unprecedented proportions. Many hundreds dead. Billions of pesos in property damage. Nearly a million homeless. Crops destroyed. Food supplies low. Transportation paralyzed. Time for a nation to pull together. But not the Philippines, not where even the weather blows political.

Government relief goods turned out to be so inadequate that victims and editorial writers complained of bureaucrats and politicians who were suspected of hoarding and taking kickbacks in the form of desperately needed supplies. What finally was distributed often was dispensed amid great fanfare and photography. Imelda made well-orchestrated forays into disaster areas to deliver packages labeled "Special Disaster Relief Project of the First Lady Imelda R. Marcos." Observed columnist Granada in the *Chronicle:* "The people just cannot seem to think of the First Family doing anything for them without getting something in return. Particularly since every act of public service . . . is repeatedly impressed on the people by their awesome propaganda machinery."

Ideology and partisan politics also affected distribution. A group of student activists handing out food and antigovernment pamphlets near Angeles City was arrested by constabulary officers, supposedly for failing to register with proper authorities. And Malacanang refused to release supplies to the Liberal party governor of the flood-ravaged province of Pampanga, insisting that goods waiting unused in a warehouse could be distributed only by a Nacionalista party congressman who was delayed in Manila tending to a sick brother.

While relief efforts floundered, the Philippine people looked heavenward for blue sky and some answers. Why so much wind and rain? Newspapers and weather reporters called it a byproduct of geography. The Philippines occupied a spot of ocean where warm, moisture-laden tropical air from around the Equator collided with cooler air from the north in something called an Inter-Tropical Convergence Zone. The result: meteorological fireworks. But others dismissed science. They blamed a curse. Manila Mayor Ramon Bagatsing, under political fire at the time for a woeful city flood-control system, insisted that the biblical flood visited on Manila was God's punishment for the theft of a religious icon from a parish church in the Tondo slums. A bejeweled statue of the Christ child, *Santo Nino,* believed to have healing powers, had been stolen and dismembered during July, sometime between the departure of Typhoon Edeng and the arrival of Typhoon Konsing. Two weeks later, its missing parts were recovered — by Imelda Marcos. Press and diary accounts said that she paid 2,800 pesos (about $400) to buy the statue's head, arms, and feet after the thieves offered to sell them to a friend of the First Lady, a Makati antique dealer.

Another media event was promptly arranged, mixing images of religion and politics and the weather. Major church leaders shunned the event, but a thanksgiving mass was celebrated at Malacanang. The reassembled icon was presented to a waiting crowd from a palace balcony. Imelda said she had faith that *Santo Nino*'s recovery "would change the unusual bad weather conditions." The statue then was "accompanied home" by Marcos and the First Lady, who led a slow procession through flooded streets to the Tondo church. Marcos, who rode in a bus while thousands walked, described the August 2 scene in his diary:

> People joined the procession, lined the streets carrying candles or placing candles on the window sills. There must have been at least 50,000. And they were mostly in tears.
>
> This faith and spiritual strength is what communism cannot conquer. . . . And I do believe in miracles. I have seen too many happen in my lifetime.

The next morning, blue sky and sunshine greeted Manila. Floodwaters seemed to be receding. Columnist Granada dubbed it sarcastically the "First Lady's Miracle" and wrote that he would not be surprised if she ran for president as the miracle candidate. Marcos dismissed critics, writing: "The talk of Manila is the miracle of Sto. Nino, with a few sour grapes as was expected. But it looks like I am not the only believer in miracles." In Baguio later, Marcos wrote that the people kept talking about "the sun that we brought to that city." It did not last long. Another monsoon blew across the archipelago, followed by severe tropical storms. In days, Manila was back underwater — still under siege from the heavens and from the terrifying work of the night bombers.

Amid all the summer storms that were making life desperate for millions of Filipinos in 1972, Marcos and his rivals waged desperate politics. On July 7, the constitutional convention adopted the Marcos-backed parliamentary system by a vote of 158 to 120. It was promptly condemned in the press. Public support for ultimate ratification was in serious doubt. Marcos wrote: "If it is not ratified, Imelda may have to run for President as there is no other candidate that can win against the Liberals. But the parliamentary form of government will save Imelda from the muckracking [*sic*] of politics."

The same day, warnings of pending martial law broke on the front pages of Manila newspapers. A secret report of Marcos's legal advisers in the military and Justice Department was recommending martial law before the 1973 elections. A *Chronicle* account said the report also called for "creation of a situation to justify" the action. It would be illegal, declared Senator Diokno. He conceded that "ambition, however, could make a travesty of legality." He accused Marcos of "building a throne with bayonets." In his diary, Marcos simply noted: "Diokno is beginning to sound off again on martial law."

The tale of a mysterious ship also dominated the headlines through the summer. The *m/v Karagatan,* a small cargo ship, was seized along an isolated Isabela shore after a protracted gun battle and bombing runs against never-seen and never-harmed enemies hiding in the jungle. The constabulary reported it found a cache of hundreds of M-14s, mortars, and explosives. Defense Secretary Enrile called it proof that a foreign power, presumably the People's Republic of China, was supporting the New People's Army. The Manila media suggested it was another concocted story to support claims of a serious Communist threat. Apparently, it was neither. Years later, Jose Maria Sison, the NPA founder, would say that his guerrillas were, indeed, in the area. However, the arms shipment was being smuggled into Isabela by agents of a local warlord. Whether the NPA was acting in some sort of partnership with the unidentified warlord remains unclear.

Real or concocted, the *Karagatan* incident gave Marcos another reason to trumpet an alarm. On July 15, he wrote: "[T]he conspiracy for subversion, insurgency and rebellion is more alarming than we originally imagined — And we are reassessing the contingency plans of the military." Once again Marcos was galled by the skeptical press that questioned his credibility and belittled military reports from the scene of the odd battle for the *Karagatan.* So, that day he also wrote: "The media, especially the newspapers, have forfeited their right to freedom of the press. They have abused it to the point where they actually seek to falsify news. . . . There must be some way to prevent these irresponsible advocates of not press freedom but press tyranny from weakening the state and the democracy that gives them the liberty that their friends, the communists, seek to destroy." He recorded a preview of his enemies list — Chino Roces of the *Times*, Amando Doronila and Ernesto Granada of the *Chronicle*, Civil Liberties Union chairman and columnist Renato Constantino. "I have a clear conscience in fighting them."

By late summer, the Marcos lobby completed its domination of the constitutional convention, defeating a motion to ban Marcos and his family from serving as president or prime minister under the new charter. Malacanang forces prevailed by a margin of twenty-four votes, 155 to 131. Eduardo Quintero, still hospitalized from the stress of his whistle-blower role in the payola scandal, was among thirty-one delegates unable or unwilling to vote. The *Chronicle* reported that silence, rather than jubilation, followed the critical vote. Pesos and special-interest politics had won for Marcos what he could claim was a constitutional convention endorsement. Now, if he had to assume dictatorial control, how could anyone say he did so to avoid surrendering office? The next day, Thursday, September 7, Marcos wrote: "The afternoon I spent in finishing all papers needed for a possible proclamation of martial law, just in case it is necessary to do so."

The summer of 1972 brought one more troubling development. In a late August cable from the Philippine embassy in Washington, Marcos was informed that senior U.S. State Department official Marshall Green "bluntly told us that the Philippine government has overestimated the aid extended by the Chinese (Red) government and the Chinese communists . . . to the local communists." Marcos was, by his description, "exercised" by Green's comments. He directed Kokoy Romualdez to contact Philippine friends in Washington and to "send word to the cabinet level and the National Security Council level that I feel that we are being misused."

In his diary entry of Sunday, August 27, Marcos angrily scrawled:

The U.S. State Department has a consistent record of error in the assessment of Asian situations and judging Red Chinese intentions. It is preposterous, therefore, for them to lecture to us on their estimate of the threat we face from the local communists. And apparently they are at it again in the Philippines.

It was the CIA position, as relayed to Marcos a year earlier, that the NPA was funded "out of the hip pockets" of Jose Sison and Commander Dante, that it was disorganized, "small and vulnerable." The CIA's assessment was that the NPA "does not pose a threat — numbering less than 100" armed insurgents. In his August diary entry, Marcos raged: "How stupid can they be?" Then, citing his secretly manipulated Supreme Court decision in which jurists ruled that a state of rebellion had existed when the writ of habeas corpus was declared, a contemptuous Marcos wrote: "Are the Americans saying that the justices are incompetent? Like all of us, supposedly?"

His strong reaction to Marshall Green's pointed remarks and the CIA's skepticism betrayed some of Marcos's profound conflicts over his relationship with the United States. He wanted its aid money but no strings on how it was used; he wanted its defense support, but he regarded the military bases as "a limitation of our sovereignty"; he wanted its official blessing for martial law if or when he chose to proclaim it, but he never quite trusted the assurances he got.

While Ambassador Henry Byroade often assured him of Nixon Administration support, Marcos kept asking him to repeat it. What did Richard Nixon think? What did the American people think? In the spring of 1972, Marcos approached Byroade again about the possibility he might suspend the writ of habeas corpus or declare martial law.

> I asked him pointblank whether the American government would at least remain neutral. He answered that his government would support my move. But I noticed a hesitancy when he said that my suspension had caused a controversy [in August 1971] indicating that he would prefer to have it avoided.

Marcos sought political allies among American business interests. And in the summer of 1972 a key Supreme Court decision was handed down giving the president new leverage with U.S. investors. As of 1974, with expiration of the Laurel-Langley Agreement dating back to independence, Americans would be banned from keeping or acquiring agricultural land in the Philippines, the court ruled. Furthermore, Americans would be subject to legal restrictions in the exploitation of natural resources and the ownership of numerous business enterprises. U.S. business officials clamored for Marcos to intercede. In August, special presidential envoy Kokoy Romualdez told a group of anxious investors in New York that Marcos was not happy with their timid support for his administration, "that the President of the Philippines was less interested in their property than in the security of the Philippines and its people which [were] threatened by the communists — and they have not helped on this danger that haunts the President; on the contrary they have belittled his fears and not extended arms and sympathy to fight the communists."

A few days later Marcos told visiting U.S. oil executives that while Americans worried about their properties and profits, the Filipino was worried about national survival. In September Marcos wrote: "The message I asked them to convey to their American bosses in business and government [was] that we would like them to help us fight the communists. Otherwise, we cannot help them. This is the line we must follow."

Late in the summer, United States Senator Daniel K. Inouye of Hawaii flew to Manila, ostensibly to inspect typhoon and flood damage and to pledge at least $30 million in disaster aid. Marcos described him as "an old friend," but confronted him almost immediately with a complaint. "I briefed him on the State Department and U.S. Embassy attempt to understate the threat posed by Communism to the Philippines." The same day he met with visiting West German Prime Minister Helmut Kohl. Marcos was critical but terse. "I felt he is a politician, not a statesman."

Inouye proceeded on field trips into the flooded regions of Luzon before returning to meet privately with Marcos. On September 1, 1972, Marcos wrote: "He confided to me that he did not merely come to see the damage caused by the calamity, but also to see the general situation. And he will carry the message that the U.S. should pay more attention to the Philippines. He also revealed that Amb. Byroade has the same thinking as I have on the communist threat." Marcos made a plea for military surplus goods from Vietnam, including helicopters, mortars, and recoilless rifles, to enhance the Philippine military's anti-subversion capabilities, he explained. And Marcos wrote: "Senator Inouye will be a great help to the Philippines."

Their conversation turned to politics. Inouye wanted to know about the martial-law option. Marcos seemed to bristle at the notion he might proclaim it to avoid a political contest.

> I immediately countered that I do not need martial law to win an election and that in the present situation anybody I supported would come out [winning]; that I would not agree to allowing the First Lady to run since it would be unfair to her. "We are too old in this game to need martial law to get votes," I said and he smiled with understanding.
>
> "However," I explained, "do not misunderstand me. If the communists sow terror in Manila — if they bomb and burn, kill and kidnap, if they use the Vietcong tactics, then I will not hesitate to proclaim martial law."

Marcos said his preference would be a simple extension of his term, but that such an option would require bipartisan support. He did not tell the visiting senator that such an option was wholly fanciful. But if that did not work out, he said, he would try to become prime minister.

Then, in comments dripping with omens, Marcos qualified his intentions:

> But I would first wipe out the communists before the new President or Prime Minister takes over so he has a chance. I need several years to build up my replacement. None of those aspiring now are fit to lead the country. Aquino and Diokno are demagogues and are communist-inclined. They would immediately set up a communist regime.... What we need is somebody who is trusted by the Armed Forces, is a liberal thinker, will fight communism and will risk not only his life but everything in this fight.

On the streets of Manila, the bombing incidents resumed soon after Senator Inouye flew home. Manila City Hall. Water mains. A power station. An unexploded bomb was found in a busy shopping emporium. Bomb threats proliferated all over the city. There was a general unease throughout Manila the night of Wednesday, September 13. But not in Malacanang. It was Bongbong's fourteenth birthday. One wing of the palace had been converted into a nightclub complete with strobe lights and posters of the president's popular, shaggy-haired son. With apparent pride Marcos wrote: "And there are more girls than boys. In fact, there are only a handful of boys and about five times of girls." But he turned immediately to more serious matters, adding: "At the rate the tension and hysteria in Manila continues, I may have to declare martial law soon. Many people are not leaving their homes. Threats to bomb and blackmail [are] rampant."

Earlier that day Ninoy Aquino had dropped a bombshell, of sorts, on the Philippine Senate floor. He revealed that he had seen a copy of a military contingency plan designated "OPLAN Sagittarius," a plan to place Greater Manila under control of the Philippine constabulary in order to enforce martial law. The breach of security among his inner circle of advisers was worrisome, but Marcos rather welcomed the publicity. "Perhaps it is best that the political opposition start a debate that will get the people used to the idea of emergency powers."

Indeed, the date had already been set. A few hours before the disco music erupted in Bongbong's wing of the palace, Marcos met across the Pasig with Enrile and a group of advisers. "We agreed to set the 21st of this month as the deadline."

Martial law was on the calendar, secretly set to occur on a date not coincidentally divisible by the president's lucky number seven. It was agreed that sufficient acts of terror and sabotage already had occurred and that public demand for restoration of peace and order was clear. All that remained to satisfy the president's oft-stated requirements for seizing authoritarian control was an attempted assassination.

Despite his fears of numerous rumored assassination plots that continued through the summer, no attempt had ever been made against the lives of the president, his family, or members of the cabinet. But neither had there been a historic fire in the Reichstag before 1933. And as of Bongbong's disco birthday party on September 13, 1972, there were still eight days to the secret martial law deadline — plenty of time to choreograph one last encounter with one more phantom urban guerrilla.

CHAPTER FOURTEEN
Some Kind of Hero

In a city already spooked by bombings and bomb threats, the awful smell that began seeping under doors and wafting through open windows was as alarming as it was repulsive. Could it be a massive gas leak? Would the air erupt in a ball of flame? Across northern Manila, workers evacuated office buildings. Frantic residents fled into the streets, gagging and vomiting from the overpowering stench. Something about it seemed reminiscent of cadavers. Down in the port district, authorities rushed to the site of a cargo mishap and what turned out to be the odor's source: a major spill of formaldehyde. It was Thursday evening, September 14, 1972. Manila had entered the last days of Philippine democracy smelling vaguely like a morgue.

For Ferdinand Marcos, the day began early with the sweet smell of moist grass out on the Malacanang golf course. After the round he retired to Pangarap for a breakfast meeting with Defense Secretary Enrile and the nation's top military officers, some of whom were told for the first time over cornflakes that martial law was no longer a contingency plan — it was their mission. And it would be a legal dictatorship. "I told [them] that I intend to declare martial law to liquidate the communist apparatus, reform our government and society, then have the ConCon ratify our acts and the people confirm it by plebiscite and return to constitutional processes . . . this would be legitimate exercise of my emergency powers under the constitution as clarified under the habeas corpus case by the Supreme Court last January." Marcos barely mentioned the Communist factor, but he emphasized what he saw as the need "to cure the ills of our society by radical means (I mentioned corruption, tax evasion, criminality, smuggling, lack of discipline, unequal opportunities), so we must keep our noses clean and submerge self-interest. I asked for any objection to the plan and there was none. . . ."

Back at the palace later in the day, Marcos received Ambassador Henry Byroade. Marcos still was stinging from Assistant Secretary of State Marshall Green's accusation that the Philippines was exaggerating its Communist threat. As Marcos wrote, the American ambassador seemed intent on soothing hard feelings. "[Byroade] explained that he kept [the] White House informed weekly of developments here — and that the communist threat was increasing."

Meanwhile, in the streets of Manila crime and disorder flourished. An editorial that morning in the *Chronicle* blamed the Marcos administration for the wave of lawlessness. Organized kidnapping gangs preyed on wealthy Chinese bankers. Armed thieves terrorized families in their homes. Cars were stolen at gunpoint on the streets. Instead of cracking down on hoodlums, complained the editorial, the government was pouring resources into fighting subversives "whose threat to society is being blown up to frightening proportions." It blamed the Marcos government for "creation of a national hysteria."

Marcos only turned up the rhetoric. He accused Ninoy Aquino of attempting to negotiate "a link-up" between the Liberal party and Sison's NPA guerrillas to overthrow a democratically elected administration. The traditional political opposition and the radical revolutionary were coming together in one grand conspiracy, in one "common plan of propaganda, logistics [and] armed support" to thwart the will of the people and to impose a foreign ideology on the Philippines. In his diary Marcos noted: "I am sure this will start another raging controversy."

On Friday, September 15, Marcos spoke to the Filipino-Chinese Chambers of Commerce, exhorting them to stand firmly against the subversives. "When [Communists] come to power," he said, "the first they liquidate will be the rich and those who have big houses." He said NPA guerrillas had been sighted in the Manila area and he warned that "something big is in the offing."

Bongbong flew off to London on Saturday, the last of the children to return to distant schools. Roaming the empty palace on Sunday afternoon, the president was overwhelmed by loneliness. He stepped into his son's room to nap on "the worst bed . . . and the lumpiest mattress" in the presidential residence. Later, with Imelda he "escaped" to the state guest house, Ang Maharlika, a few blocks from Malacanang where he spent the evening reading histories of the Kennedys, Chou En-lai, and the state of Israel. That night he wrote: "The departure of our children has made the palace a ghostly unbearable place."

Manila was a caldron of rumor and suspicion as the new week began. Since Ninoy Aquino's disclosure of "OPLAN Sagittarius," the specter of martial law was everywhere — in political debate, in editorial columns, in the travel plans of prominent Marcos enemies. Senator Sergio Osmena, Jr., a survivor of the Plaza Miranda bombing and a bitter Marcos critic, flew out of Manila International Airport for California the same day that Ferdinand and Imelda escorted Bongbong onto a jetliner for London. Radical commentator "Bomba" Arienda took two bodyguards and a gun and slipped away to await the future in the countryside, moving from one rural village to another. Certainly, it took no special gift of clairvoyance to see Manila's immediate future. One member of a prominent sugar family angled a palace appointment on Monday, September 18, to assure the president that he and his relatives were behind him, even if martial law was declared. In his diary Marcos observed: "One thing about this man, he has a good nose for survival."

Across town at Quezon City Hall, an afternoon session of the constitutional convention was being called to order on the fourteenth floor. Delegate Jose Nolledo was late. He waited in a crowd on the ground floor for one of the express elevators to whisk him fourteen stories to his place in the chamber. But when the doors opened, two men in uniforms of the Philippine constabulary burst out. What was their rush? Jesting, he asked aloud if they had planted a bomb. A few minutes later, a blast ripped through the public restroom just outside the meeting hall. Delegates dove for cover under their desks. A second bomb exploded in a sixth-floor restroom. Twenty people were hurt.

In his diary, Marcos made no mention of the suspicious constabulary officers or of other press reports that a man believed to be in the military was among those arrested. Indeed, there was increasing media speculation that Marcos was behind many of the bombings. He may have been acknowledging such reports when on Monday night he wrote about meeting to finalize more plans for martial law with top military advisers. "They all agreed the earlier we do it the better because the media is waging a propaganda campaign that distorts and twists the facts and they may succeed in weakening our support among the people if it is allowed to continue. So, after the bombing of the ConCon, we agreed on the 21st without any postponement."

Marcos again increased the rhetoric against Aquino. On Tuesday, September 19, the president accused his rival of playing a double-agent game — not only conspiring to link up with the Communists, but also secretly providing intelligence information about the NPA to the government. It was the second half of the allegation that sent chills through friends of Aquino. Was Marcos planning to have Ninoy killed?

The *Free Press*, which had named the senator their 1971 "Man of the Year" for successfully challenging Marcos after the Plaza Miranda bombings, started work on a cover story questioning whether the president was setting up Aquino for assassination. Speculation was that if a military agent or anyone else gunned down the Liberal leader, Marcos would blame it on the Communists. He not only would be rid of his most threatening rival, but he could even use the violence to help justify a declaration of martial law. Publisher Teodoro Locsin ordered a front cover for the *Free Press* edition of September 30: a picture of Ninoy Aquino standing in the cross hairs of a gunsight.

Aquino rose to make what would be his last speech from the floor of the Philippine Senate on Wednesday, seeking recognition on a point of personal privilege. The president, Aquino said, was laying the groundwork for an administration plot to liquidate him. "I would now like to enter these words into our records," he said. "Should I be assassinated, my blood would be [on] the hands of those who set me up for the kill."

In white *barong* and black horn-rimmed glasses, Aquino addressed the president of the Senate, but he was speaking to the packed spectator gallery behind him and to the national audience beyond the chamber as he concluded: "I do not know what fate awaits me. For the last five years I have discharged my duty as God and my conscience have shown me the way. . . . If this situation prevails, if Mr. Marcos pursues his subversion of our fundamental institutions, even our form of government, to keep himself in power, then I pray to God that He give me the strength to resist the embraces of the forces of darkness."

On Thursday, September 21, 1972 — the day that Ferdinand Marcos had selected to be the official Day One of his dictatorship — a delegation of Ilocano congressmen hurried to the palace for an early meeting. They were anxious about the latest Aquino statement to the press. He had predicted martial law within forty-eight hours. His military sources alerted him, Aquino had explained. It was a sign, perhaps, of Aquino's current credibility that his staunchest political foes believed him. He had been right, after all, about the existence of the secret military operations plan for Manila, "OPLAN Sagittarius." He had good sources in the palace. Too good. Congressman Joe Aspiras of La Union asked the president if it was true, that martial law was less than forty-eight hours away. "Of course Imelda and I denied it," Marcos wrote in his diary.

Ambassador Byroade arrived soon after, at 11:15, "apparently interested to know whether there would be martial law," Marcos wrote. What the president did not know was that the American ambassador already had seen a draft of the secret Malacanang orders, obtained by the CIA from a palace insider the day before. Byroade had promptly telephoned Marcos to arrange an appointment. His call literally interrupted the work of martial-law planning. Marcos and Enrile "were working on the list of target personalities," the president's enemies list. The secretary of defense was using names from that list to fill out the blank lines on a stack of fresh arrest warrants.

Byroade's primary mission was to seek delay. He was convinced there would be "a hell of an uproar back home if [Marcos] tampered with democracy" — especially since Marcos was so clearly unpopular. The two men met, as they usually did, alone in the president's small private office. Byroade sat in his usual chair. "He always put me in the same chair, so I knew which ones were bugged," the ambassador would recall later.

The morning meeting seemed to go well for both men, with each one hearing what he wanted to hear from the other. According to the diary account, Marcos acknowledged the obvious, telling Byroade that he was considering martial law and that it was "intended to primarily reform our society and eliminate the communist threat." Of the ambassador's response to the prospects for martial law, Marcos wrote: "He seemed to favor it. . . . But he suggested that a proclamation before the American elections may be used by [George] McGovern, the Democratic presidential candidate, as proof of the failure of [Nixon's] foreign policy."

When Byroade suggested to Marcos that the proclamation's delay would be useful, the president said he cautioned the ambassador. "I told him I did not want it said that he was intervening in internal matters of the Philippine government. And that no decision has been arrived at, but that I was under pressure and there seemed to be no other solution. He agreed . . . ," Marcos wrote.

However, Byroade left the palace Thursday morning with the understanding that he had persuaded Marcos to wait at least until November. "I wouldn't say Marcos lied to me outright," the ambassador said years later. "I don't think he said, for example, that he was *not* going to do anything. But he gave me the impression that he was concerned about the same things I was concerned about — negative public reaction in the States. He made it fuzzy enough that I thought he was probably going to wait."

In a confidential cable to Washington the next day, Ambassador Byroade advised: "For the time being, possibly for the next six weeks, the likelihood of martial law declaration has lessened." And he made a similar observation to Kokoy Romualdez within a few hours of the Marcos meeting. Byroade had discussed with Imelda's brother, the governor of Leyte, the possibility Kokoy would go to California to help the Nixon reelection campaign. "There are 200,000 Filipino votes and California is crucial," Marcos noted. But Marcos expressed puzzlement at Byroade's account of their meeting as Kokoy reported it. "[H]e told Gov. Romualdez . . . that his impression was that martial law would be proclaimed after the [American presidential] elections. How he came to arrive at this conclusion I can only guess. But this man cannot make logical deductions. I must be wary."

He retained some doubts about how the United States would respond to the reality of his declaration. Byroade's warnings underscored one of the imponderables: the potential effect of America's election politics on Nixon's ultimate reaction to events in Manila. After all, it was Marcos's view that American public opinion primarily was forcing the U.S. government out of Vietnam. He feared American public opinion could do mischief to his cause, as well. Marcos dispatched his Annapolis-trained executive secretary, Alejandro "Alex" Melchor, to Washington. "I asked [him] . . . to use his American contacts to see the U.S. does not oppose us."

At Plaza Miranda Thursday afternoon, thousands of demonstrators calling themselves the Movement of Concerned Citizens for Civil Liberties packed the square and the rooftops surrounding it to sing, wave flags, and hoist banners protesting the threat of martial law. Marcos took no note of them in his diary, but he did express concern about Aquino and his apparent "pipeline" to highly confidential palace strategy. "He seems to know that the proclamation will be made this weekend," Marcos wrote. "We have to check this. It is dangerous."

It was after 2:00 A.M. when Marcos finished his diary entry. September 21 was now history. He had not declared martial law. The decree was ready — refined, reviewed, and retyped at least twice. But there remained the missing element of an assassination attempt. A triggering mechanism, so to speak. The final excuse.

Friday evening, September 22, radio and television stations were first to report the news: Defense Secretary Juan Ponce Enrile had been ambushed. According to the official story, Enrile had left his office at Fort Aguinaldo as usual, heading home at about 8:00 P.M. in his blue Ford sedan trailed by the customary security escort car. On Fordham Street behind the Wack Wack Golf Course, gunmen in another car suddenly opened fire on the Ford. The secretary told reporters that his driver "slammed on the brakes and jumped out, firing at the car, which sped away." The driver was unharmed. Enrile himself was saved, he explained, because on that evening he happened to be riding with his guards in the escort car. "God saved him," declared Christina Enrile, the secretary's wife. Years later, Enrile would say he was nowhere near the shooting, that he had ordered his men to shoot up the empty sedan. The assassination attempt was a sham. But that night in his presidential diary, Marcos recorded the fiction:

> It was a good thing he was riding in his security car as a protective measure. His first car which he usually uses was the one riddled by bullets from a car parked in ambush. He is now at his [Defense Department] office. I have advised him to stay there. And I have doubled the security of Imelda. . . . This makes the martial law proclamation a necessity.

Imelda returned to the palace at 11:35 P.M. in the president's bulletproof Electra. Marcos already had signed the martial-law order. General Ver had ringed the palace in extra security. But no overt military action had yet been taken in the city. All over Manila the streets were full of blue Metrocom cars and vans, cruising around the offices of newspapers and television stations, circling the homes of political opposition leaders. Martial law hovered, undetected, waiting to settle on the nation.

There was reason for delay. Marcos needed one man, the first name on his list of "target personalities" — Ninoy Aquino. The senator's defiant conduct a year earlier after the president's suspension of the writ of habeas corpus had been most instructive. The image of Aquino marching from hospital to hospital after the Plaza Miranda bombing had, as the *Free Press* observed, "crystallized the people's timid resentment against the Marcos Administration into an unshakeable determination to resist. The people fixed their eyes on Ninoy." On the night of September 22, 1972, Marcos could not afford to let Aquino ignite resistance by word, deed, or image. So, he waited.

At the *Free Press,* Teddy Boy Locsin had just returned to his typewriter after catching a late screening of the Charles Bronson film *Red Sun* at the Luneta Theater. One of the blue Metrocom cars was outside when he arrived. For the past month, the publisher's son had noticed that the Delta Motors automobile plant was turning out a lot of blue cars. Almost nothing, it seemed, but blue cars. Now the streets of Manila were filled with those blue cars. Inside, a Metrocom officer said he and his men were there to protect the newspaper against left-wing agitators. Teddy Boy shrugged. There had been similar visits in previous days. The young editor returned to his partially written article about Aquino's warnings of martial law.

At the Hilton Hotel, Colonel Romeo Gatan knocked at the door of room 1701. Inside, Aquino was conducting his last meeting as a Philippine senator, a congressional conference committee session on tariffs and taxes. His arrest was polite and swift. His friend Sonny Osmena, the young senator from Cebu, stood in the middle of the room in disbelief as Aquino disappeared out the door. Marcos had what he needed. The military plan was activated. It was just after midnight. Democracy was transformed into dictatorship.

Back at the *Free Press,* Teddy Boy was on the phone when the Metrocom officer slapped the receiver from his ear. "We have martial law," said the man protecting the paper from left-wing agitators. Everyone out. By order of the president, the *Free Press* was closed. Teddy Boy rushed out to look for his father.

Times publisher Chino Roces heard the news in his telephone-equipped car. It was a call from his wife. A Metrocom raiding party was at the door. Their Quezon City home was surrounded. They had a warrant for his arrest, signed by Enrile. Roces drove immediately to Camp Crame and surrendered to constabulary authorities.

It was shortly after midnight that editor Doronila called his *Chronicle* office to check on the last edition. A clerk answered. Everyone else had been sent home. By whom? Soldiers. The newspaper was closed.

Across Manila, raiding parties arrived in the darkness to arrest others on the president's list. They found Senator Diokno at his home. He surrendered without resistance. So did Senator Mitra. But Luis Mauricio, publisher of the *Graphic,* which had carried some of the most lurid coverage of the Dovie Beams affair, was dragged from his home. And an anti-Marcos delegate from the constitutional convention, in bed with a serious illness, was forced to the rapidly filling gymnasium of Camp Crame to spend the next several nights on a cot.

The telephone ringing next to Ambassador Byroade's bed awoke him from a sound sleep. It was Richard Usher, the Philippine desk officer at the State Department in Washington, calling to ask about early press reports that martial law had been declared. Tanks and truckloads of troops were sweeping through downtown Manila, Usher informed the ambassador. Byroade snapped on a bedside lamp, suddenly wide awake. "I thought I talked him out of that," he said.

In the predawn hours leading up to 5:00 A.M., Sonny Osmena waited to be arrested. The young senator, who still limped from his Plaza Miranda bomb wounds, was an outspoken Marcos critic. If his good friend Ninoy and so many others were being arrested, Osmena was sure he too was on the list. He stayed home so he could be found easily. He packed a few personal items. Sitting in a dimly lighted home with his wife, the senator listened for sounds of military trucks. Then, he heard it. There had been false alarms twice before, neighbors coming or going, but this time the commotion was unmistakable. He embraced his wife once more, then opened their front door. The crew of a garbage truck wished him good morning. Osmena was beginning to feel neglected.

Teodoro Locsin was not forgotten, but the *Free Press* publisher was allowed to sleep through the night. He was ready to surrender at 7:00 A.M., a toothbrush and some books packed in an overnight bag for the trip to Camp Crame. A military car came to fetch him at his door, where Teddy Boy bade his father good-bye. "Daddy, they're taking our country away from us."

Manila awoke to an eerie national silence. *Chronicle* publisher Eugenio "Geny" Lopez, Jr., aboard the family yacht *Miss Iloilo* off the shore of Batangas south of Manila, could not raise a signal on his portable radio. He wanted to hear the morning news normally broadcast over the family-owned radio station. But that part of the radio dial was dead. He turned the dial. More silence. Finally, he found one station broadcasting popular music, the voice of Filipina singing favorite Nora Aunor. But no news. No commercials. Geny suspected a radio malfunction and asked the ship's captain to tinker with it. Why did it receive only one station? The answer arrived by helicopter. The military aircraft buzzed the yacht, anchored just offshore, then landed on the beach. Two men in air force uniforms jumped out and called to Geny. They were friends. One asked: "Do you know what happened? Martial law." Lopez thanked them "for dropping by to tell me." The young publisher considered sailing for Hong Kong. His powerful but ailing father, Ining Lopez, already was in a San Francisco clinic for medical treatment, beyond the reach of a Marcos arrest warrant. But Geny, filled with trepidation, ordered a course for Manila.

On Saturday, September 23, 1972, the president of the Philippines awoke as Dictator Ferdinand Marcos. If things went badly as the day wore on, General Ver was responsible for the president's emergency escape. It was one of the contingency plans. But there was no sign of resistance. In fact, in his diary that evening Marcos noted that "things have moved according to plan." He wrote specifically, and with apparent satisfaction, about the arrests of Aquino, Diokno, Mitra, Chino Roces, and Teddy Locsin. During that first night and morning, fifty-two out of the two hundred target personalities were taken into custody. Among those missing was "Bomba" Arienda, still hiding in the rice fields of Batangas, listening for hints of public resistance.

There was no broadcast news of any kind throughout the day, except for an announcer's voice periodically interrupting the music to say the president soon would address the nation. Finally, after overcoming the technical difficulties of getting a television station back on the air, Marcos appeared on the nation's TV screens at 7:15 P.M.

"My countrymen," he began gravely, "I have proclaimed martial law in accordance with the powers vested in the president by the constitution. . . . I have had to use this constitutional power in order that we may not completely lose the civil rights and freedoms which we cherish.

"I assure you that this is not a precipitate decision, and that I have weighed all the factors. . . . Now, the limit has been reached, for we are against the wall. We must now defend the republic. . . . To those guilty of treason, insurrection, rebellion, [martial law] may pose a grave danger. But to the ordinary citizens, to almost all of you whose primary concern is merely to be left alone to pursue your lawful activities, this is the guarantee of that freedom that you seek. All that I do is for the republic and for you."

He had prayed for God's guidance, Marcos assured his people. And he asked them to pray for him. "I am confident that with God's help, we will attain our dream of a reformed society, a new and brighter world."

It seemed to be the realization of Ferdinand's dream, the fulfillment of his messianic visions. Marcos, the savior of the Philippines, preserving Philippine democracy by preventing its exercise. But to be certain there was no meaningful objection, he took a few precautions: imposing a general curfew, banning free speech and free assembly, authorizing arrests without warrants, outlawing labor strikes, ordering the surrender of firearms, and declaring "rumor mongering" to be a crime comparable to treason.

With all criticism abruptly silenced by the mass arrests of political opponents, journalists, liberal priests, and student activists, Marcos created the instant illusion of popularity. Overnight, street demonstrations stopped. Political debate stopped. Newspaper editorials stopped. Democracy stopped.

But at the same time, how peaceful it seemed Manila had become. Overnight, too, the bombings stopped. Crime stopped. Private armies were being disarmed. Indeed, there were more signs of public relief than resentment. In the rice paddies, Arienda grew increasingly disillusioned. Was no one ready to fight for freedom? In Manila, among political leaders dismayed by the passivity of their countrymen, arose a common lament: "We are a nation of 40 million cowards and one son of a bitch!"

Some early advice came in from Earl Mazo, a White House adviser and biographer of Richard Nixon. He recommended that Marcos "immediately meet the press . . . and explain that this is not a dictatorship." The American Chamber of Commerce of the Philippines cabled Marcos that it "wishes you every success in your endeavors to restore peace and order, business confidence, economic growth and the well-being of the Filipino people and nation." There was no criticism from Washington. Byroade was surprised. Later he conceded: "I vastly over-estimated the reactions."

Marcos was elated by the response. Virtually no opposition. He did not wait for further reaction from foreign leaders or the foreign press. After two days of peaceful martial law, he declared victory. In his diary on Monday, September 25, 1972, Marcos wrote: "I am some kind of hero!"

EPILOGUE
The Last Delusion

Ferdinand Marcos called his new government "constitutional authoritarianism," still seeking to justify in legal terms his grab for power. He looked to the Supreme Court once again to ratify his actions. But this time, unlike 1971, rather than petition the court, he issued a threat. Five of the president's appointees were summoned to Malacanang on Sunday and Monday, the days immediately following his declaration of martial law. He told Justice Fred Ruiz Castro that "there must be no conflict between the two separate departments of Justice and the Executive, for it would be embarrassing to both." With the other justices, Marcos was more menacing. In a palace meeting also attended by Defense Secretary Enrile and Justice Secretary Vicente Abad Santos, the president bluntly told jurists:

> [I]f necessary I would formally declare the establishment of a revolutionary government so that I can formally disregard the actions of the Supreme Court.
>
> They insisted that we retain a color of constitutionality for everything that we do. But I feel that they . . . do not understand that a new day has dawned.

Marcos used the first hundred days of martial law to establish his grip firmly not only on the Supreme Court, but on all the centers of power. Doors to the Senate chambers were padlocked. The military, his key to control, received a series of pay raises and bonuses. He handed out distinguished service medals to every member of the armed forces. The constitutional convention, with its most ardent anti-Marcos delegates either imprisoned at Camp Crame or fleeing to exile, not surprisingly approved a new charter tailored precisely to the president's demands.

During those early days, Imelda Marcos commissioned noted Philippine composer Felipe de Leon to write a hymn and an anthem to celebrate the "New Society." The works were performed in October by the Manila Philharmonic to a rave review by the president: "Inspiring and moving."

But as the initial shock of martial law wore off, the nation began to show signs of recalcitrance. Crime was back — and what Marcos saw as greed, frivolity, and arrogance. Conspicuous consumption remained a problem. "The quiet, slow slide into the old society is now perceptible," he acknowledged near the end of 1972. "Even Mao Tse-tung spoke of the return of reaction in a letter to his wife several years after the 1949 victory of his revolution. Thus, the need of the Cultural Revolution." Marcos, too, was ready to impose harsher measures. And he could see he would need more time. "We need a longer period of gestation of the New Society. Otherwise, it will be aborted."

In fact, the Marcos dictatorship would retain power for more than thirteen years. It was a period marked by unprecedented graft and corruption. Unrestrained by an independent legislature or a free press, Marcos and his wife looted billions of dollars from the impoverished nation's treasury. The Marcoses' own financial records, many of which were seized by agents of the U.S. Customs Service in 1986, showed that the president held secret ownership in virtually every industry in the nation — from mining operations and insurance agencies to pineapple plantations and automobile distributorships. He owned hidden shares of shipping lines, construction companies, hotels, and banks. Some Philippine cement producers had to kick back to Marcos the equivalent of fifty cents for every bag of cement they sold. Even war-reparations payments from Japan were channeled into the private bank accounts of Ferdinand and Imelda, some of which, like those in

Geneva, Switzerland, were hidden behind such Marcos aliases as "William Saunders" and "Jane Ryan."

It was clear from the beginning that Marcos considered the nation something of a personal preserve — to have, to exploit, and even to offer as a token of love to his wife. On the occasion of their wedding anniversary, their first under martial law on May 1, 1973, Marcos penned an untitled poem:

> *To my beloved Imelda,*
> *On our nineteenth year of wedded life we are long past ceremonial gifts and*
>   *words,*
> *For you I have plumbed the depths of joy and sorrow.*
> *Even you, Imelda, of the delicate cameo-like beauty, have felt the pain of*
>   *tears — the threat of death ever close.*
> *So, to us, things and creatures have no meaning except as symbols.*
> *Therefore, I shall offer no gift of worldly price — no gold, no gems,*
> *But my whole life's work I tenderly hold to lay lovingly at your feet, with*
>   *adoration, the New Society — the new Philippines.*
> *All my dreams, a bright and brave new world.*
> *Forever I shall love you. — Ferdinand*

Not only did Marcos give his wife "the new Philippines" in a figurative sense, he made her an even more powerful political partner as well. She was named governor of the newly created regional government of Metro Manila. She joined the cabinet as head of the liberally funded Ministry of Human Settlements. By the early 1980s, her spending sprees were legendary — from Manhattan skyscrapers to Rodeo Drive jewelry.

The dictator period also was marked by the rise, finally, of a real Communist threat. From the outset, martial law was the single greatest enlistment incentive in the history of the New People's Army.

On the day that martial law was declared, Jose Maria Sison was hiding out in the northern mountains with a poorly armed band of a few hundred followers. Their influence did not extend beyond the rural areas in two or three northern provinces. While Marcos was warning that the NPA probably had about ten thousand rifles, Sison says they had no more than three hundred rifles — hardly a threat to the Philippine nation in 1972. But that changed. Dictatorship fertilized the revolution. Student leaders like Edgar Jopson, who once carried nothing more dangerous than placards in street demonstrations, fled the political repression of martial law to carry a gun in the NPA. By the end of the Marcos dictatorship, the NPA was active in more than sixty provinces and had about twenty thousand full-time, well-armed guerrillas. "We should allow them to gather strength," he had written in February 1970, "but not such strength that we cannot overcome them." Ironically, rather than save his nation from a phantom Communist menace, Marcos — like a political Dr. Frankenstein — actually had given life to a revolution monster.

Meanwhile, the president's attempt to destroy Ninoy Aquino, his chief political rival, was having mixed results. The imprisoned senator smuggled out letters and tracts condemning the Marcos dictatorship. One lengthy treatise, dated January 26, 1973, called on Filipinos to topple the dictator who was "making a mockery" of Philippine democracy. With Marcos critics jailed and free press, free speech, free assembly, and due process suspended, Aquino said Filipinos retained only "the freedom to concur, the freedom to conform." His pleas rallied little overt support, and only three months into his long imprisonment the disheartened Aquino acknowledged: "What is disconcerting, however, is how Mr. Marcos staged his palace coup . . . [with] not a whimper from the Filipinos." Still in jail years later, he told a friend: "I judged Marcos correctly, but I misjudged the people."

Ninoy Aquino remained in jail through the remainder of the decade, at one point condemned to death for treason. He staged a prolonged hunger strike in 1975, explaining in a letter to his wife, Corazon: "Let Mr. Marcos realize that there are still Filipinos who are prepared to suffer and lay down their lives for a cause bigger than their own physical survival." In the end, prison may have kept Aquino off any presidential ballots, but in his enforced isolation he was reemerging as a political rival to the president — as an international hero, a symbol to human-rights advocates everywhere.

There was pressure in Washington to cut off financial aid to the Marcos government unless Aquino was freed. The Philippine president, apparently making only sporadic diary entries by that time, was provoked on February 17, 1978, to write: "Today is a day . . . I shall remember . . . as the day the American government tried to pressure me to . . . release Ninoy Aquino." Marcos resisted, he noted with what seemed to be some irritation, because "I would lose my credibility as a nationalist and leader if I submit to American pressure . . . and worse, I would lose my self-respect."

Two years later, in May 1980, Marcos backed down. Aquino was released after more than seven and a half years in prison to undergo medical treatment in the United States. But pressure continued to mount for Marcos to restore democracy. His authoritarian rule generated an anger in Manila that was revealed in dark humor. In one martial-law-era story, a visitor to Malacanang approaches the entrance where an indifferent guard asks, "What is your business?" The visitor answers, "I've come to kill the president." The guard waves him toward a crowd nearby, saying, "You'll have to fall in line."

Early in 1981, in honor of a visit by Pope John Paul II, Marcos finally announced that he was lifting martial law. It was only for show. Little changed. Marcos retained the power to rule by decree. Later, in June, he held the nation's first presidential election since martial law. It, too, was for show. With many boycotting the election and virtually no opposition, Marcos won 86 percent of the vote.

U.S. Vice-President George Bush attended the inauguration and, during one of the festive dinners, delivered an exuberant toast that would rankle human-rights advocates for years to come. Bush, raising a wineglass toward Marcos the dictator and mastermind of martial law, said: "We love your adherence to democratic principle and to the democratic processes."

At the close of traditional Inauguration Day ceremonies in Luneta Park, Marcos was serenaded by a thousand-voice male choir singing a stirring version of the "Hallelujah Chorus" from Handel's *Messiah:* "And he shall reign for ever and ever. . . ."

It is clear from earlier entries in the diary that Marcos intended to rule for as long as he felt that his country needed him. And in 1982 "for ever and ever" seemed likely tenure. Marcos believed he was popular. He believed he alone could prevent a Communist takeover of his nation. That he believed his own myths and fabrications was especially apparent at the end of the year.

In September 1982, the San Francisco–based *Philippine News* — largest of the Filipino-American newspapers — published a well-researched article by a retired Philippine army officer who called the Marcos war record a fraud. Bonafacio H. Gillego, the author, who also had been a delegate to the constitutional convention until forced into exile by martial law, included a statement from one of Marcos's wartime commanding officers saying that he considered Marcos to be "the greatest impostor that World War II has ever produced." The story produced a spate of other articles in the Philippines and around the world that continued for months questioning the heroic claims of Ferdinand Marcos.

The president was stung by the reports. On January 1, 1983, seemingly convinced of the truth of the stories he had invented decades before, a sad and self-righteous Marcos wrote:

> I had sought to protect the sacredness and preciousness of my memories of the war with the sanctity of silence. So, I had refused to talk or write about them except in an indirect way when forced to as when I offered my medals to the dead for I believed all such medals belonged to them.
>
> But the sanctity of silence has been broken by the pettiness and cynicism that overwhelms the contemporary world. And the small souls whose vicarious achievement is to insult and offend the mighty and the achievers have succeeded in trivializing the most solemn and honorable of deeds and intentions. Their pettiness has besmirched with the foul attention the honorable service of all who have received medals and citations in the last World War. They have . . . made me their special target as the most visible of those who offered blood, honor and life to our people.
>
> So, I must fight the battles of Bataan all over again. We must walk our Death March in the hot April sun once again. . . . For we bleed and die again. This time in the hands of men who claim to be our countrymen.

His delusions of heroism were not the last to be challenged. Marcos's health was failing. In 1983 he was forced to undergo two kidney transplant operations, conducted secretly in the basement of Malacanang, where a modern medical facility was installed so that few would know of his weakened condition. It was during that period that an apparently healthy Ninoy Aquino, recovered from successful heart bypass surgery, announced he was returning to the Philippines. No one could more effectively challenge Marcos's delusions of political popularity than the now internationally famous Aquino.

It can be argued that the Marcos dictatorship was mortally wounded on the tarmac of Manila International Airport on August 21, 1983.

That was the day Aquino returned home from U.S. exile, stepped foot on his native land, and immediately was shot in the head. Marcos was blamed. Neither a controlled press nor a controlled legislature could control the national rage. Marcos, then confined to bed with his ailing kidneys, was forced to relinquish some authoritarian controls. Pressure to hold open elections mounted. And despite continuing friendly support from President Ronald Reagan, growing numbers of critics in the United States clamored for reforms as a condition for retaining huge financial aid from America. Again Marcos resisted, but from that August day forward he was presiding over the steady decline of his regime.

The end came in February 1986. A sickly Marcos, his face puffy from the effects of his illness, claimed victory in an election that the whole world knew he had lost to Ninoy's widow, Corazon "Cory" Aquino. Indeed, election fraud notwithstanding, he likely lost by a landslide in the actual balloting. Millions of Filipinos poured into the streets of Manila to proclaim Cory their president. Even the loyal Marcos military abandoned him. Defense Secretary Enrile and General Ramos defected and proclaimed Aquino the victor. Enrile said he had personally faked at least 350,000 votes for Marcos. Now, Caesar's Brutus had joined the conspirators. In the streets, there was a remarkable and peaceful spectacle — unarmed throngs led by nuns, priests, and housewives were staring down tanks and heavily armed troops. No shots were fired. Military defections multiplied. Still, Marcos held Malacanang.

One of those who had come to see the president in the latter days of his reign was an old friend, Henry Byroade. Recalling that visit years later, the retired ambassador said: "[Marcos] was a very vain man . . . a very confident guy. He refused to accept that he was unpopular. Even the last time I saw him, just before his downfall, he still showed no lack of confidence that he was the boss or that he wouldn't always be the boss."

But Marcos finally was alone with his delusions of popular support. Abandoned by the American government and his own key military leaders, the ailing president could hold back history no longer. Still, there was time for one more extraordinary ritual: a defiant inaugural ceremony. At the very hour of exile, Marcos took the oath of office one last time. As he stumbled through an inaugural address, at times his voice barely audible and his swollen eyes making it difficult to read his own speech, family and friends gathered in grim silence around him. A child in the crowd, one of his granddaughters, noticed without understanding that everyone seemed so sad. Then, a last appearance at the palace balcony. Ferdinand and Imelda waved to a chanting group of loyalists in the garden below and sang one last duet for the crowd: "Because of You."

Marcos left Malacanang with his family that night aboard an American military helicopter, still insisting he was the lawfully elected president of the Philippines. He retired to luxurious but discontented exile in the hills above Honolulu, still plotting a triumphant return to his country, still awaiting another chance to save the Philippines.

Instead, he found himself a prisoner of paradise. U.S. State Department officials, after learning in 1987 about covert schemes to fly Ferdinand and Imelda back to Ilocos Norte to lead a rebellion against the Aquino government, confronted Marcos in Honolulu and told him bluntly that he would not be allowed to leave the island of Oahu. Colonel Arturo Aruiza, a longtime military aide who witnessed the humbling encounter, said later: "They wanted Marcos to stop plotting or planning or hoping or dreaming."

Then came the criminal indictment. In October 1988, a federal grand jury in New York charged the deposed dictator and his wife with fraud and racketeering. U.S. prosecutors based the indictment on alleged conspiracies and a pattern of criminal conduct dating back to the imposition of martial law in 1972. It was in the aftermath of that legal action — faced with an order to appear at a local FBI office for fingerprinting and personal writing samples — that the last of Marcos's stubborn delusions finally may have been dashed.

Colonel Aruiza, who supervised security at the family's residential compound in Makiki Heights, was summoned to Marcos's bedroom and told to prepare for the FBI visit. The former president's vigorous legal battle to quash the court order had failed. In his book, *Malacanang to Makiki*, Aruiza recalled the moment:

> As soon as he saw me at his bedroom door, he said, "Make the necessary arrangements for Friday." Before I could answer, he looked away, but not before I caught, in that fleeting moment, etched on his face, the look of surrender, of defeat, of resignation. . . .

Marcos never stood trial. After months of slipping into and out of comas, he died on September 28, 1989.

In ceremonies at a hillside cemetery, Bongbong — now a young man of thirty-one — called his father a man "touched by God" who was conspired against by "alien forces . . . too blind to see his vision." The young Marcos told mourners that his father had been given the choice in 1986 to kill his countrymen or kill himself. Said the son, Marcos "remained true and saved his country by stepping down."

Marcos had wondered how he might be remembered by history. He had speculated about the eulogies and tributes that might be paid to him upon his death. And fifteen years before leaving Malacanang he had written in his diary: " 'This is your principal mission — save the country . . .' God seems to be saying to me."

But the visions he described in that March 6, 1971, diary entry and his distant musings about posthumous tributes gave no glimpse of what eventually was to be — international scorn, rejection by his own countrymen, and a place in history among notorious thieves and tyrants.

In the end, however, looking back on the bloodless "People Power" uprising that toppled the Marcos dictatorship, both his devoted son and his legions of critics could agree on one final assessment:

That on February 25, 1986, Ferdinand E. Marcos finally saved his country — "by stepping down."

About the Other Players

Aquino, Benigno "Ninoy" — Imprisoned longer than any of Marcos's political rivals and at one point sentenced to death, he became an international symbol of Marcos repression and human-rights violations. From prison, in papers smuggled out a page at a time by his family, Aquino wrote: "While . . . I am surrendering my body, my spirit will never tolerate nor compromise with injustice, immorality and dictatorship." After Aquino suffered a heart attack in the spring of 1980, Marcos was pressured both at home and by the Jimmy Carter White House to release the ailing prisoner for humanitarian reasons. Ninoy was allowed to leave the country after more than seven years in prison to undergo coronary bypass surgery in Dallas. He remained in U.S. exile, teaching at Harvard University's Center for International Affairs, until his fateful return to Manila on August 21, 1983.

Aquino, Corazon "Cory" — The widow of the dictator's martyred political rival — the woman Ninoy Aquino called "the healing oasis in the desert of my prison" — successfully united anti-Marcos forces in a December 1985 "snap" presidential election. She was denied victory only by flagrant and violent fraud. But a bloodless citizen uprising called the "People Power Revolution" forced Marcos into exile and swept Mrs. Aquino into Malacanang. She served as president from 1986 to 1992, surviving a number of failed coup attempts.

Arienda, Roger "Bomba" — The radical political commentator who spent eighty-three days in jail during Marcos's 1971 crackdown after the Plaza Miranda bombing was imprisoned for more than eight years under martial law. He was one of the few martial-law detainees actually convicted of a crime, in his case possession of firearms and inciting to sedition. After preaching Marxism in jail for three years, he became a born-again Christian. He was released on Christmas of 1980, and was sometimes called to Malacanang to pray with Ferdinand and Imelda.

Beams, Dovie — The actress who was the "other woman" in Manila's most sensational sex scandal later married a Los Angeles nightclub owner and dabbled in California real estate investments. When Malacanang was abandoned by the Marcoses in 1986, pictures of Dovie defaced with obscene drawings were found in Imelda's bedroom. In 1988, Dovie was sentenced to eight years in federal prison along with her husband, Sergio de Villagran, after their convictions on multiple counts of bank fraud.

Byroade, Henry A. — The American ambassador to the Philippines when martial law was declared stayed on until replaced by William Sullivan in the summer of 1973. Thereafter, he served a tour in Pakistan before retiring from the U.S. foreign service to his home outside Washington, D.C.

Castro, Fred Ruiz — The Supreme Court jurist who acted as a spy for President Marcos inside the court's private chambers was elevated to chief justice in 1976 and died in office in 1979.

De Vega, Guillermo "Gimo" — The palace aide who helped manage the president's bribery campaign in the constitutional convention also was alleged to have offered Tibo Mijares a bribe not to testify about Marcos corruption before a U.S. congressional committee in 1975.

The U.S. Justice Department was investigating the matter when de Vega was gunned down in his Malacanang office by a mysterious assailant.

Diokno, Jose W. — The Nacionalista senator who broke with Marcos after the Plaza Miranda bombing was among the first government critics arrested the night martial law was declared. He spent two years in jail. When he died of cancer in 1987, President Cory Aquino declared ten days of national mourning and eulogized him as "a giant of a man [who] braved the Marcos dictatorship with a dignified and eloquent courage."

Doronila, Amando "Doro" — The *Manila Chronicle* editor was arrested and held for seventy days after martial law and then lived in exile for several years in Australia. When the Marcos regime fell, Doro returned to the Philippines to resume editing the resurrected *Chronicle*.

Enrile, Juan "Johnny" Ponce — The longtime Marcos confidant helped plan and execute martial law. He was rewarded for his loyalty, gaining substantial holdings in the coconut, lumber, and banking industries while serving for sixteen years as secretary of defense. Eventually, he was regarded as the third wealthiest man in the Philippines (after Marcos and crony Eduardo Cojuangco). Enrile defected in February 1986, supporting the "People Power Revolution" that brought down the regime. He became President Aquino's first secretary of defense but was fired later in 1986 after a failed coup attempt by military officers loyal to Enrile. He was elected to the Senate in 1987 and became a leader of the Aquino opposition. He also became a born-again Christian and tried to mount a presidential campaign in 1992 as a new Enrile. Despite initially heavy spending, however, he generated little popular support and was forced to withdraw. Rather than mount a nationwide campaign to defend his Senate seat, Enrile retained a place in Philippine politics by winning election to Congress.

Granada, Ernesto — The *Chronicle* columnist was arrested and held for a time at Camp Crame. During most of the Marcos dictatorship he lived in exile in California, continuing to work there for the Lopez family who had published his Manila paper.

Ileto, General Rafael "Rocky" — A onetime chief of the army under Marcos, Ileto's resistance to early martial-law plans prompted the president to move him into a harmless deputy chief of staff office. Later, he was moved out of the country, given what was then an unimportant ambassadorial assignment to Iran. In civilian life he was a pig farmer who Marcos, in apparent puzzlement, once declared "prefers his pigs to politicians." Later, in an interview, Ileto would shrug: "My hogs support me, and I find them more sincere." After Marcos fell, Ileto served President Aquino as defense secretary during 1987 and then became national security adviser for the remainder of her presidency. Through it all, he maintained his piggery.

Ilusorio, Potenciano "Nanoy" — One of the original Marcos cronies, a longtime friend and golfing buddy of the president, Ilusorio lost his friend and much of his wealth in retaliation for his role in the Dovie Beams scandal. Imelda blamed him for bringing the actress to Manila. After the scandal broke, he was *persona non grata* at Malacanang and never played another round of golf with Marcos. Imelda referred to him by a derogatory Tagalog term meaning "pimp."

Jopson, Edgar — The Ateneo University scholar and activist who led anti-Marcos student demonstrations in 1970, joined the Communist New People's Army after martial law. He was captured and reportedly tortured, but he escaped after a few months by bribing a guard. In the summer of 1982, he was hunted and gunned down by a constabulary raiding party in Mindanao. Church leaders said he was executed. Ateneo afforded him a hero's memorial, despite objections from military leaders.

Kalaw, Eva Estrada — The Liberal party senator injured at Plaza Miranda rushed back to Manila from Hong Kong after learning about martial law. She was an early leader of the vocal opposition, declaring that her dazed and disorganized party "must take a stand against this [authoritarian] government." Jailed Liberal leader Ninoy Aquino, who called her *"Atche"* (big sister) out of personal affection and because their grandmothers were sisters, was cheered by her otherwise futile political struggle. He later said that Eva Kalaw "is the only man in the senate." It was a tribute.

Locsin, Teodoro "Teddy," Sr. — The publisher of the *Philippines Free Press*, who had endorsed Marcos for reelection in 1969 but then criticized the corruption and militarization of his second term, was held in jail for three months. He refused to sell the paper's name to cronies of the president. Later, Locsin was one of those who, in 1983, tried to dissuade Ninoy Aquino from returning to Manila. "I asked what do you expect to do? He said, 'I will talk to Marcos. I will ask him to restore our liberties. I believe there is something good in this man and I will address that goodness.' And I said, 'Have you gone over his record!'" He blamed Marcos for the assassination. In a 1991 interview he said: "I think [Marcos] killed Ninoy to prove to himself that he was powerful." After Marcos fell, Locsin resumed publication of the *Free Press*.

Locsin, Teodoro "Teddy Boy," Jr. — The young editor of the *Free Press* was married a few months after martial law was declared. His father was released from prison in time to attend ceremonies. After Marcos was ousted, Teddy Boy served as Cory Aquino's press secretary and speechwriter. He left government to publish the *Daily Globe*, "the newspaper for the changing times."

Lopez, Eugenio "Geny," Jr. — The youthful publisher of the *Manila Chronicle* and the son of perhaps the richest man in the Philippines in 1972 was arrested two months into martial law and convicted of conspiracy to assassinate the president. He denied any involvement in such a plot. After five years in prison he made a daring escape, masterminded by a brother-in-law from San Francisco, and lived in California until the fall of the Marcos regime. In 1986, he returned to Manila to reclaim family properties stolen by Marcos and his cronies and to restore the *Chronicle* after a fourteen-year absence.

Lopez, Eugenio "Ining," Sr. — The head of the wealthiest family in the Philippines was in San Francisco undergoing medical treatments when martial law was declared. To win his son's release from prison, he agreed to sell his $400 million stake in Meralco, the Manila electric utility, for only $1,500 to Imelda's brother, Kokoy Romualdez. But his son was not released. Ining died of cancer in 1975, two years before his son's escape. Besides losing Meralco, the Lopez family lost seven television stations, twenty-one radio stations, and the *Chronicle*'s presses.

Marcos, Ferdinand E. "Bongbong," Jr. — As a young playboy, the president's only son seemed to have little interest in politics. Nonetheless, at his father's insistence he was named governor of Ilocos Norte. He fled Manila with his parents and spent much of his time in exile touring nightclubs in New York. His return to Manila in November 1991 was a boisterous celebration that upstaged his mother's carefully managed homecoming a few days later. Reports of trouble between mother and son were encouraged when Bongbong stayed for a time in the home of a rival of Imelda's for the presidency, Eduardo Cojuangco, Jr., a wealthy former crony of his father. The young Marcos then ran for a seat in Congress — the same seat for the village of Batac that his grandfather had lost to Julio Nalundasan and the same seat his father had won to launch his political career. His easy victory in his father's old "Solid North" required Philippine politics once again to make room for a Ferdinand E. Marcos.

Marcos, Imelda Romualdez — Once the most powerful woman in the Philippines, the late president's widow returned to Manila in November 1991 to be fingerprinted and face charges of tax evasion and other criminal allegations that she looted her nation. Earlier, she was acquitted of fraud and conspiracy charges in a New York federal court. Imelda returned to Manila in a chartered Boeing 747 dressed in the white of innocence. She was greeted by crowds of well-wishers and others, many of whom were paid 150 pesos each (about $5.20) to show their enthusiastic support. She occupied the $2,000-per-day penthouse floor of a luxury hotel while complaining that she was on the brink of poverty. Almost immediately, sounding more like a politician than a criminal defendant, she dusted off some of her late husband's old campaign slogans. "This country can be great again," she said in speeches soon after her return. Finally, in 1992 she returned to the political arena, singing and campaigning across the Philippines in a bid to reclaim the presidential palace. She won little support. Imelda spent much of election day in a Manila cathedral praying before

Our Lady of Consolation. It became clear that her prayers would not be answered when she lost in Leyte, her home province. Imelda finished fifth among seven candidates. She said she was a victim of vote fraud. Thereafter, she continued to campaign for permission to bring home from Hawaii the body of her dead husband for the hero's burial that he had been denied by the Aquino government.

Mijares, Luis "Boyet" — The teenaged son of Marcos propagandist Primitivo Mijares was killed in 1977 after receiving a mysterious telephone call that his missing father was alive. The sixteen-year-old boy's gruesomely mutilated body was found outside Manila, the apparent victim of torture and execution.

Mijares, Primitivo "Tibo" — The Marcos confidant, ghostwriter, and propagandist, who compared his role to that of Hitler's Joseph Goebbels, defected from the Marcos government in 1975 after a falling out with Imelda's brother, Kokoy Romualdez. Later that year, in dramatic testimony in Washington before a congressional committee, he blew the whistle on corruption, graft, and repression in the Marcos administration. He said that Marcos, through palace aide Guillermo de Vega, had offered him a $100,000 bribe not to testify before the U.S. congress. His book, *The Conjugal Dictatorship*, was published in 1976. Soon after it came out, Mijares disappeared while on a mysterious trip to Manila. He was never seen again.

Osmena, Sergio, Jr. — The Liberal senator, one of those who nearly died in the Plaza Miranda bombing, had been plotting to have Marcos assassinated by a team of American hitmen when martial law was declared. While the plot never resulted in an actual attempt against the president, its participants were discovered and forced to flee. One was arrested. Osmena already was out of the country when martial law was declared and the plot revealed thereafter. In apparent retaliation by the Marcos government, Osmena's son Sergio III was jailed for five years along with Geny Lopez. The senator, who lost to Marcos in the 1969 presidential race, was the son of a former Philippine president and obsessed with winning Malacanang himself. He died in exile in California.

Quintero, Eduardo — The constitutional convention delegate and former ambassador who exposed the Marcos bribery campaign only to find himself charged with crimes left his Manila hospital bed soon after martial law was declared to flee the country. When he died in 1984 he was living in San Francisco, working on a book he intended to call "The Imelda Marcos Envelopes."

Ramos, General Fidel V. "Eddie" — The Marcos cousin and chief of the Philippine constabulary at the time of martial law turned out to be a key figure in the fall of the Marcos regime. His defection along with Enrile, in February 1986, deprived the Marcos dictatorship of united military support and thereby sealed its doom. Ramos became chief of staff of the Philippines armed forces under President Corazon Aquino and, later, her secretary of defense, standing beside her despite recurring military coup attempts by younger officers. In 1992, Mrs. Aquino rewarded his loyalty by endorsing Ramos in his bid for the presidency. In a crowded field of contenders that included Imelda Marcos, Ramos eked out an election victory with barely 25 percent of the vote. When he was sworn in after nearly a month of vote-counting, he became the first Protestant elected to lead the predominantly Catholic nation.

Roces, Joaquin "Chino" — The publisher of the *Manila Times* continued to be a critic of Marcos after his release from prison, despite the fact that he lost his newspaper. In 1985, he became a familiar sight around Manila wearing a Ninoy Aquino T-shirt and pushing a shopping cart filled with petitions. Cory Aquino had told him she would run for president only if Chino could get two million signatures. He did. He also collected millions of pesos in small donations from citizens supporting Mrs. Aquino's candidacy. After Marcos fell, Roces returned to journalism and was working on the *Chronicle* when he died.

Salonga, Jovito — The Liberal senator, who lost an eye and for a time was expected to die from other critical injuries sustained in the Plaza Miranda bombing, became the original chairman of Cory Aquino's Presidential Commission on Good Government. The agency was created for the ambitious task of tracing and attempting to recover billions of dollars in stolen Philippine assets scattered around the world in property investments and secret bank accounts controlled by the Marcoses or their cronies. Salonga later became president of the Senate, one of the most influential offices in the restored Philippine democracy. And he was an unsuccessful candidate for president in 1992.

Sison, Jose Maria — The founder of the Communist party of the Philippines and the New People's Army was captured in 1977 and imprisoned until Marcos fled into Hawaiian exile. In 1986, President Aquino declared a general amnesty for all political prisoners, setting Sison free. The onetime English lecturer resumed a teaching career at the University of the Philippines, then began an international speaking tour in which he continued to criticize the Manila government. Aquino revoked his passport in 1988. Since then, he has lived in exile in the Netherlands.

In September 1992, Sison and members of his family were among two dozen plaintiffs who sued the Marcos estate in United States District Court, Honolulu, claiming monetary damages for incidents of torture, political imprisonment, and denial of human rights. The American jury ruled that the Marcos regime had engaged in systematic torture and human rights abuses that also resulted in the deaths and disappearances of thousands of Filipinos.

Tatad, Francisco "Kit" — The presidential press secretary at the time of martial law was a true-believer in the Marcos "New Society" but said he became disillusioned by the corruption and elitist politics. Tatad had a final falling out with the president when he insisted on running for a political office against a Marcos-preferred candidate. Later, Tatad published *Newsday*, one of the many daily newspapers that flourished in Manila after press freedom was restored with collapse of the Marcos regime.

Ver, General Fabian — The Ilocano chief of palace security was promoted rapidly from chauffeur and bodyguard to become the president's most trusted military aide. He was appointed armed forces chief of staff in the early 1980s. Allegations linked him to the Aquino assassination in 1983. He was tried and acquitted along with twenty-five others in December 1985, in a sham trial that helped unite political support for the candidacy of Cory Aquino. A post-Marcos Supreme Court voided the acquittal. Ver, by then a fugitive, was believed to be living in Malaysia or Indonesia. The general's son, living in exile, was chief of security for Imelda Marcos prior to her Manila return late in 1991.

Notes and Sources

Particularly useful for historical background throughout this book were Stanley Karnow's Pulitzer Prize–winning book *In Our Image*; Raymond Bonner's highly acclaimed *Waltzing With a Dictator*; Katherine Ellison's richly detailed *Imelda: Steel Butterfly of the Philippines*; and Carmen Navarro Pedrosa's ground-breaking profile, *Imelda Marcos*. The works of many other writers also were consulted for background on specific events and characters, as will be detailed in the following pages.

Reference books of value were Gregorio F. Zaide's two-volume *The Pageant of Philippine History*, *The Philippine Legislative Reader* edited by Renato Valasco and Sylvano Mahiwo, Victor J. Sevilla's three-volume *Justices of the Supreme Court of the Philippines*, and the *Philippine Almanac*.

All interviews cited in these pages, unless otherwise noted, were conducted by the author. Diary entries used in the text but not specifically identified there by date are included at the end of each set of chapter notes.

The Diary: An Introduction

This chapter is based entirely on analysis of the diary and on the author's original reporting — first, for the *Los Angeles Times* and, subsequently, in the preparation of this book. The diary photocopies obtained by the author show that Ferdinand Marcos was diligent in recording almost daily entries in his journals for the first five years, from the beginning of 1970 through the end of 1974. Apparently, he made only sporadic entries in later years.

Diary entries:
Page xiii — "You are the only person": March 6, 1971.
P. xiii — "I often wonder": Oct. 8, 1970.
P. xiv — "History should not": May 24, 1971.
P. xiv — "Make history": Dec. 19, 1971.
P. xv — "I am president": April 3, 1971.

Prologue: September 22, 1972

To reconstruct key moments in this chapter, the author relied in large measure on the vivid firsthand accounts provided by various participants. Considerable detail came from interviews with the following: former presidential press secretary Francisco "Kit" Tatad and his onetime assistant Larry Cruz; Philippine Senator John "Sonny" Osmena; the Locsins, Teodoro Sr. and his son, Teddy Boy, who were publisher and editor, respectively, of the *Philippines Free Press* on the night of September 22, 1972; Amando "Doro" Doronila, then editor of the *Manila Chronicle*; Antonio Roces, Jr., then publisher of the *Manila Daily Star*, and Henry A. Byroade, then U.S. ambassador to Manila.

Especially useful were accounts by onetime palace insider Primitivo Mijares, as described in his book *The Conjugal Dictatorship of Ferdinand and Imelda Marcos*. He related, for example, his observations of the president's telephone conversation with Juan Ponce Enrile on the eve of martial law.

Mijares is a particularly curious character of recent Philippine history. On one hand, he was an unprincipled journalist whose credibility as a reporter was crippled by his acceptance of bribes, an all-too-common practice in Manila. After being forced to resign from the *Manila Chronicle* in 1972, he joined the Marcos administration and became the president's chief propagandist and ghostwriter. At the time, he also wrote for the Marcos-controlled *Daily Express*. But after a falling out with Ferdinand and Imelda in 1975, Mijares defected and took his inside knowledge to the United States Congress. He created something of an international sensation when in testimony before a House subcommittee Mijares disclosed publicly for the first time extensive details of Marcos administration corruption. A few months later he disappeared — the victim, it still is widely suspected, of foul play.

Just before his 1976 disappearance, however, Mijares released his book. It is an often rambling and ranting, poorly constructed document and was dismissed in some circles at the time because of the tarnished journalistic reputation of its author. Nonetheless, it must be noted that significant aspects of Mijares's book have been corroborated in the years since — by the statements and admissions of other Marcos aides, by palace records discovered after Marcos fled Manila, by court documents disclosed in criminal and civil actions against the Marcoses in the United States, and by the works of independent scholars, researchers, and journalists. Furthermore, this author found contents of the Marcos diary lending additional credence to key Mijares observations.

Other firsthand accounts helpful in reconstructing scenes in this chapter came from the books of long-time Philippines Civil Liberties Union official and University of the Philippines professor Hernando J. Abaya, *The Making of a Subversive: A Memoir*, and former *Manila Chronicle* editor Rodolfo T. Reyes, *Memoirs of a Newsman*.

Diary entry:
Page 8 — "This makes martial law": Sept. 22, 1972.

One: The First Coffin

In recounting early stories about Ferdinand and Imelda Marcos and about Philippine history prior to 1970, when the president's diaries began, the author was aided especially by the works of Karnow, Bonner, Pedrosa, and Ellison. Other very valuable sources were Manuel F. Martinez, who wrote *Aquino vs. Marcos: The Grand Collision*, and Sterling Seagrave's *The Marcos Dynasty*.

The book *Reportage on the Marcoses 1964–1970*, perhaps best described as a third-person diary written with the obvious cooperation of the Marcoses, also was a significant source of detail for this chapter. The ancedote-rich book is attributed to Quijano de Manila, a pen name used by Philippine journalist-biographer Nick Joaquin. The book also contains a brief reference to the Marcos diary, recounting a moment in the spring of 1970 when the president retrieved his journal to show the biographer what he had written a few weeks earlier about the student protesters who had stormed Malacanang.

Also somewhat useful were two books by unabashedly pro-Marcos biographers — *Marcos of the Philippines* by Hartzell Spence (an updated version of Spence's original *For Every Tear a Victory*), and Victor G. Nituda's *The Young Marcos*, a very friendly biography written by the palace aide as a special gift for his president and political benefactor.

Official records of the Julio Nalundasan murder and subsequent trial, conviction, and appeal of Ferdinand Marcos have been widely reported. Some of the most detailed treatments appear in the works of Bonner, Seagrave, and Spence.

Accounts of the exaggerated Marcos war record came from stories published early in 1986 by the *New York Times* and the *Washington Post*, from
Bonner, and from the very detailed 1987 book *The Marcos File*, by Charles C.
McDougald. Much of that work stems from original research in Washington's National Archives in 1985 by Dr. Alfred McCoy, an American professor of history in Sydney, Australia, who discovered the records.

It is interesting to note that at various times throughout the diary Marcos
refers to his war experiences with reverence, as if believing his own myths. The
diary versions of his war exploits represent an especially sharp contrast to the
versions that researchers later would uncover in U.S. military records suggesting that Marcos had been a wartime profiteer and, possibly, a collaborator
with the Japanese occupation forces. Nonetheless, in one typically heroic diary
entry on January 3, 1970, Marcos wrote: "During the war in some critical
phase of a battle I always asked myself what could I do which others dare not
do and which would change the tide of battle."

The story of Ferdinand's involvement with American actress Dovie Beams
has been widely reported by Pedrosa, Ellison, Bonner, Seagrave, Mijares, and
others. Elements also were reported in various Manila magazines and newspapers. By far the most lurid version of the not-so-secret affair was provided
by Hermie Rotea, with significant help from the actress, in his 1984 book,
Marcos's Lovey Dovie. Rotea's account includes transcripts of two private meetings with Marcos that Dovie secretly recorded, portions of which were played
for the Manila media in 1970. The author also interviewed Potenciano
"Nanoy" Ilusorio, the longtime Marcos friend responsible for bringing Dovie
to Manila.

Additional background on origins of the leftist movement and Communist revolutionary leaders came from William Chapman's book, *Inside
the Philippine Revolution*, and from Alfredo B. Saulo's *Communism in the
Philippines, An Introduction*. The author, in 1991, also interviewed Jose Maria
Sison, a founder of the Communist party of the Philippines and the revolutionary New People's Army. Also useful was the unpublished transcript
of a 1989 interview of Sison recorded for a Philippine television docu-
mentary produced by Kristina Luz Rose and the Asian Television Corporation (ATV).

This chapter also used details from Nick Joaquin's 1987 book, *The World of
Rafael Salas*, written with the cooperation of the former Malacanang executive
secretary, and from *The CLU Story*, a history of the Philippines Civil Liberties
Union written by Professor Hernando J. Abaya.

Information for this chapter also was provided by other sources interviewed by the author. In addition to those already named, the interviews
were conducted with former general and national security adviser Rafael

"Rocky" Ileto; former general and chief of staff Romeo Espino; *Manila Chronicle* publisher Eugenio "Geny" Lopez, Jr.; Mrs. Manuela R. Ablan, the widow of onetime Laoag mayor Roque Ablan, Sr., and the mother of Congressman Roque Ablan, Jr.; Teodoro Locsin and his son, Teddy Boy, of the *Philippine Free Press*; and Senator Agapito "Butz" Aquino, brother of the martyred Benigno "Ninoy" Aquino.

Diary entry:
Page 27 — "I start a daily written record": Jan. 1, 1970.

Two: Another Coffin

In addition to Marcos's diary descriptions, much detail about the violence that followed Marcos's State of the Nation address to Congress in 1970 came from extensive press accounts of the period, particularly those published in the *Manila Chronicle*, the *Times*, and the *Free Press*. This chapter also benefits from descriptions provided by Roger Arienda in a book that includes details of his dealings with Marcos and of his personal role in the riots, *Free Within Prison Walls*, with Marichelle Roque.

The president's meetings with student leaders also are detailed in Joaquin's book, *Reportage on the Marcoses 1964–70*, and in *Aquino vs. Marcos — The Grand Collision*, by Martinez. Additional information about those sessions was provided by press accounts and interviews with former Marcos press secretary Kit Tatad and onetime student activist Nelson Navarro. Descriptions of the president's anxious reaction to the rioting also came from the Tatad interview.

Background on Henry Byroade used here and elsewhere in the book came from interviews with the former U.S. ambassador and from Bonner, Karnow, and press accounts.

Diary entries:
Page 29 — "But I have been asking myself": Jan. 3, 1970.
P. 30 — "I could not go into the car": Jan. 26, 1970.
P. 31 — "[H]e says Imelda and I": Jan. 9, 1970.
P. 31 — "I can feel the confidence": Jan. 9, 1970.
P. 32 — "The invocation was in poor taste": Jan. 26, 1970.
P. 34 — "He seemed stunned": Jan. 27, 1970.
P. 35 — "The pattern of subversion": Jan. 28, 1970.
P. 35 — "meet force with force": Jan. 23, 1970.
P. 36 — "I am certain": Jan. 28, 1970.
P. 36 — "If I want to be": Jan. 28, 1970.

Three: Night Frights

In addition to the diary accounts, this chapter relies on numerous independent sources for details about what was taking place inside and outside Malacanang during the rioting that came to be known as the "Battle of Mendiola." Especially useful was extensive news coverage and analysis in the Philippine and foreign press. Also invaluable were the books *Reportage on the Marcoses 1964–70* and Arienda's *Free Within Prison Walls*.

Interviews with Tatad, Ileto, and Congressman Roque Ablan, Jr., added helpful descriptions of Marcos and of what took place inside the palace. Student activist Nelson Navarro added details from beyond the gates of Malacanang.

An additional and somewhat ironic reference to "Joe," the palace spy and apparent agent provocateur planted among the student demonstrators, appears in the diary on March 22, 1970. Marcos described a scheme for using another diary, a journal kept by Joe, that would be tailored to implicate anti-government agitators in illegal activities. The president wrote: "Convinced Joe to update his diary and to then confirm his handwriting when a raid with search warrant seizes his diary with which he is [apprehended] with the others who will also be searched and arrested simultaneously."

Given the president's own self-serving, exaggerated, and sometimes invented diary accounts, this entry is an intriguing example of his willingness to use a diary to plant information.

Diary entries:
P. 41 — "Permission to fire on intruders": Jan. 30, 1970.
P. 44 — "urging students to attack": Feb. 4, 1970.
P. 46 — "Most felt there should be": Jan. 31, 1970.
P. 47 — "I had forgotten": Jan. 31, 1970.
P. 47 — "If I let these fears deter me": Jan. 31, 1970.

Four: The Total Solution

Besides the diary, sources consulted for details reported in this chapter include former presidential press secretary Tatad, former generals Ileto and Espino, former Philippine Communist leader Jose Maria Sison, and former U.S. ambassador Byroade.

The text of Ninoy Aquino's speech on the Senate floor came from the book *Aquino vs. Marcos: The Grand Collision*, by Martinez.

Valuable independent sources of detail regarding official perceptions (or misperceptions) of a Communist menace and its impact on domestic Philippine policy during the early 1970s were the books by Bonner, Karnow, Seagrave, and Alex Bello Brillantes, Jr., *Dictatorship & Martial Law*. Also useful were numerous articles published in the *Manila Times*, *Chronicle*, and *Free Press*.

The president's rather simplistic views on communism were recorded in the February 1, 1970, diary entry that he dedicated to his children. It is particularly intriguing when read with historic hindsight, knowing that less than three years after writing about what he regarded as the evils of communism, Marcos would impose many of those same evils on the citizens of his country. A complete text of those diary entries follows:

Why I Am Fighting Communism

1. Because it does not believe in God. It believes that everything that happens is brought about by man alone. It believes in the theory of dialectic materialism. I believe in God.

2. Under communism, a man has no rights. He is a creature of the state. It is the state that is glorified, not man. So man becomes a slave under communism.

3. Under communism, a man has no freedom. In contradistinction to democracy where individual freedom is sacrosanct, communism does not allow such simple liberties as freedom of thought, speech and religion among many others. There is no such thing as dissent or debate or dialogue.

4. Correspondingly, under communism a man may own no land as he may not own any production goods. The cry of land for the landless is a mere shiboleth, for the land belongs to the state and the farmers are only slaves of the state. . . .

5. Communism is a totalitarianism or a dictatorship by the elite who have acquired power through force, killing, murder and coercion. Prime examples are Stalin and Mao Tse-tung.

6. Correspondingly, the common people that communism is supposed to serve do not have any share in government nor in decision-making. Communism does not allow such simple processes as an election or voting or political campaigns. Everything is dictated by the few or the man on top who got there by force and violence.

7. The common people, the laborers, farmers and the employees, cannot rise beyond their level. They cannot send their children to school to become lawyers, doctors, engineers, teachers or attain any profession they may wish. The state, meaning the ruling elite, determines what the people become. There is no alternative.

8. Communism gives no inducement to genius, talent, perseverance and hard work. Everybody is pulled down to a common wage or salary except the rulers who live in a state of luxury and privilege.

9. Communism ostensibly seeks to eradicate the ruling or influential oligarchies. But it succeeds in only replacing them with a worse group — the ruling or influential cliques and elite who actually rule without the approval or consent of the people. These group [*sic*] of elitists cannot be changed except by violence or force — by a revolution.

10. Communism ostensibly seeks to drive away the foreign colonialists — in the Philippines, the Americans. But it would place the Philippines under a new alien power — Red China, which is worse. Our country should be free and not dominated by any alien power.

11. Communism believes in violence as the principal weapon of policy or of change. "Power comes out of the barrel of a gun," is its principal dictum. Every time there has been change in a communist country, there has been killing, arson, pillage and destruction — wasteful, merciless and senseless. In contradistinction to this, democracy offers change through the democratic process of elections and free speech in the open market of ideas. The process may be creaky, unwieldy and sometimes frustrating, but comparatively, it is humane, Christian, wiser, more democratic and less wasteful.

Let us improve the house we now have, we call democracy — for it has defects. But let us not burn it down.

Government infiltration of student demonstrations during the *First Quarter Storm* was widely reported in the press. Brillantes provided details about palace agents acting as provocateurs in the riots, wearing Band-Aids for identification.

The *Free Press* of February 7, 1970, quoted the unidentified Liberal party senator saying, ". . . the first president to be stoned."

According to Bonner, President Johnson never got over his dislike of Marcos and told William P. Bundy, then the State Department's assistant secretary for East Asia, that he would "have your head" if Bundy ever let Marcos get near LBJ again.

Diary entries:
Page 51 — "It seems clear now": Feb. 2, 1970.
P. 51 — ". . . dollars for hearts": Sept. 29, 1970.
P. 51 — "We must unmask": Feb. 3, 1970.
P. 51 — ". . . strange capacity": March 8, 1971.
P. 52 — "We must calm everybody down": Feb. 2, 1970.
P. 53 — "It has saddened me": Feb. 6, 1970.
P. 54 — "I feel that ultimately": Feb. 4, 1970.
P. 54 — "A little more violence": Feb. 21, 1970.

P. 55 — "He said they would": Feb. 5, 1970.

P. 55 — ". . . recast the plans for a total solution": Feb. 9, 1970.

P. 56 — "I dissuaded them from infiltrating": Feb. 12, 1970.

P. 56 — "For a time I secretly hoped": Feb. 12, 1970.

P. 57 — "Blas is an enigma": Feb. 12, 1970.

P. 57 — "He said he is willing to fight": Feb. 15, 1970.

P. 58 — "We should allow them": Feb. 17, 1970.

P. 58 — "The congressmen who visited": March 4, 1970.

P. 59 — "are all for a dictator": Feb. 21, 1970.

P. 59 — "Those crazy Americans": Feb. 20, 1970.

P. 60 — "I have that feeling": Feb. 17, 1970.

P. 62 — "But he did not seem": March 7, 1970.

P. 62 — "I have my misgivings": March 7, 1970.

P. 62 — "As the number": March 7, 1970.

P. 63 — "Superb acting": March 1, 1970.

P. 63 — ". . . a little lumpy": Feb. 28, 1970.

Five: Divine Whispers

Substantial details of Pope Paul VI's eventful visit to Manila and the background of would-be assassin Benjamin Mendoza were obtained from numerous Philippine and foreign press accounts, including *Time* magazine, *Newsweek*, *U.S. News & World Report*, the *Far Eastern Economic Review*, the *New York Times*, and the *Manila Chronicle*.

Details of Imelda's spring trip to Rome in 1969 came from *Reportage on the Marcoses 1964–70*.

Marcos's criticism of Philippine church leaders was revealed not only in the diary but in various press accounts.

For additional background on *anting-antings* and local superstitions, the author consulted a book by Richard Arens, *Folk Practices and Beliefs of Leyte and Samar*.

Diary entries:

Page 64 — "I have to cut them down": Nov. 25, 1970.

P. 67 — "Some nuns have even coerced": April 12, 1970.

P. 68 — "I hope the media does not": Oct. 29, 1970.

P. 69 — "And I am strengthened": March 24, 1970.

P. 70 — "[E]ven in the United States": Nov. 26, 1970.

P. 72 — "This has been an eventful day": Nov. 27, 1970.

P. 72 — "My karate chop": Nov. 27, 1970.

P. 72 — "I feel that I have been": Nov. 27, 1970.

P. 73 — "There was no hesitation": Nov. 27, 1970.

P. 73 — "This was the only slip": Nov. 27, 1970.
P. 73 — "It was worth the pain": Nov. 27, 1970.
P. 74 — " 'Runs in the family' ": Dec. 3, 1970.
P. 75 — ". . . I must risk comfort": Jan. 7, 1971.

Six: Sex, Lies, and Audio Tapes

The opening account of Imelda viewing the film *Maharlika* was based on a description of the episode from Louie Nepomuceno, the movie studio executive originally hired to edit the film. He described the exclusive Malacanang showing in a 1989 videotaped interview with Kristina Luz Rose of Asian Television Corporation, a transcript of which was provided to the author by Mrs. Rose.

Details of Marcos's romantic involvement with the actress became widely known thanks in part to sometimes outrageous newspaper and tabloid reports published from late 1970 through 1971. Books with additional background on the Dovie affair, and other affairs involving the president, include those by Ellison, Pedrosa, Mijares, and Seagrave.

Providing the most intimate and lurid detail for this chapter, as in the earlier chapter mentioning the Dovie affair, was Rotea's book, *Marcos's Lovey Dovie*. Rotea, a Philippine journalist who in 1970 wrote an award-winning book describing military brutality during the *First Quarter Storm* student demonstrations, fled the Philippines almost immediately after his original book was published, out of fear, he said, of Marcos retaliation. After working with Miss Beams for several months during the early 1970s, developing what was to be her book about the Marcos affair, the writer and actress had a falling out. A decade later, as the Marcos regime was teetering in the aftermath of the Aquino assassination, Rotea published his own book. Key elements were transcripts that he had retained of Dovie's secretly recorded tapes of her last Marcos meetings. For a time, she threatened to sue him for taking her diary, a tape recording, and their unfinished manuscript.

Additional detail about Marcos's involvement with Dovie came from interviews with Potenciano "Nanoy" Ilusorio, the president's longtime friend and original financial backer of the *Maharlika* film. His accounts corroborate significant details in the Rotea book. The Dovie episode ended up costing Ilusorio his friendship with Marcos. Ilusorio said Imelda still blames him for introducing the president to the actress.

The account of a 1969 Vatican visit during which the Marcos daughters asked Pope Paul VI to "bless" Imelda with the birth of another son came from *Reportage on the Marcoses 1964–70*.

In the midst of the Dovie Beams scandal, Marcos continued to write about having another child with Imelda. On December 13, 1970, after describing the couple's emotional airport greeting of Bongbong returning from school in London, Marcos wrote: "And [Imelda] whispered to me, 'You were right, we have lost a child. He is now turning into a man. We can no longer baby him.' I answered, 'We will just have to have another child to baby!' This has been a happy day!"

Results of the 1969 presidential vote were not immediately certified by election officials because losing candidate Sergio Osmena filed a legal challenge. That appeal was not resolved until after martial law was declared in 1972, by which time Osmena was living in exile in California and President Marcos was the Philippine's dictator.

In 1991 interviews, Teodoro Locsin and his son, Teddy Boy, described how Dovie's picture ended up on the cover of their *Free Press*. The elder Locsin described Imelda's angry call to his wife.

For a time, the Locsins had been close to the Marcoses. The president hosted a dance party for the *Free Press* in August 1969 at which, Teddy Sr. recalled, "I danced the twist with Imelda." The Locsins later that year endorsed Ferdinand for reelection. Meanwhile, Teddy Jr. was wooed continuously by the president to serve as his press aide. When the rioting broke out in January 1970, Marcos called the Locsin family to Malacanang. "Imelda wanted us to stay at the palace," Teddy Sr. recalled. But with the growing violence and militarization, the nation's worsening economic troubles and new evidence of administration corruption the Locsins and their *Free Press* became outspoken critics of the president. Their friendship promptly withered.

Background on Delfin Cueto and accounts of his death were published in Manila newspapers. Additional details about the man Marcos tried to use as an alibi — the other "Fred" — and Cueto's pursuit of Dovie Beams to Hong Kong can be found in Seagrave's book.

The story of Supreme Court Justice Fred Ruiz Castro's hostile response to being greeted as "Fred" during the Dovie Beams scandal was related in an interview with Ilusorio.

Besides diary references, Dovie's psychiatric records have been described in the books of Ellison and Rotea. The documents, some from Dovie's divorce files in Tennessee, were made public in Manila originally in the *Republic Weekly*. The tabloid was a pro-Marcos publication that in 1971 produced the scathing ten-week series attacking Dovie and publishing nude pictures of the actress that she said were taken by Marcos.

That Marcos was a notorious womanizer and that the Dovie affair was only one — albeit a long-running affair — has been disclosed by numerous writers, including Ellison, Pedrosa, Mijares, and Seagrave (who also cites diplomatic dispatches expressing Washington's concern over a Marcos affair in the late 1960s with a U.S. military officer's wife).

The text of a personal note to Imelda written in a book by Arthur F. Burns was quoted by Marcos in his diary.

Diary entries:
Page 77 — "And we are impotent": Nov. 10, 1970.
P. 84 — ". . . mauled [him for] no reason": Jan. 22, 1970.
P. 84 — "The demonstrators (some ten of them)": Jan. 22, 1970.
P. 89 — "There is an indication": Nov. 12, 1970.
P. 89 — ". . . find out what the participation": Nov. 12, 1970.
P. 90 — "Imelda has resolutely stood by me": Nov. 11, 1970.
P. 91 — "We were irritated by some posters": Dec. 25, 1970.

Seven: New Year's Delusions

Accounts of the Crisologo assassination were carried in several Manila publications. Particularly useful in reconstructing the killing were detailed stories in the *Free Press* and *Chronicle*, both of which also had reported on crime and violence in the province, the bloody, long-running feud between Crisologo and his nephew's family, and the fiery attacks on two villages that had voted heavily for Crisologo's rival nephew in a previous election.

Additional details about Crisologo's political, financial, and personal relations with Marcos were disclosed in books by Mijares and Seagrave.

Diary entries:
Page 96 — "[H]ow unreasonable Crisologo has become": Aug. 1, 1970.
P. 97 — "There goes a friend": Oct. 18, 1970.
P. 98 — "The truth is": Oct. 20, 1970.
P. 98 — ". . . the beginning of the implementation": Oct. 18, 1970.
P. 99 — "Crisologo is dead": Oct. 20, 1970.
P. 99 — "So I assured him": Oct. 18, 1970.

Eight: Dictator Dreams

The *Manila Chronicle*'s explosive revelations of vast Marcos corruption appeared in the paper beginning in January 1971. A daily feature of the editorial pages was a cartoon depiction of a school classroom in which a teacher stands before his pupils, all of them eagerly raising their hands to answer the question of the day. One day it is: "Who is the richest man in Southeast Asia?" Another day it is: "Who is the biggest Filipino depositor in a Swiss bank?" And: "Who has the largest collection of diamonds and precious gems in Southeast Asia?" And: "Who buys dresses from Nina Ricci at $3,800 each?" Meanwhile, appearing on the news pages of the paper were stories exposing the financial interests of Ferdinand and the early spending habits of Imelda.

Of course, official graft and corruption in the Philippines did not have its origins in the Marcos administration. In a 1991 interview, Eugenio "Geny" Lopez, Jr., now publisher of the *Chronicle*, said he and his late father launched the 1971 editorial attacks on Marcos not because they were outraged by mere graft, but because of the enormity of it. "If Marcos had just skimmed $20 million off the top and done a good job of governing, it probably would have been OK," Lopez said. He also said that details of the extent of Marcos corruption first were revealed to his father by Rafael Salas, the president's highly regarded first-term executive secretary. "That's when the paper turned against Marcos," Lopez said. (See also chapter Ten.)

Marcos's corruption has been widely reported in the U.S. and Philippine press, and considerable detail emerged in testimony and court documents submitted during Imelda's 1990 federal fraud trial in New York. The subject also is treated extensively in many books, including those by Karnow, Bonner, Mijares, and Seagrave. By far the most detailed information on Marcos's corruption, however, is contained in Ricardo Manapat's book, *Some Are Smarter Than Others — The History of Marcos' Crony Capitalism*.

Press accounts, particularly stories in the *Chronicle*, provided details about the Corpuz raid and the security responses of the Marcos entourage.

Diary entries:
Page 101 — "This is your principal mission": March 6, 1971.
P. 102 — " 'I have learned' ": March 6, 1971.
P. 103 — "The opinion is developing": Feb. 10, 1971.
P. 104 — " 'We cannot understand why' ": Jan. 13, 1971.
P. 105 — "My tummy shows": Jan. 3, 1971.
P. 106 — ". . . one of those green pornographies": Aug. 22, 1970.
P. 107 — "Saw the movie 'Waterloo' ": March 13, 1971.
P. 107 — "will of the commander": March 7, 1971.
P. 107 — "provoke violence by the communists": March 3, 1970.
P. 107 — "felt that if there was": March 21, 1970.
P. 108 — ". . . I go through these days": March 21, 1971.

Nine: Democracy in Traction

Besides extensive press accounts of the Plaza Miranda bombing, much of the detail about the incident used in this chapter came from 1991 interviews with two of the bomb blast's prominent victims: Liberal party Senate candidates Eva Kalaw and John "Sonny" Osmena. Also providing background for this chapter were interviews with former generals Espino and Ileto, Nelson Navarro, Kit Tatad, and Ambassador Byroade.

Press accounts of the time also were used to examine public reaction to the bombing. And several books provided useful background on the legal, political, and diplomatic fallout from Marcos's actions suspending the writ of habeas corpus after the bombing. Among those consulted for this chapter were Bonner, Brillantes, Karnow, Martinez, Mijares, and Seagrave.

Particularly valuable was Arienda's firsthand account of his arrest and imprisonment during that period, described in his book *Free Within Prison Walls*.

In a telephone interview in 1992, Byroade said he was not surprised to hear that Marcos had reacted angrily when told that the ambassador had questioned his popularity after the Plaza Miranda bombing. "He would think I was saying the same thing to Washington — and he wouldn't like that."

While the diary provides unprecedented detail about the extent of Justice Castro's secret meetings and intelligence-sharing with the president, Marcos in 1979 publicly disclosed that they had consulted privately. His comments were made during a eulogy at the jurist's 1979 funeral. Also, Brillantes quotes other Supreme Court jurists acknowledging private meetings with the president. Chief Justice Concepcion, informed of those meetings, told Brillantes: "That is direct interference on the Court!"

Accounts of bombings during the court deliberations and Mitra's quip come from Mijares and various press sources.

General Garcia's comments about peace and order in the Philippines appeared in Mijares, attributed to the June 1, 1971, editions of the *New York Journal of Commerce*.

Despite repeated Marcos assertions in the diary that Imelda's popularity would make her a sure winner in any political contest, Martinez reported that polls of that period in 1971 showed she had less than 18 percent support nationwide. When she finally ran for the presidency in 1992, she got even less support and was badly defeated.

Martinez quoted the Filipino commentator who said Marcos campaigned as if his political life and fortune depended on it.

Diary entries:
Page 113 — "Sen. Aquino who was absent": Aug. 22, 1971.
P. 115 — "Today I must plan my life anew": Sept. 16, 1971.
P. 115 — "Columnists and commentators": Sept. 7, 1971.
P. 116 — "I could feel I was": Sept. 11, 1971.
P. 116 — "The suspension has taught us": Sept. 7, 1971.
P. 117 — "What an arrogant ingrate": Aug. 3, 1971.
P. 117 — "[S]he owes her political career": July 28, 1971.
P. 117 — "And to think": Sept. 8, 1971.
P. 119 — "so that it will hit": Sept. 16, 1971.

P. 119 — "even the honorable justices": Oct. 1, 1971.

P. 120 — "The doctrine of review": Oct. 7, 1971.

P. 122 — "do not now constitute": Jan. 11, 1971. (Note: The author believes this entry was made on Page 40 of the 1971 diary, although Marcos did not date or number this diary page. It was received in sequence between page 39, which opened the January 11 entry, and page 42, which Marcos noted as a continuation of the January 12 entry that presumably began on a missing page 41.)

P. 123 — "cry 'fraud' and give all kinds of excuses": Sept. 6, 1971.

P. 124 — "my wealth, dictatorial tendencies": Oct. 23, 1971.

P. 124 — "was dull — all speeches": Nov. 6, 1971.

P. 124 — "Instead of dull speeches": Nov. 7, 1971.

P. 125 — "The initial reports of the voting": Nov. 8, 1971.

P. 125 — "For two years now": Nov. 8, 1971.

P. 126 — "For the last several days": Nov. 14, 1971.

Ten: A Glimpse of the Rubicon

In addition to the diary, sources of details for this chapter include various Manila press accounts.

Books by Brillantes and Martinez indicate that the public and Marcos's rivals did not fully appreciate the significance of the Supreme Court ruling in favor of the president. Arienda's book provided additional detail about his response to imprisonment and his release.

Malacanang palace ledgers obtained by the author and first disclosed in articles published by the *Los Angeles Times* detailed Marcos cash payoffs to dozens of Manila journalists up to the final hours of the regime. Other accounting documents used in civil and criminal cases against the Marcoses in U.S. federal courts also showed that the Marcoses paid the travel expenses of Manila journalists and provided them with spending money on trips abroad, long an unacceptable practice in the United States.

Interviews that contributed to this chapter include those with Teodoro and Teddy Boy Locsin, Ileto, and Espino.

In a series of articles published through much of 1970, the *Philippines Free Press* documented the dramatic militarization of the nation. The stories, most of them by Napoleon G. Rama, who later served as a delegate to the constitutional convention, provided details used in this chapter.

Diary entries:

Page 127 — "all over town": Nov. 9, 1971.

P. 128 — "sees in me himself": Nov. 27, 1971.

P. 128 — "the best way": Dec. 5, 1971.

P. 128 — "[P]oor Ricky": Dec. 5, 1971.

P. 128 — "should not be allowed": Dec. 30, 1971.

P. 128 — "by imprisonment or worse": Dec. 30, 1971.

P. 128 — "These are dangerous men": Dec. 30, 1971.

P. 128 — "setting me up like a Ngo Dinh Diem": Nov. 14, 1971.

P. 128 — "I am convinced": Nov. 16, 1971.

P. 129 — "unreliable as a participant": Sept. 14, 1971.

P. 129 — "I believe democracy": Jan. 6, 1971.

P. 130 — "I can see that most": Sept. 28, 1971.

P. 130 — "empire within the Republic": Jan. 17, 1971.

P. 130 — "The . . . TV and radio": March 10, 1971.

P. 130 — "the best defense against communism": March 20, 1971.

P. 131 — "the media and the communists": May 1, 1971.

P. 131 — "vituperation and vicious fault-finding": May 2, 1971.

P. 131 — "I must counsel": May 2, 1971.

P. 131 — "What would the dead": May 9, 1971.

P. 131 — "From the vantage point": Jan. 2, 1971.

P. 132 — "change the attitude": Nov. 27, 1971.

P. 132 — "His son . . . said": Oct. 14, 1970.

P. 134 — "This merely means": Dec. 11, 1971.

P. 134 — "all trooped into the bedroom": Dec. 12, 1971. [Note: Marcos misdated the entry as "1972."]

P. 134 — "[T]he decision to suspend": Dec. 12, 1971. [Note: same as above.]

P. 136 — "I have a feeling": Dec. 24, 1971.

P. 136 — "Peace and order": Dec. 24, 1971.

P. 137 — "strikingly apropos": Dec. 26, 1971.

Eleven: The Constitution Con

In addition to writing about some of his lobbying efforts in the pages of his diary, Marcos also saved an extensive collection of correspondence from aides who were responsible for executing his lobbying campaign in the constitutional convention. From the same sources who provided access to the diary, the author obtained numerous copies of those memos, letters, and reports. Many of the documents are addressed to the president. Some are written on the president's stationery and signed by his executive assistant, Dr. Guillermo "Gimo" de Vega.

Eduardo Quintero's dramatic statement to the convention and his subsequent ordeal as the target of a Marcos government counterattack received extensive press coverage which provided much of the additional detail for this chapter.

Other valuable sources of information about the convention were Martinez, Brillantes, and Abaya.

The diary shows clearly from its earliest pages that Marcos wanted very much for the constitutional convention to change the national charter to permit him to run again for the presidency. The option of running Imelda in 1973 if his own two-term limit could not be voided was discussed publicly, and in the diary, first in 1970 and often throughout 1971 and 1972. All of which makes a diary entry of March 4, 1971, particularly puzzling.

It was a Thursday evening in the palace. Younger daughter Irene was playing the piano. Imelda and daughter Imee were reading Bongbong's latest letter from boarding school in London, describing his first snow. It was an idyllic family scene and Marcos wrote that he was "exhilaratingly happy." But he also wrote: "Imelda and I have been planning together. We look forward to retirement from politics in 1973."

It seems clear from the host of contradictory diary entries, both before and after, that Marcos never seriously contemplated retirement — as must be clear by the summer of 1971 when he flatly declared in the diary that Imelda would have to run in '73 if he could not retain power. Also see the final diary entry of the chapter (May 25, 1972) in which Marcos wrote that he expected to be killed if he retired.

Additional details about Imelda's trip to Iran and Washington, D.C., came from press accounts in Manila and from books by Bonner, Ellison, and Karnow.

While U.S. officials were skeptical, if not totally disbelieving, that the People's Republic of China was exporting revolution to the Philippines, officials might have been alarmed to read a brief diary entry on May 3, 1970, that seemed to suggest Marcos was eager for a U.S.-China war. Noting Nixon's dramatic escalation of bombing attacks in the Vietnam war, Marcos wrote: "Nixon is under attack from some of the U.S. congressional leaders, but he did the right thing and if he pushes it through, he may become a great President because it is just possible that if Red China reacts violently and starts war, that may be the end of Red China. I believe Russia will keep quiet about it and let Red China stew in her own sauce."

Diary entries:
Page 141 — "If the Cons. Con.": July 8, 1971.
P. 141 — "will not mount a rebellion": Jan. 28, 1972.
P. 147 — "jumped on us": May 25, 1972.
P. 147 — "[A]t the first impact": May 22, 1972.
P. 148 — "The lucky discovery": May 31, 1972.
P. 149 — "I am now convinced": May 25, 1972.

Twelve: A Death in the Family

Ellison was an additional source of useful details about Imelda and the public skepticism surrounding reports of her miscarriage.

The author also consulted a University of California obstetrics and gynecology expert to analyze technical details contained in the diary.

Mijares described why the success of a parliamentary government bill in the constitutional convention was so important to Marcos.

Press accounts were sources of additional detail about the fetus burial.

Diary entries:
Page 152 — "A little underhanded": Jan. 4, 1972.
P. 152 — "detente may release": Jan. 16, 1972.
P. 152 — "interpreted as some kind": March 15, 1972.
P. 152 — "I asked him what": Nov. 21, 1970.
P. 153 — "a small frog": Jan. 8, 1972.
P. 153 — "She was cautious": March 15, 1972.
P. 153 — "Kosygin found her charming": March 16, 1972.
P. 154 — "Spiritual Exercises": March 29, 1972.
P. 155 — "I asked the Lord": March 29, 1972.
P. 157 — "Imelda is in pain": May 26, 1972.
P. 157 — "was insistent on issuing": May 30, 1972.
P. 157 — "We still hope": May 31, 1972.
P. 157 — "Without her noticing": June 2, 1972.
P. 158 — "I have shed no tears": June 2, 1972.
P. 159 — "I hope the public": June 3, 1972.
P. 159 — "Most picturesque and sad": June 19, 1972.
P. 160 — . . ."pledged loyalty to me": June 16, 1972.
P. 160 — "was mobbed by thousands": June 21, 1972.
P. 160 — "democratic ways will not solve": June 22, 1972.
P. 160 — "Resolved that since no one": June 24, 1972.
P. 160 — "They asked me": June 20, 1972.
P. 161 — "I do not intend": June 20, 1972.

Thirteen: Summer Storms

Local press accounts provided details about the bombings and floods that plagued Manila through the summer of 1972. Newspaper stories also were sources of detail about flood relief controversies and about the recovery and return of the *Santo Nino* statue.

The story of the mystery ship *m/v Karagatan* was drawn from the author's interview with Sison and from other published accounts, including many in the Manila press. Bonner and Seagrave also added useful information, though conflicting conclusions. Seagrave called it "a sham." Bonner, citing two unnamed Communist sources, said it was a botched attempt to smuggle weapons into the Philippines for the revolution. Sison, in his interview with the author, suggested the third version outlined in this chapter.

Marcos felt a certain kinship with President Richard M. Nixon who, like the Philippine president, was the object of considerable press criticism — especially after the Watergate break-in during the summer of 1972. Several months later Lloyd Hand, a visiting former White House protocol officer and future U.S. ambassador to the Philippines (in 1977), told Marcos during a round of golf that Nixon was unlikely to survive the scandal. In response, then-dictator Marcos wrote: "I believe the U.S. Press has just about set back the American nation in prestige and credibility [so] they may not be able to recover."

The full text of Marcos's September 21, 1971, letter to daughter Imee follows:

> My sweet adorable scramble-brained eldest daughter who claims the temperament of a *prima dona* and the objectivity of an Oxford Don, you have just written one of the most touching letters in the history of the generation gap. We read it while we were having dinner and I am afraid the soup received some lachrymal dilution. But this dire confession must never be revealed to our critical public until twenty years after my demise!
>
> We dig you, Bongbong and Irene. But then hindsight is always much wiser than foresight so here we are setting down in paper what we should have said in the first place.
>
> But there is no need to for worry. The Marcoses and the Romualdezes are an indestructable [*sic*] lot. No amount of abrasive confrontations, nor morose soliloquys [*sic*] or agitated non-intellectual discourse will erase them from this world. . . . So we will survive. And so will you. . . . So, you have just shown us up as a little infantile. But I do not know of a more enchanting way of being unmasked nor by a more charming person! (Cheers)
>
> So, my darling talented and precocious daughter, you and Bongbong and Irene are exactly what we wanted our children to be — give and take a little on the personality dimensions.
>
> And we will all keep our eyes open for the booby traps that have been planted along the way. Without losing that spontaneity that gives grace to living.
>
> Your mother and I have been engaged in self-assessment (what does the Marxist call it — self-criticism) and introspection. So you see your genes are showing off — rather splendidly, I would say.

But do not be too overly cruel with yourselves. . . . In this case the fault may lie in the old fogies for not immediately appreciating the situation. . . . You must forgive the old their rigid and set ways. And we must understand the ways of the young. . . .

We love you always,

Your dad —

Diary entries:

Page 162 — "My answer was": Feb. 20, 1972.

P. 163 — "I told him": April 11, 1972.

P. 165 — "may have raised": Sept. 11, 1972.

P. 165 — "So there is hysteria": Sept. 10, 1972.

P. 166 — "guaranteed to stop": Nov. 17, 1971.

P. 166 — "I told [them]": Aug. 11, 1972.

P. 167 — "whether I am there": Jan. 9, 1971.

P. 167 — "He is too carefree": June 12, 1972.

P. 167 — "We have some problems": Feb. 28, 1972.

P. 167 — "Irene has lost nine pounds": May 9, 1971.

P. 168 — "seriously proposed and discussed": March 9, 1971.

P. 170 — "The talk of Manila": Aug. 3, 1972.

P. 170 — "the sun that we brought": Aug. 8, 1972.

P. 171 — "If it is not ratified": July 7, 1972.

P. 171 — "Diokno is beginning": July 7, 1972.

P. 172 — "bluntly told us": Aug. 27, 1972.

P. 173 — "How stupid can they be?": Aug. 27, 1972.

P. 173 — "Are the Americans": Aug. 27, 1972.

P. 173 — "I asked him pointblank": May 24, 1972.

P. 174 — "that the President": Aug. 31, 1972.

P. 174 — "The message I asked": Sept. 6, 1972.

P. 174 — "I briefed him": Aug. 28, 1972.

P. 174 — "Senator Inouye": Sept. 1, 1972.

P. 175 — "I immediately countered": Sept. 1, 1972.

P. 175 — "But I will first wipe out": Sept. 1, 1972.

P. 175 — "And there are more girls": Sept. 13, 1972.

P. 176 — "Perhaps it is best": Sept. 13, 1972.

P. 176 — "We agreed to set": Sept. 13, 1972.

Fourteen: Some Kind of Hero

Press accounts provided additional background on the formaldehyde spill, the bombing of Quezon City Hall where the constitutional convention was convened and other bombings that continued around Manila, the arrest of a constabulary officer, and the last Plaza Miranda rally before martial law.

Descriptions of Ninoy Aquino's last appearance before the Senate came from Martinez and press coverage.

The absence of a free press hampered research into the early hours of martial law. However, several interviews provided significant detail for this chapter, especially those with Amando "Doro" Doronila; Teodoro and Teddy Boy Locsin; John "Sonny" Osmena; Eugenio "Geny" Lopez, Jr.; and Ambassador Byroade.

Books that also were helpful in describing individual experiences at the implementation of martial law include those by Abaya, Arienda, Martinez, Mijares, and Reyes. The works of Karnow, Bonner, and Seagrave also were very useful.

One significant element that is *not* in the diary may help resolve a diplomatic mystery. Nowhere in the diary pages did Marcos ever mention a telephone conversation with President Nixon. In fact, the only references to contacts with the United States appear to be through Ambassador Byroade. In his book, Bonner asserted that such a call linking the chief executives preceded the martial law order and in the conversation Nixon gave his personal approval in advance to Marcos's planned military takeover. Nixon has denied it and no record of such a call has been found in White House records. It seems unlikely to the author that Marcos would have omitted from his diary an encounter of such significance when he did, in fact, note meetings on the same subject with Byroade. It should be noted also that in this section of the author's diary collection there are no missing pages. Thus, the Marcos omission seems to lend support to the Nixon version over Bonner's.

Despite Marcos's description of Byroade's discussions with his brother-in-law Benjamin "Kokoy" Romualdez, the ambassador said in an interview that he did not recall asking Romualdez to campaign for Nixon in the California Filipino community. "I didn't have much respect for Kokoy. And I don't think he would have been much help to Nixon. Maybe I was trying to flatter him, but I certainly wouldn't have wanted Kokoy campaigning for me!"

The common lament, that "we are a nation of 40 million cowards," came from various interviews and appears in Joaquin's profile of Senator Salvador Laurel.

Diary entries:
Page 177 — "I told [them]": Sept. 14, 1972.
P. 178 — "[Byroade] explained": Sept. 14, 1972.
P. 178 — "common plan of propaganda": Sept. 16, 1972.
P. 179 — "The departure of our children": Sept. 16, 1972.

P. 180 — "They all agreed": Sept. 18, 1972.
P. 181 — "Of course, Imelda and I": Sept. 21, 1972.
P. 182 — "He seemed to favor it": Sept. 21, 1972.
P. 182 — "I told him I did not": Sept. 21, 1972.
P. 182 — "He told Gov. Romualdez": Sept. 21, 1972.
P. 183 — "I asked [him]": Sept. 20, 1972.
P. 183 — "He seems to know": Sept. 21, 1972.
P. 184 — "It was a good thing": Sept. 22, 1972.
P. 187 — "things have moved": Sept. 23, 1972.

Epilogue: The Last Delusion

Among the constitutional convention delegates arrested in the immediate aftermath of martial law was Napoleon Rama, the *Free Press* writer who published stories about the militarization of the Philippines. According to Brillantes, more than twenty delegates were arrested or forced into exile. Others went into hiding or reassessed their opposition.

Interviews with Kalaw, who was locked out of the Senate, and with Sison, whose radical ranks multiplied with the advent of martial law, also contributed to this chapter.

Besides the records seized by U.S. Customs agents in Hawaii and turned over to federal prosecutors in New York, vast amounts of documents detailing Marcos graft and corruption were discovered in the Philippines by Corazon Aquino's Presidential Commission on Good Government. The author reviewed court records, PCGG records, and Manapat's detailed book for additional information used in this chapter.

Press accounts and books by Karnow, Martinez, and Bonner were particularly useful providing background about efforts to free Ninoy Aquino. The author obtained a copy of the lengthy 1973 response to martial law that Aquino had drafted in prison. Karnow was the source of the Aquino quote to a friend about overestimating the Filipino people.

Teodoro Locsin, in an interview, related some of the dark humor inspired by martial law.

Bonner's account of 1982 disclosures about Marcos's fraudulent war record provided additional detail for this chapter.

For details of the December 1985 snap election and the ultimate final hours of the Marcos regime, this chapter benefited from extensive press coverage and from accounts in Karnow, Bonner, and Seagrave.

Of particular value in describing the last scenes inside Malacanang was Colonel Arturo C. Aruiza's partisan but effective book, *Ferdinand Marcos: Malacanang to Makiki*, an account of the Marcoses' fall and exile written by the president's longtime loyal military aide. Aruiza was a source of detail about the inaugural ceremonies on February 25, 1986, the deposed president's response to legal problems in Hawaii, and the cemetery rites in 1989.

Although Ferdinand died before he could face trial in New York, federal prosecutors pursued their fraud and conspiracy case against Imelda in the spring of 1990. Jurors acquitted Mrs. Marcos, some of them telling reporters afterward that they could not hold the widow responsible for the crimes of her husband. If Ferdinand had been in the courtroom, one juror told the *Los Angeles Times*, he would have been convicted.

Diary entries:
Page 189 — "There must be no conflict": Sept. 25, 1972.
P. 189 — "if necessary I would": Sept. 24, 1972.
P. 190 — "Inspiring and moving": Oct. 17, 1972.
P. 190 — "The quiet, slow slide": Dec. 17, 1972.
P. 192 — "We should allow them": Feb. 17, 1970.

About the Other Players

In addition to diary material and information obtained from newspaper and magazine articles, the following sources also were helpful in providing background for this list:

1. Ninoy and Corazon Aquino — Martinez.
2. Roger Arienda — his book, and a conversation with the author in Manila.
3. Dovie Beams — Rotea, Ellison, and an interview with Teddy Boy Locsin.
4. Henry Byroade — interview with the author.
5. Fred Ruiz Castro — Sevilla.
6. Guillermo de Vega — Mijares and Seagrave.
7. Jose Diokno — Bonner.
8. Amando Doronila — interviews with the author.
9. Juan Ponce Enrile — Seagrave and Manapat.
10. Ernesto Granada — Reyes.
11. Rafael Ileto — interview with the author.
12. Potenciano Ilusorio — interviews with the author.
13. Edgar Jopson — Ellison.
14. Eva Estrada Kalaw — interview with the author.
15. Teodoro Locsin, Sr. — interview with the author.
16. Teddy Boy Locsin, Jr. — interviews with the author.
17. Eugenio "Geny" Lopez, Jr. — interview with the author.
18. Eugenio Lopez, Sr. — Bonner, Seagrave, and Reyes, as well as interview with Geny Lopez.

19. Ferdinand "Bongbong" Marcos, Jr. — Karnow and author's interviews with friends of the Marcos family during Imelda's criminal trial in New York.

20. Imelda Marcos — court records and interviews with *Los Angeles Times* Manila correspondent, Bob Drogin.

21. Luis Mijares — Seagrave.

22. Tibo Mijares — Seagrave and Reyes.

23. Sergio Osmena — Karnow, Bonner, and interview with his nephew, Senator John "Sonny" Osmena.

24. Eduardo Quintero — Brillantes and Martinez.

25. Fidel Ramos — Bonner.

26. Chino Roces — Reyes.

27. Jovito Salonga — Bonner.

28. Jose Maria Sison — interview with the author.

29. Francisco Tatad — interview with the author.

30. Fabian Ver — Bonner and Seagrave.

Bibliography

Abaya, Hernando J. *The CLU Story: Fifty Years of Struggle for Civil Liberties*. Quezon City: New Day Publishers, 1987.

_____. *The Making of a Subversive: A Memoir*. Quezon City: New Day Publishers, 1984.

Aquino, Benigno S. "Ninoy," Jr. *Testament From a Prison Cell*. Los Angeles: Philippine Journal, 1988.

_____. "Tomorrow May Be Too Late," a 39-page paper prepared in prison, dated Jan. 26, 1973.

Arens, Richard. *Folk Practices and Beliefs of Leyte and Samar*. Tacloban City: Divine Word University, no date.

Arienda, Roger "Bomba," with Marichelle Roque-Lutz. *Free Within Prison Walls*. Quezon City: New Day Publishers, 1983.

Aruiza, Arturo C. *Ferdinand E. Marcos: Malacanang to Makiki*. Quezon City: ACAruiza Enterprises, 1991.

Bello, Walden, and Severina Rivera, editors. *The Logistics of Repression*. Washington: Friends of the Filipino People, 1977.

Bonner, Raymond. *Waltzing With a Dictator*. New York: Vintage Books, 1988.

Brillantes, Alex Bello, Jr. *Dictatorship & Mutual Law*. Quezon City: Great Books Publishers, 1986.

Chaffee, Frederic H., and others. "Area Handbook for the Philippines." Washington: U.S. Government Printing Office, 1969.

Chapman, William. *Inside the Philippine Revolution*. New York: W. W. Norton, 1987.

Diokno, Jose W. *A Nation for Our Children.* Quezon City: Claretian Publications, 1987.

Doyle, William. *The Oxford History of the French Revolution.* Oxford: Clarendon Press, 1989.

Ellison, Katherine. *Imelda: Steel Butterfly of the Philippines.* New York: McGraw-Hill, 1988.

Fabros, Wilfredo. *The Church and Its Social Involvement in the Philippines, 1930–1972.* Quezon City: Ateneo de Manila University Press, 1988.

Fleming, Gerald. *Hitler and the Final Solution.* Berkeley: University of California Press, 1984.

Friend, Theodore. "Friendly Tyrants: An American Policy Dilemma—Marcos and the Philippines." *Orbis, A Journal of World Affairs* (Fall 1988).

———. "Marcos and His Critics: What Marcos Doesn't Say." *Orbis, A Journal of World Affairs* (Winter 1989).

Gagelonia, Pedro A., editor. *The Marcos Mind: A Vision of Greatness*, a selection of quotations from Marcos speeches. Rizal: Navotas Press, 1975.

Gleeck, Lewis E., Jr. *Dissolving the Colonial Bond: American Ambassadors to the Philippines, 1946–1984.* Quezon City: New Day Publishers, 1988.

Joaquin, Nick. *The World of Rafael Salas.* Manila: Solar Publishing, 1987.

———. Doy Laurel in Profile. Manila: Lahi, 1985.

———. *Reportage on the Marcoses 1964–70.* Published under the pen name Quijano de Manila. Rizal: National Book Store, 1979.

Karnow, Stanley. *In Our Image, America's Empire in the Philippines.* New York: Random House, 1989.

———. *Vietnam: A History.* Middlesex: Penguin Books, 1984.

Kirkpatrick, Jeane J., editor. *The Strategy of Deception.* New York: Farrar, Straus, 1963.

Manapat, Ricardo. *Some Are Smarter Than Others — The History of Marcos' Crony Capitalism.* New York: Aletheia Publications, 1991.

Manchester, William. *American Caesar.* Boston: Little, Brown, 1978.

Manglapus, Raul. *A Pen for Democracy.* Washington: Movement for a Free Philippines, 1983.

Marcos, Ferdinand E. *Today's Revolution: Democracy.* Manila: no publisher, 1971.

———. *The Democratic Revolution in the Philippines.* Englewood Cliffs: Prentice/Hall International, 1974.

———. *Revolution From the Center.* Hong Kong: Raya Books, 1978.

———. *Five Years of the New Society.* No city: no publisher, 1978.

———. *Progress and Martial Law.* Manila: no publisher, 1981.

———. "Marcos and His Critics: A Defense of My Tenure." *Orbis, A Journal of World Affairs* (Winter 1989).

Marcos, Imelda Romualdez. *The Compassionate Society.* Manila: National Media Production Center, 1977.

Martinez, Manuel F. *The Grand Collision: Aquino vs. Marcos.* Hong Kong: AP&G Resources, 1984.

McCoy, Alfred W. *Oligarchy: Filipino Families and the Politics of Survival.* Unpublished report presented at the Association for Asian Studies annual meeting in San Francisco, 1988.

McDougald, Charles C. *The Marcos File*. San Francisco: San Francisco Publishers, 1987.

Mijares, Primitivo. *The Conjugal Dictatorship of Ferdinand and Imelda Marcos I*. San Francisco: Union Square Publications, 1976.

Nituda, Victor G. *The Young Marcos*. Manila: Foresight International, 1980.

Pedrosa, Carmen Navarro. *Imelda Marcos*. New York: St. Martin's Press, 1987.

Psinakis, Steve. *Two Terrorists Meet*. San Francisco: Alchemy Books, 1981.

Reyes, Rodolfo T. *Memoirs of a Newsman*. Manila: Rod T. Reyes Media Services, 1990.

Romulo, Beth Day. *Inside the Palace*. New York: Putnam's Sons, 1987.

Rotea, Hermie. *Marcos' Lovey Dovie*. Los Angeles: Liberty Publishing, 1983.

Saulo, Alfredo B. *Communism in the Philippines, An Introduction*. Quezon City: Ateneo de Manila University Press, 1990.

Seagrave, Sterling. *The Marcos Dynasty*. New York: Harper & Row, 1988.

Selochan, Viberto. *Could the Military Govern the Philippines?* Quezon City: New Day Publishers, 1989.

Sevilla, Victor J. *Justices of the Supreme Court of the Philippines*, vols. I–III. Quezon City: New Day Publishers, 1984–1985.

Spence, Hartzell. *Marcos of the Philippines*. No city: no publisher, 1981.

Tatad, Francisco S. *Marcos of the Philippines*. Manila: Department of Public Information, 1975.

Valenzuela, Wilfredo P., editor. *Know Them: A Book of Biographies*, vol. III. Manila: Dotela Publications, 1968.

de Vega, Guillermo C. *An Epic*. Republic of the Philippines: no publisher, 1974.

Velasco, Renato, and Sylvano Mahiwo, editors. *The Philippine Legislature Reader*. Quezon City: Great Books Publishers, 1989.

Zaide, Gregorio F. *The Pageant of Philippine History*, vols. I & II. Manila: Philippine Education, 1979.

Index